THE LORE OF
Sportfishing
Spinning & Baitcasting

GC

Photography

Erwin Bauer; cover, pages 78, 101, 156-157, 193, 195 (top), 232-233, 234.
Håkan Berg; pages 22, 25, 26, 28-29, 32, 35 (top), 36-37, 40 (top), 60-61, 63, 65, 66-67, 69, 71, 72-73, 74, 77, 78-79, 80, 81, 82-83, 84, 86-87, 88, 101, 103.
Rudolf Bischoff; page 119.
Bill Browning; pages 59, 193.
Göran Cederberg; cover (inset), pages 8-9, 12, 13, 14, 15, 41, 47, 93, 164, 165, 180, 180-181, 182, 183, 200-201, 205, 207, 228-229.
Martin Falklind; pages 187 (top), 209 (top), 210-211 (bottom), 226-227 (bottom).
M. L. Giovannetti; page 104-105.
Herman J. Gruhl; pages 111, 179.
Jens Ploug Hansen; pages 20-21, 24, 27, 34, 35 (bottom), 37, 50-51, 52-53, 58-59, 87, 90, 92, 94-95, 96, 97, 100, 128, 129 (right), 130, 134-135, 136, 140-141, 143, 152-153, 158, 166-167, 168, 169, 170-171, 173, 174-175 (bottom), 176,177, 178-179, 182 (inset), 187 (bottom), 188, 190, 192-193, 196-197, 198-199 (top), 203, 204, 205, 206-207, 208-209, 209 (bottom), 210-211 (top), 212-213, 215, 219 (right), 226-227 (top).
Heinz Jagusch; page 137.
Per Ola Johannisson; pages 224, 230-231.
Christer Johansson; cover (inset), pages 16-17, 27, 38-39 (bottom), 49, 126-127, 129 (left), 131, 142, 147, 154, 155, 161, 162-163, 211, 216-217, 218, 219 (left).
Peter Kirkby; pages 83, 191, 195 (bottom).
Steen Larsen; endpapers, pages 19, 40 (bottom), 42-43, 48, 51, 89, 132-133, 144-145, 172, 174-175 (top), 189, 198-199 (bottom), 201, 214, 220-221, 222-223.
Munir Lotia; page 10.
Tommy Pedersen; page 225.
Doug Stamm; cover, pages 38-39 (top), 70, 79, 121, 124-125, 133, 138, 139, 148-149, 149, 150-151.

The Lore of Sportfishing
has been originated and produced by
Nordbok International, Gothenburg, Sweden.

Editorial chief:
Göran Cederberg

Design, setting & photowork:
Munir Lotia, Designia

Illustrations:
Ulf Söderqvist together with Peter Grahn (p. 41, 107),
Thommy Gustavsson (p. 184) and Munir Lotia (116, 232)

Nordbok would like to express sincere thanks to all
persons and companies who have contributed in
different ways to the production of this book.

World copyright © 1994
Nordbok International,
Box 7095, S - 402 32 Gothenburg, Sweden.

First published in the USA in 1998 by
CHARTWELL BOOKS, INC.
A Division of **BOOK SALES, INC.**
114 Northfield Avenue
Edison, New Jersey 08837

ISBN 0-7858-0919-8

Printed in Portugal 1998

THE LORE OF
Sportfishing
Spinning & Baitcasting

SPINNING & BAITCASTING – THEN AND NOW
EQUIPMENT FOR THE SPORT • CASTING TECHNIQUES • ARTIFICIAL BAITS
NATURAL BAITS • THE ENVIRONMENTS OF FISH • FISHING IN FRESH WATERS
FISHING IN MARINE WATERS • WHEN, WHERE, AND HOW

**CHARTWELL
BOOKS, INC.**

Göran Cederberg has been the project leader for this book. He planned and elaborated it, coordinated the illustration material, and adapted the contents to an international public. With long experience and deep enthusiasm as a sportfisherman, Göran Cederberg has also edited many multilingual productions such as *The Complete Book of Sportfishing*, *The Complete Book of Flyfishing* and *The Complete Book of Trolling*. He has been chief editor of the Swedish sportfishing magazine *ESOX* as well as contributing articles and photography to sportfishing media in Sweden and elsewhere.

Jens Ploug Hansen was an internationally familiar Danish sportfishing journalist and photographer. Extraordinarily productive, he devoted much of his life to travel, photography and writing countless articles and volumes about all kinds of sportfishing. Already in the 1970s he made a reputation as one of the finest European sportfishing photographers, and he produced many films on aspects of the sport in the past ten years. Most of the present book has been written by Jens Ploug Hansen, but his eventful life and admirable career ended a few months before the publication, and it can only be wished that he too had seen these pages.

Contents

E very day millions of sportfishermen all over the world devote themselves to spinning and baitcasting. This enormous popularity owes, of course, to the extraordinary diversity of this way of fishing and its ability to challenge the majority of well-known fish species. Moreover, spinning with artificial and natural baits is both simple and effective – which is probably one of the main reasons why spinning and baitcasting tends to be the obvious choice, for beginners as well as many experienced fishermen, when catching a great variety of fish in fresh and marine waters alike.

A characteristic of spinning and baitcasting is that the baits are cast out. This is true no matter whether we fish with spoons, big plugs, small spinners and jigs – or with natural baits on tackle, presented with sinkers, floats and other casting weights. Another basis of the sport is that it focuses almost exclusively on predatory fish, the species which at times are primarily active in hunting all kinds of small fish. Baits that are more or less deceptive – through their shape, movement, colour, smell, sound, consistency or even taste – are meant to imitate the predator's prey as realistically as possible and thus tempt it to bite.

The garden of greed-provoking baits is forever flowering with new creations, and today we see a nearly indescribable range of artificial lures. Equipment, fishing methods, and baits are continually being developed and refined for adaptation or perfection with regard to new waters, species and techniques. In short, there is plenty of experimentation to find optimally attractive "fish foolers": baits which, at least to our eyes, should be irresistible to the quarry. Now and then, entirely novel inventions appear – and sometimes they hit the jackpot. Genuinely rewarding baits soon earn a reputation for being "killers".

The fish, however, are not always impressed by innovations and this may be just what challenges us, or perhaps what spices the brew in the brine or brook we cast our baits on. Fine catches can still be made with old worn spoons, plugs and spinners. And here is a sign that the fishing results are determined chiefly by the fisherman's knowledge and experience. In addition, it is a fact that natural baits are superior in many situations to even the best-made imitations. A seasoned and well-informed practitioner, with gear that looks far from "modern" to many of us, often lands a lot more fish than does a novice who is armed to the teeth. Correct presentation of the bait will remain the hallmark of successful enthusiasts.

Unlike equipment, experience cannot be bought with money – it has to be acquired through actual fishing. By means of his or her technique in retrieving baits, the fisherman must give them life and offer them at the depth or place where the fish are then located. Consequently, the catch depends on learning how to fish for various species rather than on having a bloated budget. Or as the ancient saying goes, a master reveals himself through his limitations.

This book will hopefully guide readers not only in choosing the right equipment and baits for the right occasions, but also in using them at the right spots with the right state of mind!

Göran Cederberg

Spinning and Bait-casting – then and now

The history of sportfishing has for many reasons come to be associated chiefly with the evolution of angling and flyfishing. Naturally, spinning and baitcasting also have a history – although a much shorter one, due to several factors. Their technical progress began only about 150 years ago, and it is primarily during the last half-century that new rods, reels, lines and lures have emerged at an ever faster pace.

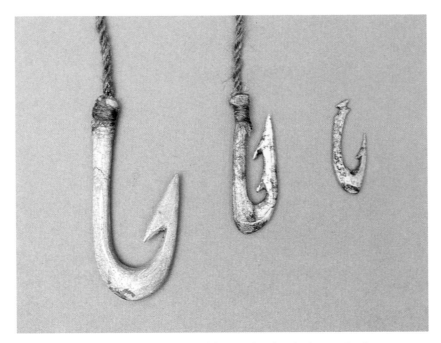

Today we see a continuous stream of innovations in technique and refinements in equipment, even if by no means all "improvements" satisfy the sportfisherman's demand for durable and functional gear. A great deal has clearly been done not just to make the fishing simpler and more enjoyable, but also to increase the chances of a rewarding catch – despite a decline of fishing in many parts of the world due to environmental damage and overexploitation of water resources.

Fish have always been an important food for people. Already thousands of years ago, our ancestors made hooks and harpoons of wood and bone. The barbed hooks shown above are about 10,000 years old, but the principle is still the same. Despite being larger and clumsier than today's much slenderer hooks, they doubtless served well as fishing equipment.

amusement, and this is among the earliest evidence that mankind had begun to experience entertainment in fishing.

Some 500 years later, around 200 AD, the Chinese were fishing with rods, lines made of silk, and hooks of metal. At this time, in addition, the Macedonians fished with artificial, jig-like baits of feather and hair. As a comparison, the manufacture of iron hooks did not arise in Europe until 300 years afterward.

From necessity to pleasure

Before going into the technical development of spinning and baitcasting equipment itself, we should look far back in time. People have fished, hunted and gathered for several hundred thousand years, but a mere fraction of this epoch has given us the privilege of being able to fish solely for pleasure. From fishing with the hands, or with plain spears and harpoons, to using modern carbon-fibre rods and advanced multiplier reels has been a long and eventful voyage.

We know that barbed hooks made of bone and wood were made as early as 30,000 BC. These were fastened to "lines" consisting mainly of animal sinews, as well as of thin tough roots and vines or certain grass species. Archaeological finds show, too, that floats – cut from bark – were used with hooks already 7,000 years ago. By 2,000 BC, Egyptian paintings illustrated fishing with hooks and elementary rods having top-knotted lines, probably using natural baits such as small fish.

The first recorded description of fishing with a rod and hook is dated to about 300 BC. In Greece, Theocritus wrote that fishing was done "with bait deceitfully dangling from the rod". It can be assumed on good grounds that he was referring to people who fished mostly for

Angling and its authors

In 1425 the famous "Treatyse of Fysshynge wyth an Angle" was written, probably by an English abbess, Dame Juliana Berners. This became part of the "Book of St. Albans" (1496), which dealt with hunting and fishing for the benefit of aristocrats. The "Treatyse" concerned both the fisherman's attitude toward nature and the sport's practical details. Besides being skillful at catching fish, he should be an idealist with a "philosophical" approach, making his own equipment and able to present baits – whether natural or artificial – as faithfully to nature as possible. The fineness of the sport was proportional to the difficulty of the catch.

A similar spirit pervaded Izaak Walton's classic "The Compleat Angler", which appeared in 1653 in England. Its subtitle, "The Contemplative Man's Recreation", reveals much about how fishermen in his day viewed (or were urged to view) the sport. The concept of sportfishing now became established, implying that fish could be caught for enjoyment, and that the experience of nature was at least as valuable as the catch.

With Walton's book, moreover, the sportfishing tradition was founded: fishing with a rod, line and hook purely for pleasure, as a source of recreation and relaxation. Yet it should be remembered that only the upper classes had such

This Egyptian painting, some 4,000 years old, includes pictures of different kinds of fish. Among the subjects in the lower section is some sort of angling. No older representations of fishing with a rod, line and hook are yet known.

The *Treatyse of Fysshynge wyth an Angle* was written as early as 1425, but its publication delayed until 1496. This illustration shows the treatise's first page as it looked in the original edition.

an opportunity for luxury. The vast majority of Europeans were then still quite poor, and forced to make better use of both fishing and fish.

Development of early reels

Equipment changed very little until the beginning of the nineteenth century. To be sure, already in the mid-1600s, village smiths had started to harden hooks for greater durability. Soon this work was adopted by needle-makers, so that the hooks became thinner and lighter, and the production grew from a handicraft into an industry. However, the sportfisherman's primary tools remained the top-knotted line of horsehair and a long, heavy rod of jointed wood. Simple reels were occasionally included, but used almost exclusively for storing the line and, perhaps, to parry a rushing fish with. The normal procedure was still to drop natural baits – and, of course, flies – on hooks into the water. Fishing by properly casting was out of the question.

Around 1770, when rods with guides had existed for some years, the first primitive baitcasting reels came to light in London. These were extremely clumsy and stiff by today's standards, allowing only a short cast. But they had a rotating spool and gearing, so they can be termed baitcasting reels. This scarcely made them ideal for casting, though, and they served principally to store the thick braided line.

Not before the level-wind was introduced, to spread the line over the whole rotating spool, did the baitcasting reel turn into a device suitable for casting. The only lines avail-

able at the time were fat, sluggish ones made of linen and cotton, which limited the casting distances. Nonetheless, these original baitcasting reels meant a kind of revolution for the growing number of sportfishermen, who – notably in the United States – fished in the sea for species such as striped bass.

A breakthrough with split bamboo

Neither were rods particularly functional, in relation to modern high-tech casting cannons. During the early 1800s, many experiments were carried out to improve the material and construction of rods. Among the ingredients tested were hickory, lancewood, and especially greenheart: a heavy, hard, durable type of wood imported from South America.

11

As in the past, it was the requirements of flyfishermen for their rods that called the tune in the work of development. Thus, the rods were long – up to 18 feet – and designed for swinging the line outward in the traditional flyfishing manner.

It took until 1846 to find a seemingly optimal combination of material and construction. The first split-cane rod was then built by an American violin-maker. This comparatively light, well-casting rod had enormous advantages over its unwieldy predecessors. Extensive manufacture was delayed for 25 years more – but by splitting bamboo cane three ways and gluing together six of the planed parts, a pliable tool with good casting qualities had at last been invented.

Also in the 1870s, lines with oil-impregnated silk were brought into use. This innovation enabled the casting distance to be tripled and, when combined with the increasingly common split-cane rod, it raised entirely new possibilities for the rod fisherman who had a baitcasting reel. On the other hand, backlash – resulting in troublesome tangled line – was more a rule than an exception during the infancy of spinning and baitcasting.

The large, clumsy reels were therefore still the main problem. In order to reach fish across the water, it was necessary to employ big casting weights. From our point of view, the enthusiastic pioneers of this sport must have had considerable obstacles to overcome. Theirs was literally "heavy fishing", placing a substantial strain on both the equipment and the body.

Already in 1884, the so-called Malloch reel was created in Perth, England. Yet not until 1905 did the first open-face fixed-spool reel of "modern" design appear. This prototype of today's much more advanced versions emerged in the English city of Bradford, and represented a giant step in the direction of lighter, more comfortable and enjoyable cast-fishing. Reels with a fixed spool gave little or no backlash, in addition to a longer cast. Obviously such a reel had decisive advantages, and further evolution of the fixed-spool reel soon began.

Artificial lures: a brief history

While the use of natural baits is probably as old as that of hooks, artificial baits – apart from flies – are relatively recent. The most traditional kind of artificial casting bait is the spoon. This may include any somewhat spoon-shaped, oval, elongated or round lure.

The two photographs show the "Allcock aerial" from S. Allcock & Co. Ltd. The reel had a rotating spool and a simple braking device. Called a centre-pin reel, this type recalls a flyfishing reel but it was used for baitcasting.

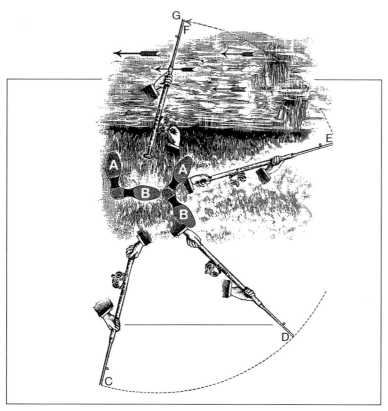

The illustration is taken from a Hardy catalogue of the early 1900s, showing the cast positions when fishing with baits such as shrimp or spinners, and with rotating-spool reels.

In 1905, Alfred Holden Illingworth patented his first casting reel with a fixed spool. This photo shows the Illingworth No.3 from 1913, which started the resemblance to modern spinning reels. In fact, the spinning reel's principles have hardly changed since then.

In fact, spoons have existed for less than 200 years, but they are still ranked very high by casting fishermen – not surprisingly, because a spoon is easy to cast and is an effective attractor. The first spoons, however, were produced not for spinning but for dragline fishing, the simplest form of trolling.

The wobbler (plug), too, originated in North America, although Finland – due not least to Lauri Rapala and the later company Rapala – has been tremendously important for the development of new, well-fishing varieties of wobbler. Initially, wobblers were made from bark and balsa wood. Meant to imitate small fish, such as vendace, they were used only for rowboat trolling. Many of today's wobblers, normally manufactured in plastic, are also quite effective as casting lures. They look, and move, ever more like their natural models, diverse preyfish, and the wobbler's appeal for both fish and fishermen seems to be growing constantly.

Spinners have been popular since the 1930s. This type of lure, with a little metal spoon rotating on an axle, is certainly effective – but unfortunately it has the weakness of being able to twist the line. In spite of that, casting fishermen often consider it superior in many situations. Through the years, numerous experiments have also been made with the spoons of spinners, for example by giving them attractive powers of sound and reflection.

These three basic types of artificial lure – the spoon, wobbler and spinner – will doubtless keep their status for a long time. Even so, the market is continually swamped with new lures, some more irresistible than others. Materials such as rubber and plastic have allowed the manufacture of incredibly lifelike imitations of, for instance, small fish and worms, which have caught loads of fish with the help of specially designed hooks and tackle. Today, in many parts of the world, jigs are regarded as an excellent complement to both spoons and spinners, as are novel types of lure built up with hair and feathers.

Granted that the experimentation with lures is always yielding fresh creations, their huge range leads one to wonder who is most fascinated by them – the fish or the fisherman. All too many new "superbaits" have displayed deep defects in practical fishing and thus been forgotten, while others have rapidly become known as real "killers". In any case, plenty of the old classics are still recognized to be effective lures. This surely indicates that the fish are less fastidious than we believe, and that success at fishing depends at least as much on the presentation as on the choice of bait.

Here are some variants of casting lures from the infancy of sportfishing.

Lauri Rapala supported himself during much of his life by fishing. To improve the catch, he began whittling lures that would imitate injured small fish, and after many attempts he created a fish-like wobbler with a durable surface coating. He sold his first wobbler in 1938, but it took ten years for the name Rapala to win fame among sportfishermen. Under the photo of him are some early examples of his wobbler – a model that is sold today as Rapala Original.

The advent of synthetic materials

During the first half of the twentieth century, equipment for spinning and baitcasting remained fairly awkward. Rods of split cane and later of steel, with silk lines and the "coffee-grinder" sort of reel, were unavoidable. Not until World War II did anything significant happen in developing the equipment. Then two inventions, each in its own manner, revolutionized spinning and baitcasting: the fibreglass rod and the synthetic line.

This was what countless sportfishermen had long awaited. Durable and robust rods, which were cheap as well, and thin but strong lines offered an unprecedented opportunity to cast far and trouble-free. The new rods were introduced by Shakespeare, an American company that launched the massive fibreglass rod in 1947. Quick to follow were the first tube-built fibreglass rods. Fishing could finally become a popular sport in the true sense of the word.

The steadily growing interest in spinning and baitcasting was shown in many ways. Development of lures accelerated, and fishing increased for various species that had fallen out of favour. Mass production of rods, reels and lines also lowered their prices, and the sport's practitioners multiplied accordingly. This in turn enabled the manufacturers to invest even more money in improving and advancing the equipment.

When carbon-fibre came into use as a rod ingredient during the mid-1970s, it was widely thought that such a "space material" could only be a complement to fibreglass. As so often, the prophets were found to be wrong. Minimal weight and unbeatable casting qualities, together with ever lower prices, meant that these rods almost replaced fibreglass rods. And the fact is that carbon-fibre outperforms fibreglass in nearly all respects. Hence, in the 1990s, development of carbon-fibre has proceeded at a raging tempo, alongside experiments with other "space-age" substances like kevlar and boron.

Our technological horizons

The days of the osier rod, silk line, and handmade hook are gone for good. After a few decades in the space age, we have witnessed amazing changes in fishing equipment. Future rods are also bound to be even better, lighter and cheaper. The same naturally applies to reels, which continue to become smaller and smoother in cast-

This multiplier reel, over 50 years old, demonstrates that the type's design remains essentially unaltered. Changes have been made chiefly beneath the skin, with lighter spools and softer brakes. In particular, the spool's inertia has been minimized, so that the previously awful tangling of line is now seldom seen.

ing, as well as supplied with diverse functional refinements. The lines are being improved by new production methods, tending to get ever thinner and more flexible – and stronger. The properties of artificial lures are being extended apace and, on the whole, the items of equipment are increasingly adapted to their purpose.

However, one cannot discuss the development of spinning and baitcasting without mentioning the growing interest in fishing from boats. Ever since the first primitive log boats began to carry people across water, different kinds of vessels have been used for fishing. Today, casting from a boat is ever more common, and the boat-borne sportfisherman has fantastic possibilities of fishing at places – such as sunken reefs and deep edges – which are inaccessible from land.

Also relevant is the echo-sounder's importance for adding

to our knowledge of the environment that fish inhabit. The more we know about bottom structures, small fish schools' movements, thermoclines, and – not least – the holding places of prey, the greater is our chance to experience fishing with both pleasure and success. It is, of course, a gross oversight to say that the echo-sounder gives the sportfisherman advantages which are almost unsporting. Knowing where the fish is in the water does not necessarily mean that it is willing to take the bait.

The fish is still the same biological creature as what our ancestors fished for. It responds to the same stimuli now as then, fighting with equal spirit, and can be just as difficult to catch. Fish do not know what goes on above the water surface, or understand technology or, therefore, allow themselves to be impressed by technical innovations.

A hungry predatory fish still eats best, and we can hardly alter that fact. Admittedly, we can improve the odds in numerous ways, but we can never change the ecological demands, and must adapt our fishing to the natural laws which have always governed fishing and fish. Yet this may be the very enchantment of the sport. Despite the new opportunities provided by technical progress, it is the fish that determines the rules of play – the same rules that all previous generations of fishermen have had to obey!

Equipment for the Sport

A fisherman does not need advanced tackle to have an exciting time at spinning and baitcasting, but the items should be appropriate and function properly. Then the fishing is both more fun and more profitable, as the casts are longer and one can retrieve with greater sensitivity. Moreover, there is less risk of losing fish that dive and fight to get off the hook.

■

No equipment is so all-round that it suffices for everything from trout and salmon to pike and bass – or for fishing in both big and small waters. One can, though, require that the gear be adapted to as many forms of spinning and baitcasting as possible. If different kinds of fishing are envisaged, several setups are therefore necessary: for example, a light one-handed rod for small waters, a light two-handed rod for larger fish and waters, and a stronger two-handed rod for heavy spinning.

Lacking the right rod and a suitable reel with correct line strength, casts that are far and exact enough cannot be made. In addition, the rod and reel must be able to guide the bait's movements while retrieving it, and to register the faintest take.

Hardly a year goes by without the tackle manufacturers announcing new refinements and clever details on rods and reels that are to render them indispensable. The really essential point is thus to evaluate one's needs, not just rely on printed advice. Indeed, those with most experience in spinning and baitcasting have learned to limit their equipment.

Rods

The development of rods has gone forward much faster than that of reels. Fibreglass rods predominated during the 1960s, and carbon-fibre rods arrived in the early 1970s. The latter were at first considered too expensive for widespread acceptance, but some years later came cheap composite rods – with a blend of fibreglass and graphite, which is now most common.

Graphite and composite rods have many advantages over the earlier fibreglass rods. They are lighter, relax faster after the cast, are more obedient when retrieving, and can better register cautious takes as well as the movements of artificial lures. A couple of years after these rods became established, the boron rod made its appearance. This contains graphite blended with boron, a metal in fibre form. It is a bit lighter than the carbon-fibre rod, but more springy and powerful.

Boron rods have never gained broad popularity, and the future market will presumably be ruled by the composite rod, whose graphite content varies from a few percent to about 80%. This type of rod is also cheaper and slightly heavier than rods of pure graphite, which is often rather expensive and beyond the means of most fishermen. Further, there are certain graphite rods with kevlar fibres that lend the shaft greater strength with a little less springiness.

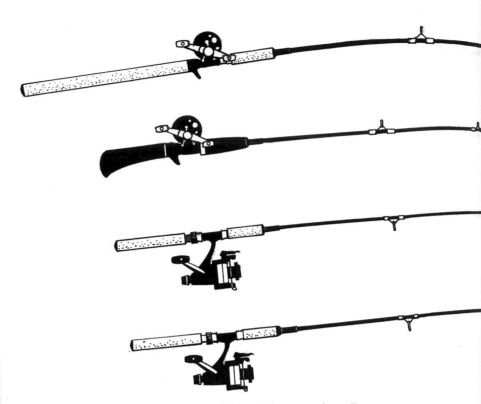

The curve formed by the rod blank under full load is known as the rod's action. At top is shown a rod with full (slow) action, whose entire blank bends in an even curve. Next come a half-action (medium) rod, where only the upper half bends, and a rod with top action. At bottom appears a rod with extra-fast action.

The rod's action

Rod action is an expression for how the rod bends during the cast and the playing of a fish. Rods with full action were once common. Here the whole rod bends in a smooth curve, from the tip to the handle. On a medium- or half-action rod, the upper part bends. Top action is rapid, where the rod's uppermost third or fourth bends. Today, many rods have progressive action, a term that is more a selling argument than a product description, as there are both full- and top-action rods with progressive action.

Rods with half action are the type that makes one happiest when spinning. Using them, the majority of artificial lures can be nicely cast out and the fish safely tired out. This type of action and rod is also the best all-round choice.

Rods with top action are excellent for casting, but are somewhat too stiff for tiring out the fish. Due to their high initial speed in the cast, a spoon or wobbler tends to rotate or shoot out, although compact spoons and pirks can be cast quite far. Neither is top action very suited to fishing with natural baits.

For spinning and baitcasting, rods with half or 3/4 action are the best all-round type, as they serve very well for both casting artificial lures and tiring out hooked fish.

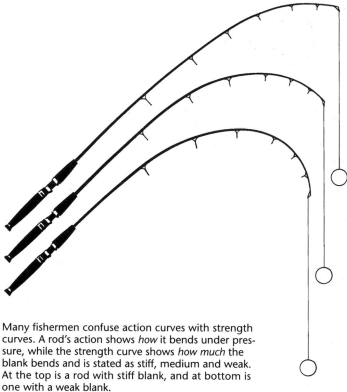

Many fishermen confuse action curves with strength curves. A rod's action shows *how* it bends under pressure, while the strength curve shows *how much* the blank bends and is stated as stiff, medium and weak. At the top is a rod with stiff blank, and at bottom is one with a weak blank.

Full-action rods are superb for tiring out fish. Yet they are a little slower at casting, and demand a special casting technique to perform optimally. Still, this rod type is ideal for fishing with natural bait, which it can cast out in a soft line curve.

Rod length

Rods can be divided into the one-handed type, 6-7 feet long, and the two-handed which is 8-11 feet long. Since the light graphite rod's explosive development, both of these types have become longer in recent decades. When fibreglass rods prevailed, excessive length often made them heavy to cast with – but the new materials are constantly changing our evaluation of rods, as well as classification of them.

In the class of 7-8 feet are several rods that can justifiably be called one-and-a-half-handed. It is possible to use them as slightly longer one-handed rods, but normally they serve as two-handed. There is plenty of room for two hands under the cast, and the bottom part is long enough to give extra power for tiring the fish. This type and length are also

very common in what may be termed light spinning, ultralight (UL) fishing, or light-tackle spinning.

Previously, light fishing meant a short rod; but nowadays the trend is toward ever lighter and longer rods even in this fishing. Blanks of 9-10.5 feet for flyfishing are rebuilt as light spinning rods, often with full action. Some are shortened at either the top or bottom, depending on which kind of spinning they are to be used for. Some such spinning rods are also factory-made, and these are well suited to long, exact casts with ultralight lures weighing 5-15 grams (1/6-1/2 ounce). Another variety is the combi-rod, applicable to both spinning and flyfishing.

Casting weight

Most rods are built for a particular casting weight. To make the rod as useful and easily sold as possible, the casting weight is often stated with a wide margin. For instance, 10-40 grams are frequently recommended on a 9-foot rod. In truth, such a rod is commonly best suited to a casting weight of 15-25 grams. It can, of course, cast with weights of both 10 and 40 grams, but then does not yield a pleasing cast, and neither does it react naturally during the cast. In order to cast artificial lures of 10 or 35-40 grams, one should instead choose a rod with a casting weight of 5-20 or 30-80 grams.

Ferrules

Most rods consist of two parts, but there are some longer two-handed rods of 11 feet that have three parts. Each joint is called a ferrule, and may be designed in different ways. A topover ferrule is most common: the rod's upper half projects down over the lower half. A spigot ferrule is among the most secure: the rod blank, built in a single piece, is cut in the middle and a short, massive graphite tube is glued into the lower part. The upper part is slid down over this spigot. On many cheap rods, the top part is simply stuck into the bottom part.

Rod guides

Ceramic guides are now standard on nearly all rods. Some years ago, ceramic guides were high-quality products from makers like Fuji and Seymo – but today many rods have guides of much worse quality. Good ceramic guides cause minimal friction and last long, but "unknown" brands can be weak and break easily. Often the latter's insert falls out or cracks form in the guide.

Ceramic guides are one-legged on light rods and two-legged on strong rods. They are also frequently bigger on spinning rods than on rods intended for multiplier reels. Remember that considerable friction occurs in the lowest guide if you use a spinning reel on a rod which is made for a multiplier reel. On spinning rods of 7-9 feet, the lowest ceramic guide should have a diameter of about 3 cm (1.2 inches).

Rod handles and reel seats

The rod handle consists of cork or foam rubber (EVA = evaporin). Both types are excellent and give a good grip. Most older fishermen doubtless prefer cork as a natural material, which insulates at least as well as EVA. Since many rods are standardized products, one often finds that an 8-foot rod, for example, has been provided with the same length of handle as a 9-footer. On quality rods, however, the rod handle's bottom part is better proportioned.

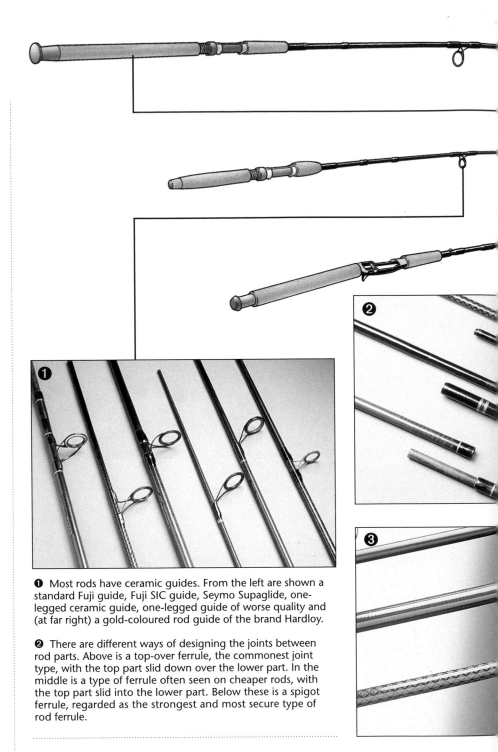

❶ Most rods have ceramic guides. From the left are shown a standard Fuji guide, Fuji SIC guide, Seymo Supaglide, one-legged ceramic guide, one-legged guide of worse quality and (at far right) a gold-coloured rod guide of the brand Hardloy.

❷ There are different ways of designing the joints between rod parts. Above is a top-over ferrule, the commonest joint type, with the top part slid down over the lower part. In the middle is a type of ferrule often seen on cheaper rods, with the top part slid into the lower part. Below these is a spigot ferrule, regarded as the strongest and most secure type of rod ferrule.

The reel seat is made of metal and/or composite material, and has two locking rings. Nowadays most rods use a screw-down reel seat: the front part of the handle has a built-in threading, which locks the reel foot. It tends to be thicker than a standard handle.

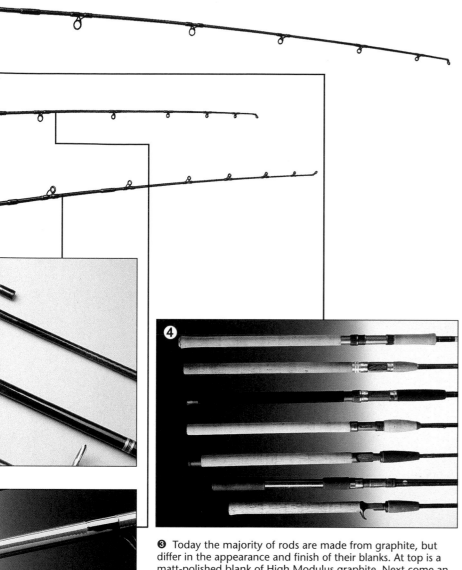

❸ Today the majority of rods are made from graphite, but differ in the appearance and finish of their blanks. At top is a matt-polished blank of High Modulus graphite. Next come an unpolished blank and a Whisker High Modulus graphite blank. At bottom is a blank of kevlar-reinforced IM6 graphite.

❹ Rod handles are now made almost exclusively of cork and foam (EVA-grip or a kind of foam rubber), and the reel seats primarily of composite and/or metal. In this photo are seven two-handed rods with different types of handles and reel seats. Except for multiplier rods with finger-hooks, most reel seats can be combined with both open-face spinning reels and multiplier reels.

On rods for multiplier reels, the seat is designed differently, even though such a reel can easily be used in ordinary seats on rods made for spinning reels. Many rods constructed for baitcasting reels have a depressed seat that allows an improved finger-grip, and commonly also a

finger-hook or a pistol-grip. Unfortunately, this kind of seat makes the rod heavier, and the blank ends in the front part of the handle, which slightly worsens the action. But on most rods for baitcasting reels, the seat is the same as on rods for spinning reels except that a finger-hook is added.

Telescopic rods

For spinning and baitcasting, telescopic rods have never been a success, apart from their great popularity in some countries like Germany. One of their disadvantages is that this construction does not give a very pleasing action. Due to the separate parts of the rod, the guides are also often too far apart, causing a lot of friction on the line – especially when playing large fish. Moreover, these rods are comparatively heavy. A telescopic rod is ideal for journeys, but the guides should always be protected by a holster during transportation.

Reels

Spinning reels and baitcasting reels are superb within their respective fields of use. A spinning reel is easiest for a beginner to operate, and it is best suited to light casting weights of 2-10 grams. A baitcasting reel, however, casts farthest with weights from 10 grams upward. This reel's structure also better conveys the feel of a fight and the contact with a fish, as the line is in direct touch with the spool during the fight. Besides, a multireel has very good power transmission and, therefore, makes it easier to fight big fish with a small reel.

On the other hand, in a headwind where the lures are readily blown sideways, problems can arise with a baitcasting reel: the accelerating force does not stop when the lure has been cast, and a backlash may well result. But while retrieving, the contact with the lure is better with a baitcasting reel. It is also quite possible to use a baitcasting reel for night fishing, yet greater attention is necessary than with a spinning reel, which works perfectly under such conditions.

Spinning reels

Anyone can learn to cast with a modern spinning reel after just a few hours' training. Sizes range from the smallest UL

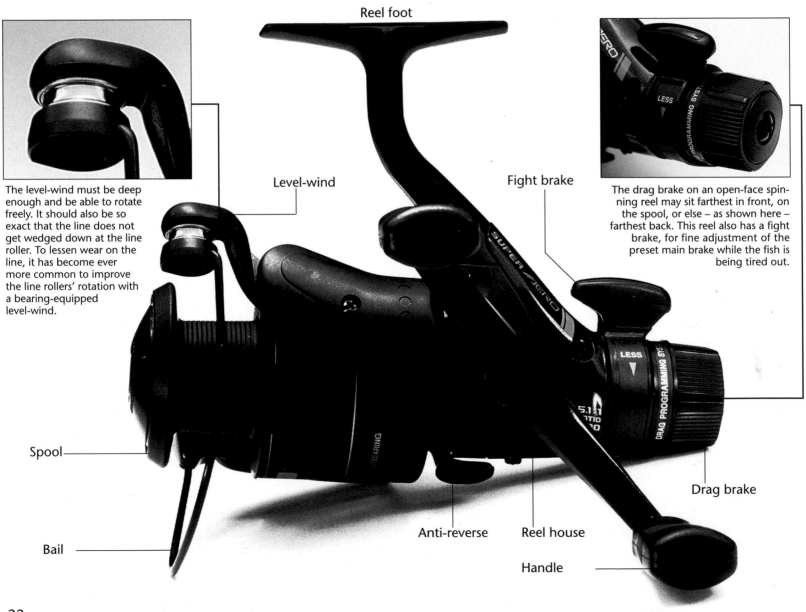

Reel foot

The level-wind must be deep enough and be able to rotate freely. It should also be so exact that the line does not get wedged down at the line roller. To lessen wear on the line, it has become ever more common to improve the line rollers' rotation with a bearing-equipped level-wind.

Level-wind

Fight brake

The drag brake on an open-face spinning reel may sit farthest in front, on the spool, or else – as shown here – farthest back. This reel also has a fight brake, for fine adjustment of the preset main brake while the fish is being tired out.

Spool

Bail

Anti-reverse

Reel house

Drag brake

Handle

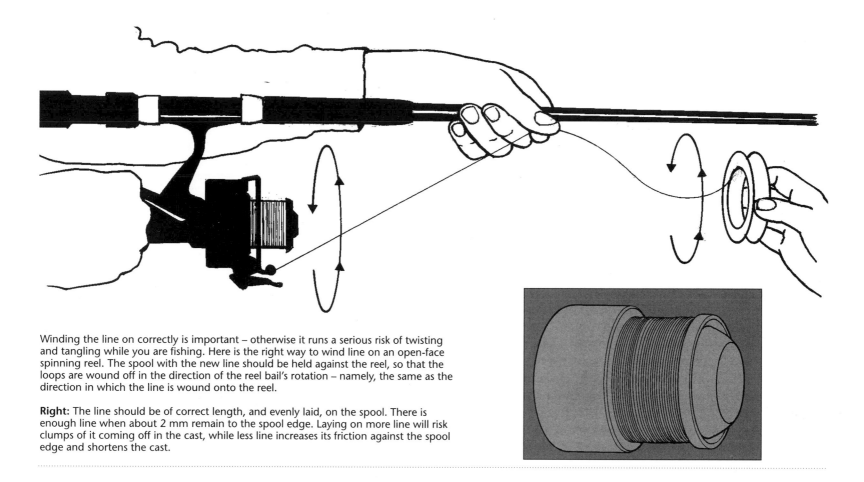

Winding the line on correctly is important – otherwise it runs a serious risk of twisting and tangling while you are fishing. Here is the right way to wind line on an open-face spinning reel. The spool with the new line should be held against the reel, so that the loops are wound off in the direction of the reel bail's rotation – namely, the same as the direction in which the line is wound onto the reel.

Right: The line should be of correct length, and evenly laid, on the spool. There is enough line when about 2 mm remain to the spool edge. Laying on more line will risk clumps of it coming off in the cast, while less line increases its friction against the spool edge and shortens the cast.

types, through fairly large reels that suit almost all fish species, to big reels for salmon and sea fishing. Nearly all spinning reels are made according to the same principle, although the drag may be placed differently and the brake discs manufactured of different materials. The spool's form and the handle's way of folding may also vary.

The design of the reel handle makes it possible to retrieve the lure with either your left or right hand. The reel may also have a few, or many, ball bearings. The number of ball bearings is often a sellers' argument, but in fact there are many examples of reels with 3-4 bearings that last longer than others with 5-6 bearings.

The material of which the reel itself is made has varied in recent decades. Most reels were once made of aluminium, followed by graphite reels during the 1970s. These, however, were not very durable and the trend is now back toward aluminium reels, although graphite reels will continue in the low-price category.

Gearing

Today the majority of reels have a helical pinion, but some – mainly German ones – still have a worm pinion. This is a simple and practical design, which at first goes a little more sluggishly than a helical pinion but soon becomes "run in". To put it briefly, the worm pinion is a quite reliable gear that can last for years, and not a few have worked for 30 years.

A gear ratio of 4:1 was previously considered relatively high, but many reels now have a ratio of 6:1 or 7:1. The ideal, though, is between 4:1 and 5.2:1. While a ratio of 5:1 should generally be preferred on small reels, larger ones may easily have 4:1. A high gear ratio is advantageous for rapid retrieval, yet always a disadvantage when playing a fish.

A double handle is ever more common, as it allows the reel to run more smoothly. But even reels with a single handle can be very well balanced, so there is little difference in running between the two types.

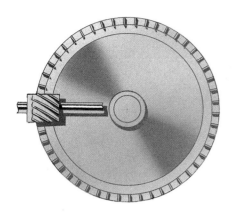

Open-face spinning reels have two types of pinion: worm (*above*) and helical (*below*). The helical, or angle, pinion is most common today. Compared to the worm pinion, it has the drawbacks of a less soft gait and a shorter lifetime, but it usually gives better contact with both lures and hooked fish. The worm pinion also tends to cost more, and to need a breaking-in period before losing its initial sluggishness.

Spool and drag

Nearly all spinning reels today have an external spool. This open-face construction, introduced in 1975 by Daiwa, was intended to prevent the line from getting caught between the spool and its housing. The spool is still one of the weakest features in a spinning reel, because a poorly designed spool can give very bad casts and allow the line to shoot off in clumps. The spool's front edge should have a sharp edge in order to lay the line up well, which of course is essential for good casts without tangling.

The Longcast spool has become familiar on many reels. It lays the line up better, and can actually yield somewhat longer casts. As a rule, the spool should be filled with line up to 2-3 millimetres from the spool edge. Too little line produces short casts, due to friction against the spool edge, whereas too much line will result in its being pulled off in clumps.

The pick-up bail, with a built-in level-wind and a line roller, is among the spinning reel's most important details. Every year, efforts are made to improve it. Some rollers are self-lubricating, while others need a drop of oil after every fishing trip to work optimally.

The drag may be placed either before or behind the housing on a spinning reel. Drag discs in the spool have a larger braking area than discs behind on the back of the reel – but more discs can compensate for a smaller area, so in practice both systems work equally well. Some reels with the drag at the back also have a fight brake, which is a fine-tuning device in combination with the preset drag brake. The fight brake is a small wing that sits on the main brake and enables it to be adjusted during the fight. Baitrunner reels have a separate device, connected to the drag at the back. One can also disengage the spool, a procedure that is useful chiefly for those who fish with natural bait.

Simple, closed-face spinning reels are most appropriate for beginners.

Closed-face spinning reels

Spinning reels with a cover over the spool and its housing were once very common, but are gradually disappearing. Here the mechanics are simple, and the casting ability mediocre. These reels are easy to handle and, for many years, were thought suitable for beginners in the low-price category, although some examples became popular among anglers. For anyone who has a great interest in fishing, the best choice of all is to invest in an open-faced spinning reel of good quality.

Some closed-face spinning reels are also used by experienced fishermen, mainly under difficult conditions where short casting is sufficient.

The open-faced spinning reel is probably the world's most widespread type of reel. It is simple to handle – not least for beginners – and gives long, safe casts. Light lures from 2 to 10-15 grams also suit it very well. No matter whether the drag sits at its front or rear, this is an effective tool for tiring out even big fish.

Baitcasting reels

In contrast to spinning reels, the baitcasting reel has a rotating horizontal spool. The handle drives the spool by means of toothed wheels, whose gear ratio depends on the kind of fishing intended. Normally the ratio is around 5:1.

Granted that many of the modern small baitcasting reels are technical wonders, the basic principle of a baitcasting reel is elementary. But a certain amount of training is needed to cast with this reel. Despite its frequently well-planned brake system, beginners in particular are bound to suffer a backlash when the spool overwinds in the cast.

Prices are often much higher for baitcasting reels than for spinning reels. Like the latter, baitcasting reels of graphite were made during the 1980s, but time has shown that aluminium reel houses are best. In terms of design, there are two types of baitcasting reel: the classic cylindrical reel with round side-gables, and the more low-profiled variety. Both types have excellent mechanics and satisfy all the requirements of spinning and baitcasting.

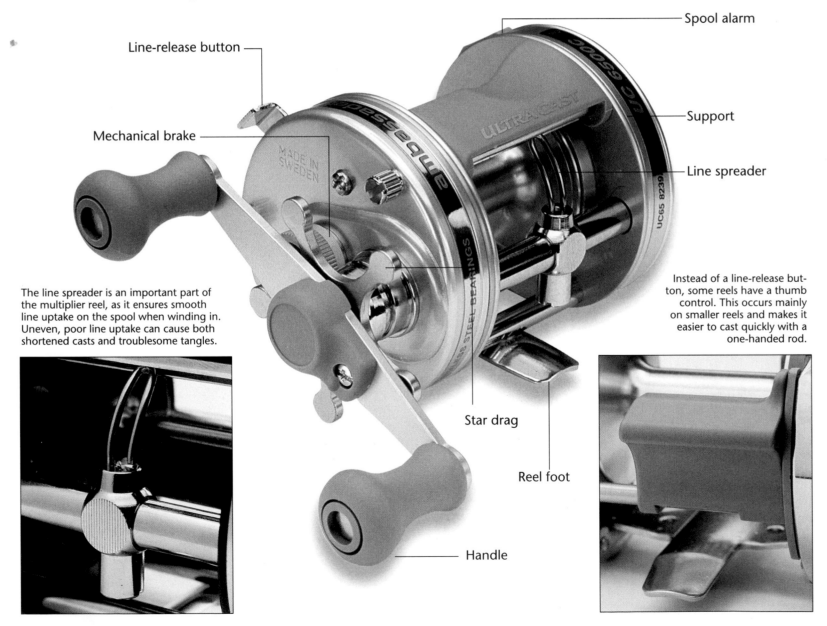

Spool alarm

Line-release button

Mechanical brake

Support

Line spreader

The line spreader is an important part of the multiplier reel, as it ensures smooth line uptake on the spool when winding in. Uneven, poor line uptake can cause both shortened casts and troublesome tangles.

Instead of a line-release button, some reels have a thumb control. This occurs mainly on smaller reels and makes it easier to cast quickly with a one-handed rod.

Star drag

Reel foot

Handle

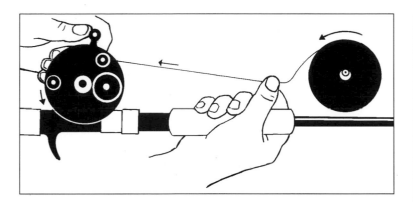

When laying line onto a multiplier reel, the line's spool should be held so as to rotate in the same direction as the reel's spool. Stick a pencil into the line spool's mid-hole for smooth turning, and keep the line stretched between your fingers while laying on. The reel is full when 1-2 mm are left to its spool's upper edge.

Below left: Most multiplier reels today have effective cast-braking systems, both centrifugal and mechanical, to lessen the risk of running the spool too fast when casting.

Care and maintenance

Reels can be damaged by salt water and dirty fresh water. Hence they should always be rinsed after a fishing trip, then dried and sprayed with silicon. Simultaneously the brakes should be loosened, as the discs may otherwise deform, making the reel's brake uneven and jerky. The handle knob and the bail springs should be given a couple of drops of oil, which will also benefit the line roller. With a baitcasting reel, you do yourself a service by putting a drop of oil on the screw. If the reel is used regularly, it should undergo a thorough service each year as well.

Lines

Nylon and monofilament lines are manufactured from a nylon raw material, consisting of tiny balls that are heated and pressed through holes of different sizes. The threads are then cooled over rollers that also stretch them, so that they become soft and elastic. Lines of good quality (and high price) are usually impregnated with waterproof substances, which settle between the nylon molecules and prevent the line from absorbing water – thus increasing the breaking strain. Lines can also be surface-treated with, for example, teflon. In sum, making a fishing line is not as simple as it may sound.

Nylon lines are measured and evaluated in terms of properties such as material strength and knot strength. Wear resistance, elasticity, stiffness, and visibility are also weighed in. Extra-strong lines, as opposed to the cheaper budget lines, consist of molecules lying straight and parallel in the direction along the line, and they use better raw material. Good lines do not absorb water, either – whereas cheap ones may suck in water up to ten percent of their weight, which makes them more porous and weak. Still, cheap lines do exist that are just as usable as expensive lines.

Knot strength and elasticity

Lines are often classified, meaning that you have a guarantee of the line breaking only at a certain load. But this raises the price, and such lines should not be bought unless you need to fish with them.

The best knots can provide a knot strength of 90-100 percent, while bad knots – or weaknesses in the knot itself – reach a knot strength of only 50-60 percent. Wear resistance also varies: some lines crack after a single snag on the bottom, or tear to pieces in the line guides after a few hours of fishing. Others, however, will last for many fishing days without a sign of weakness.

When you hook and fight a wild fish on a short line, elasticity is essential. But on a long line, lack of resilience is best. Some lines, in any case, stretch by at least 15-30 percent if they are wet. Generally, soft lines are more elastic than stiff ones.

Coloured and transparent lines

There are really three main types of coloured line: transparent, coloured, and fluorescent. Transparent white, and blue or green coloured, are the most common lines. A fluorescent

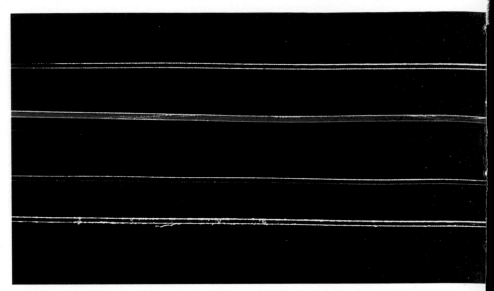

Above: Four types of monofilament line (0.20 mm) are highly magnified here. From the top down are a colourless transparent line, easily seen in the air but almost invisible underwater; a fluorescent line; a coloured transparent line; and an ordinary colourless transparent line.

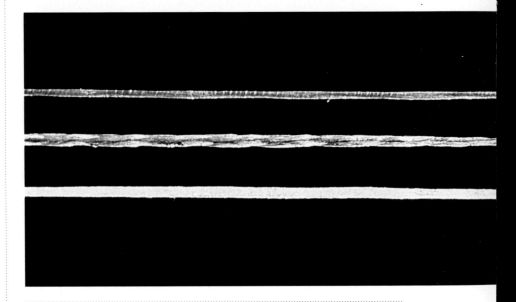

line is easily visible, which can be an advantage if trolling and fishing from a boat, when the rods stand close together and you want to be able to see the line clearly in the water. For spinning and baitcasting, some fishermen dislike a fluorescent line, believing that it makes the fish suspicious. Others think this unimportant – and yet they often tie a piece of ordinary transparent line on the end of the fluorescent line. Nevertheless, only in certain kinds of fishing has a fluorescent line been found to yield worse catches than the transparent type, or than ordinary light-green and light-blue lines.

It is always difficult to give good advice on which type of line to use, but the broad rule should be to choose soft lines

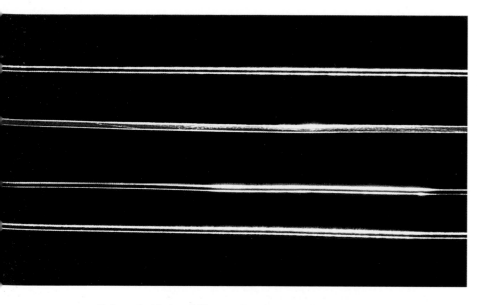

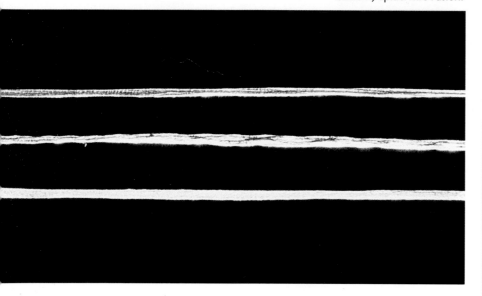

Below: Braided multifilament lines are becoming ever more common, as they combine small diameter with very high test strength. Here are three different kinds (0.20 mm), highly magnified: FireLine (at top), Corastrong and (at bottom) Spiderwire Fusion.

for small reels. A stiff line does not lie so well on such a spool, and can easily lift off during the cast – perhaps resulting in a tangle. During cold and frost, it is best to fish with soft lines, since a stiff line then has a greater tendency to break.

Lines age at different rates. Sunlight, continual dampness, and chemicals can destroy a line. Neither should it come in contact with oil, mosquito spray, petrol and the like. Preferably store it in a dark place, and check it at regular intervals even while fishing. Especially the outermost metres of line are loaded hard during the cast, and by snags on the bottom, so they should be discarded before each new fishing trip.

Braided lines

The new braided multifilament lines are characterized by a very high breaking strain in relation to their diameter. They consist of many fibres, and were introduced by a German company that called its line Corastrong. The fibres, termed coramid, probably contain kevlar. Other, competing line manufacturers use fibres designated as spectra. Both of these line types, which are comparatively expensive, often come in blends with different fibre materials, to improve their knot strength and applicability.

These lines have rapidly won popularity, and will undoubtedly become even more widespread as their prices sink. Regarding cost, a common practice is to fill the reel partly with cheap nylon line, before winding on the expensive multifilament line.

The weak points of multifilament lines are the knots. One can recommend the Trilene knot, but a Uni-knot should be used for the nylon back-line. These lines also have certain weaknesses during frost, mainly due to ice formation.

Multifilament lines perform best on spinning reels, as the accelerating force on a baitcasting reel – combined with the nonresilient line – can cause serious tangling. However, special spools have been developed for these lines, and are likely to gain still more users. Since the line is almost completely inelastic, the fish must be fought under even pressure, with the drag set loose.

When a bottom snag occurs, the line should never be wound about your hand – it easily cuts into flesh. Tangles and backlash may be difficult to fix with these lines. A great and immediate advantage when spinning, though, is that bottom snags come off easily. Another is that the casting distance can be increased considerably, as the line's strength is so high in relation to its diameter. Hence one can fish with a thinner line.

New lines, whose fibres are joined by binder substances, are also growing in popularity. The best known are FireLine and Spiderwire Fusion. But such lines have a somewhat lower breaking strain than the above-mentioned spectra and kevlar lines. No matter which type of line is selected, braided lines are definitely the lines of the future for certain forms of fishing.

Knots

No part of the spinning fisherman's "chain" of equipment is stronger than its weakest link – the knot. Incorrect or poorly tied knots can decrease the breaking strain by up to half. Still, there are dozens of knots that have survived for decades despite their weaknesses. The best approach is to learn three or four durable knots well, and thus be able to tie few but secure knots.

The spool, or arbor, knot comes in handy when the line is to be tied on the spool of a multireel or spinning reel. It is really just a simple three-turn clinch knot. The traditional clinch knot itself can be improved by giving the line an extra pass through the eye. This results in a so-called Trilene knot, with a breaking strain of 95-100 percent.

The Rapala, Duncan or Uni-knot is used primarily for wobblers and small bait. The knot is pulled into a loop, so that the lure obtains a better and more lively gait.

The blood knot applies when two lines are to be joined – even lines of unequal diameter. The difference should not exceed 0.10 mm, but otherwise the thin line is laid double. One end can then also be retained to hold an artificial imitation lure.

The double Uni-knot, too, is very practical and, in this case as well, one leader is suitable for an imitator.

The surgeon's knot is a double overhand knot, also convenient for joining two lines.

Even the sliding Uni-knot is used for an imitator. It has an advantage in that the fish cannot snap the leader during a take or fight, since the knot slides.

The "dropper knot" is one of the simplest imitator knots, but it serves best for small fish, as the knot strength does not quite match that of an ordinary blood knot or the double Uni-knot.

Whichever knots you use, they should be moistened with saliva, before being pulled tight under constant pressure. Almost all knots are tied with several turns, and these should of course slide neatly into place against each other – for if some turns lie over others, the knot may cut itself off. As a rule, knots are always tied with at least five turns, but three are enough when using 0.70-mm or thicker line.

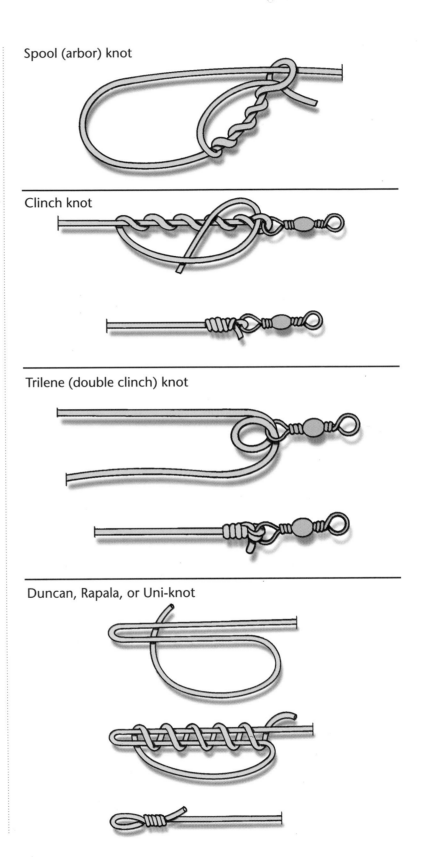

Spool (arbor) knot

Clinch knot

Trilene (double clinch) knot

Duncan, Rapala, or Uni-knot

Double Uni-knot

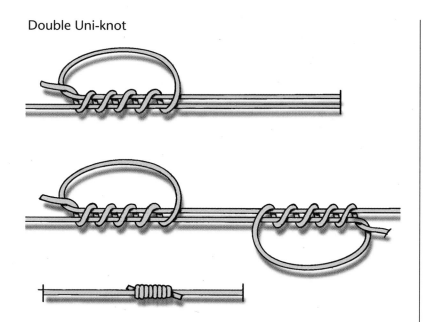

Blood knot

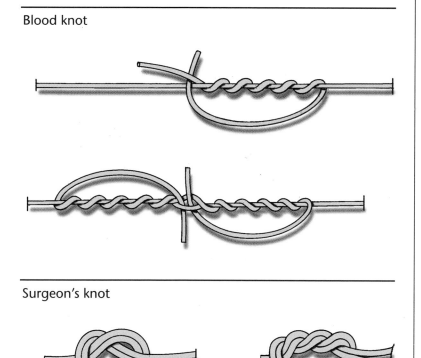

Surgeon's knot

Sliding Uni-knot

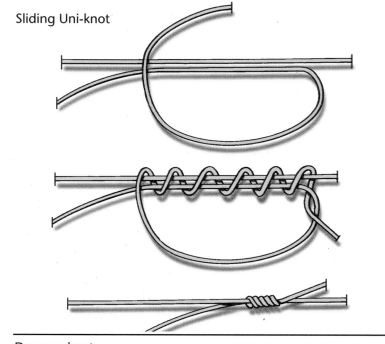

Dropper knot

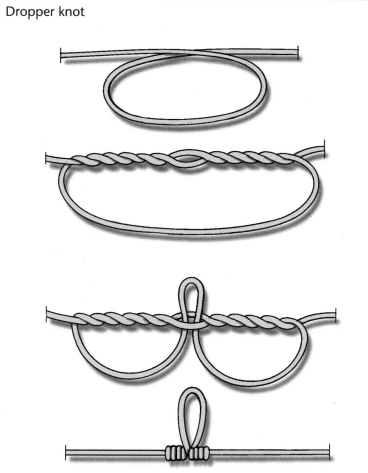

Hooks

The hooks used for artificial lures are not necessarily suitable for fishing with natural bait. This is because fish take artificial and natural baits in different ways. When fishing with lures, the fish are often hooked superficially – in the hard parts of the mouth. Natural bait is frequently swallowed, so that the fish is hooked in the soft parts of the mouth or in the throat. Moreover, the hooks for a natural bait must be adapted to its softness, since too thin a hook can easily come loose from the bait during the cast.

Most artificial lures are provided with treble hooks. Yet some have a single hook, usually due to local circumstances – such as a ban against treble hooks because they risk hooking the fish in the wrong way. Single hooks also occur on certain spoon and pirk lures in coastal fishing for cod and sea trout. The treble hook's size, though, depends on the lure's. A good rule is that the treble hook should be wider than the lure, but this does not apply to some slender lures.

One seldom hooks a predatory fish with all three hook tips. If one does, however, the fish is in great danger of being lost, as it is not hooked equally well – for more force is needed on three hooks than on a single hook. When spinning, therefore, some fishermen replace their treble hooks with single hooks. The latter also give more lifelike movements to the lure, and a single hook is easier to free from water plants and seaweed.

Thick and thin hooks

Treble hooks vary in their material thickness. The stronger ones are used for large predatory fish, while very thin ones are meant for small predators. The shaft may be either short or long, and the hook gap either wide or narrow. Hooks with a long shaft and narrow gap penetrate more easily, whereas a short shaft and wide gap is best for fishing with natural baits.

The smaller the barbs are, the more securely the fish is hooked. In other words, big barbs do not guarantee that the hook will keep its grip. Barbless hooks have increased their appeal to flyfishermen, and will surely also see greater use in spinning. The hook tip should be freshly whetted, and so sharp that it readily catches on a fingernail. Short hook tips are best for fish with hard mouths, and long ones for soft-mouthed fish.

In practice, you must be prepared to replace the treble hooks on certain types of artificial lure. Some of them are specially made for musky, large pike or heavy marine fish, and these lures are provided with extra-strong hooks that do not grip as securely in other, more soft-mouthed predatory fish. For the latter, thinner treble hooks are used instead. Before starting to fish, one should always check the lure's movement to see whether it has changed after the hooks were replaced.

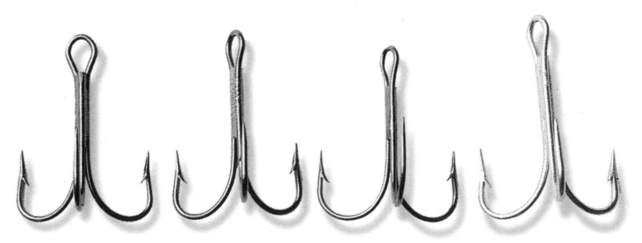

Treble hooks are the most common, and often obvious, choice for spinning. But this group includes many variants to choose between. Here are some examples of different types: thin and thick metal, wide and narrow gap, short and long shaft, as well as a browned and a galvanized treble hook.

Treble hooks

A treble hook's size must be suited to the given fishing situation. It often helps to replace existing hooks with, for example, smaller or thinner hooks. This all-round hook is shown at scale 1:1.

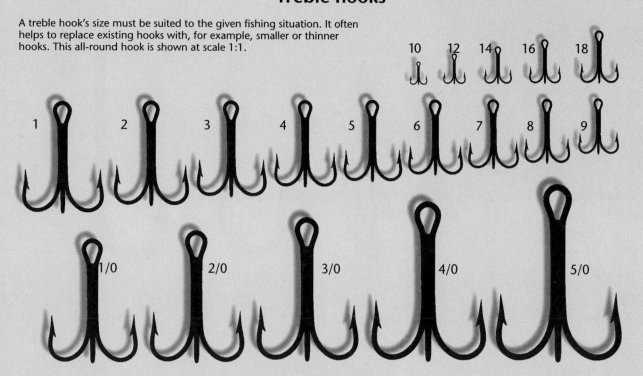

Single hooks

The main uses of single hooks are in spinning and casting with natural bait. They also suit fishing with lures, as in abundant underwater vegetation or in order to give the lure livelier movements. These hooks are shown at scale 1:1.

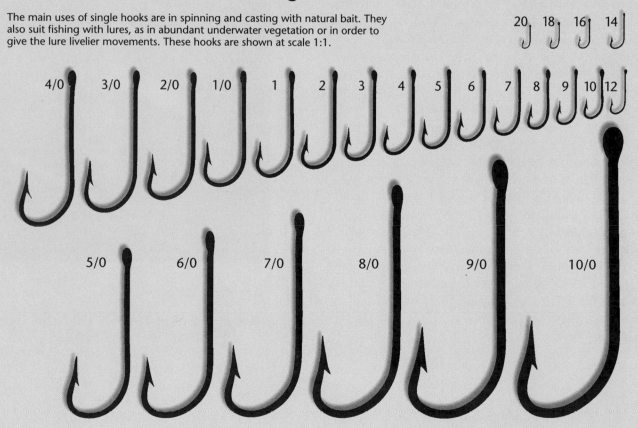

Parts of the hook

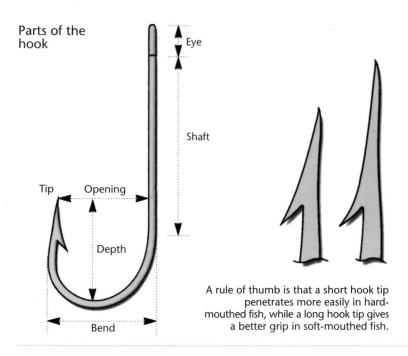

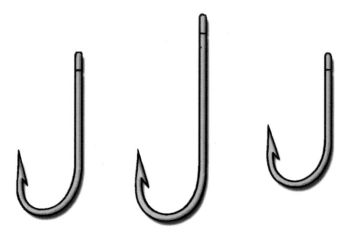

A rule of thumb is that a short hook tip penetrates more easily in hard-mouthed fish, while a long hook tip gives a better grip in soft-mouthed fish.

The same hook can have different shaft lengths. Those shown here have a normal – standard – shaft length (at left), a long shaft (middle) and a short shaft (right).

The hook's finish

Several sorts of finish or surface treatment occur on treble hooks. The most common is browning, a form of lacquering that protects the hook from rust. This hook type is easy to sharpen with a whetstone. Hooks that are nickel-plated, or otherwise galvanized, are more resistant to rust and salt water. Often, too, these are stronger and a little harder to whet, so many people use a diamond or metal file on such hooks. But opinions differ about stainless hooks, since they continue to "fish" for a long time if lost in the water.

Some treble hooks may be coloured. Gilded ones are normally used on small spinners and spoon lures – when fishing for trout, bass or perch – as their gold colour seems to be attractive. Treble hooks can also be decorated with hen-hackle feathers, or another kind of "skirt" or covering, which attracts the attention of predatory fish.

Treble hooks for natural bait have a relatively wide gap and short shaft. Some anglers prefer small treble hooks of strong material with inward-bent tips. Others think the fish are hooked better if the hooks are bent a bit outward, to get a grip more quickly on the predator.

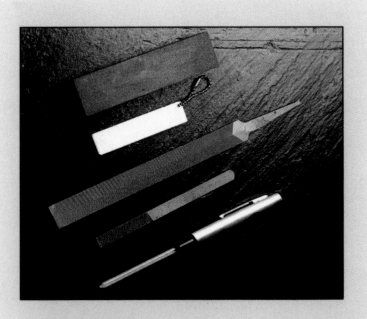

Sharp hooks

Regardless of which type of hook one chooses, the tip has to be sharp and there are two ways of sharpening it: all-round whetting, or whetting at two angles so that a sharp edge is created, which cuts into the fish during a strike or take.

Swivels, snaps, split rings

It is perfectly feasible to avoid using a swivel, whose only real purpose is to prevent the line from twisting. Tests have shown that swivels do not work as intended – but they are fine to tie the line on. There are also several other causes of line twist: when the bait rotates, when the line is wrongly wound up on the reel, and when the drag is so loosely set that the line does not go onto the spool of a spinning reel while being wound in as you play a fish.

Even small swivels are extremely strong and can be used for all kinds of light spinning for little predatory fish. Big fish such as pike and salmon, though, call for stronger and tested swivels. A ball-bearing swivel is reliable and works as it should – if you need a swivel at all. Too large a swivel can easily ruin the well-adjusted movement of small lures. There is no problem with tying the line directly to a split ring, as long as you check that the knot is not at the ends of the threads: otherwise the line may get stuck between the spirals and be cut off.

Rapid changing of baits is done by means of snaps without swivels. These snaps can also be placed in the eye of a wobbler or, for example, in a drag or spinner. But many small lures perform best if the line is tied directly to them – with a locking knot.

Bait snaps come in different types. Familiar brands are Berkley's CrossLok, Sampo and Rosco, quite suited to heavier and more demanding fish. Other, brandless, snaps are best used only for lighter spinning. Swivels with snaps are also common, but even they can often destroy the movement of a small bait.

Influence on the bait's movement

Split rings are either galvanized or browned, such as Mustad's oval rings, or else made of stainless steel. Most split rings are durable and do not have the weaknesses that occur in swivels and snaps. The delicate movements of small wobblers can be maintained by attaching a little split ring, to which the line is then knotted. Some drags, however, are burdened with too heavy split rings: here again, a more lively movement is achieved by replacing these with more modest rings.

Not-a-Knot is a completely different type of bait lock, invented by Berkley and nowadays copied by others – even sportfishermen who can easily bend a piece of stainless

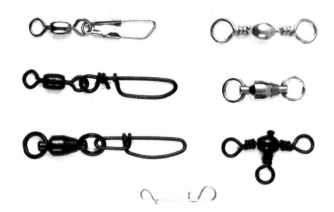

Swivels and snaps. (*Left, from top:*) Standard snap, Rosco snap, Berkley CrossLok. (*Right, from top:*) Standard swivel, Sampo ball-bearing swivel, three-way swivel. (*Bottom:*) A bait lock of the Not-a-knot type.

steel wire. The line is then wound around the lock. Virtually maximum knot strength is attained with this bait lock, which comes in various sizes and can serve for both light and heavy spinning.

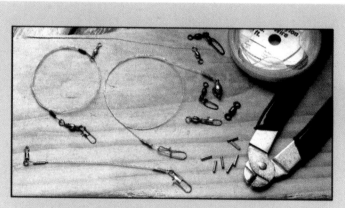

Wire leaders

Leaders are employed in spinning and baitcasting mainly to catch pike, musky and other strongly toothed fish species, where multistrand steel leaders with nylon coating or other surface treatment are necessary. But nylon-coated leaders are soon destroyed by the teeth of fish, so leaders without such coating are best. Using pliers, you can make your own simple leaders from wire, sleeves, swivels and snaps. Excellent and durable leaders can also be knotted from nylon line of 0.60-0.70 millimetres.

Landing equipment

Immediately before the fish is landed, the reel's anti-reverse is activated. The drag is released and the fingers are used as a fine brake on the spool. At this particular stage, many fish have a habit of making their final dive or some other surprising manoeuvre. In some fishing situations, no landing equipment is needed at all, for example if the beach enables you to walk slowly backward and heave up the fish – such as salmon and sea trout – onto land. Moreover, a salmon can be grabbed by the narrow part of its tail, thus nearly paralyzing the fish and keeping it still. Smaller species like perch, if caught from a boat, can be simply lifted aboard with the leader or a slightly bent fishing rod.

Nets

For almost every fish species, a net is splendid. There are nets both for small trout and for big fish of 20-25 kilograms (9-11 lbs). Small, short-shafted nets are chiefly suited to wading in minor waters with lesser fish. Such nets are made of wood or tubes, so that they float. Telescopic and collapsible nets, however, are more common. These do not occupy so much space, but their trapping mechanism is seldom very good. Besides, the net's meshes tend to tangle in its hoop. This type of net comes in nearly all sizes. Large boat-nets are superb when landing pike, salmon and musky, for instance, though they can be difficult to handle if one is alone.

The gaff

Gaffs are most popular among salmon and sea-trout fishermen. In some countries, such as Sweden, they are also used for pike fishing. A gaff is not an especially humane tool to land fish with – at least in hands that lack experience. Yet it is often the only applicable tool under difficult conditions, as in salmon rivers or when you are alone at cramped and inaccessible fishing spots. Gaffs come in both fixed and telescopic forms, but also in pocket versions. The latter, in some cases, can actually land fish of 10-15 kilograms without any problem. Salmon are normally gaffed over the neck, so that one of the large main arteries is punctured at the same time. Pike can be gaffed in this way too, although many of us prefer to set the hook in the lower jaw. It should, however, be noted that gaffs are forbidden in certain places.

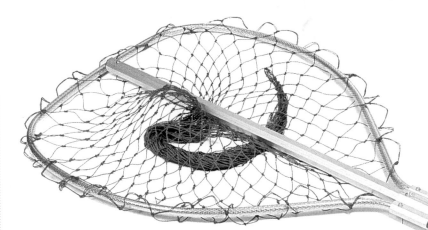

Big nets with an insertable shaft, for landing fish such as large salmon and pike, are relatively heavy and difficult to transport, so they are often called boat-nets. When landing a really large fish, you should – to avoid breaking the net shaft – never lift the fish up, but pull it with the net over the railing.

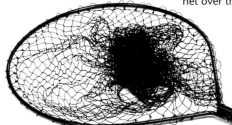

Folding and collapsible nets do not take much space and are easiest to carry, hanging from your belt or fishing-bag. They are used chiefly in boats or when fishing from land, where a long shaft is needed to reach the fish.

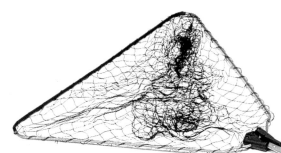

Telescoping nets are helpful when a longer shaft may be required, as on rough shores and where rich vegetation can impede landing fish. Non-collapsible telescoping nets are best suited to fishing from a boat.

Short-shafted nets serve mainly in situations that do not demand such a long reach, as when wading or fishing from a float-ring or small boat and, therefore, near or in the water.

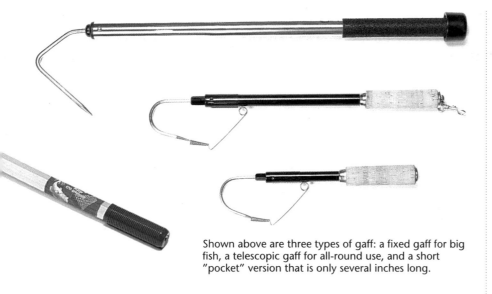

Shown above are three types of gaff: a fixed gaff for big fish, a telescopic gaff for all-round use, and a short "pocket" version that is only several inches long.

The tailer

A tailer – or snare – is a more humane landing tool and has been developed for salmon fishing. It requires some training for proper use, but is excellent for fish weighing 3-4 kilograms upward. It consists of a shaft with a wire device that is cocked into a noose and drawn over the salmon's body, between the tail and dorsal fins. Then the tailer is pulled a little upward and forward, whereupon the mechanism is released and the noose slides down onto the salmon's tail spool, locking it. Sometimes the noose releases too soon and must be cocked again. While a tailer can be used by one individual, two are best – one to guide the fish and one to operate the tailer.

When landing with a net, be sure to place it in the water in good time and then lead the fish into it. Do not poke it toward the fish, which otherwise may panic and fight free.

In the right hands, a gaff is both humane and effective as landing gear. Pike can be landed by setting the hook in the thin skin just behind the lower jawbone, then lifting the fish straight up.

Boat equipment

For many people, equipment and methods are the keys to better fishing and larger catches. In practice, though, knowledge of the bottom conditions, the water depth, and the fish's territory is far more important. In short, fishing from a boat widens your horizons!

A nautical chart that reveals shoals and reefs, deep edges and depths, thus decreasing the time wasted at less productive fishing spots, is quite essential. But charts in combination with an echo-sounder are ideal. During just a few years, small LCD echo-sounders have been adopted by boat fishermen all over the world. They not only show the bottom, its type and conditions, the depths and thermoclines, but also reveal current edges, algae, small fish, schools of fish – and, not least, predatory fish. The cheapest sounders have certain limitations, yet the better models can provide much valuable information.

Lacking access to an echo-sounder, a sounding-line is among the simplest tools for measuring depths and registering types of bottom. It is made from 20 metres of spun line, with a bead marking every metre. Instead of beads, knots can be tied. A lead sinker of 200-250 grams (7-9 ounces) is tied to the line's end. By measuring the depth – possibly with the help of a chart – you can quickly locate many fine fishing spots, such as deep edges and shoals. Thanks to the heavy sinker, you can also feel whether the bottom is of sand, stone, clay or mud.

Once you find a good place – or want to mark an underwater cliff or the top of a shoal that you intend to fish off – a marker or two can be very useful. There are several types of simple, floating H-shaped markers. Some of these should always be carried in the boat.

Small, light boats of rubber (and aluminium) are easy to handle, and thus very useful if you fish in different waters. Their disadvantage is crowding on board when more than two people are fishing. But with well-planned, portable equipment, they become handy "fishing machines" for small waters and can even be transported on a car roof.

Thanks to a boat, entirely new opportunities for fishing open up – especially on wider waters, where the best spots can seldom be reached from land even by a fine caster. As in all fishing, the secret of success is to acquire good knowledge about the fish's holding places and the conditions of depth, bottom and temperature.

Rod holders are not only much-appreciated when trolling, but can also be beneficial in catching baitfish. Alternatively, rods can be parked in them during a coffee pause!

An electric motor is wonderful for travelling noiselessly in confined waters. It is easy to mount and to handle, and has enough steering and driving power for short distances, as well as for correctly placing the boat in relation to fish and fishing spots. As a means of transport, however, it has its drawbacks – particularly in windy weather and for long trips. Electric motors are environment-friendly, and come in both hand- and foot-steered versions, but they do not eliminate the need of a petrol engine for fast, safe transport on open waters.

The figure-of-eight

When spinning and baitcasting from a boat, it often happens that fish – not least the real predators, such as pike and musky – follow the lure without taking it. If they follow up to the boat's edge, you should not lift the lure from the water, but move it around with the rod tip. By doing this in a figure-of-eight next to the boat, you can coax a bite. But first release the reel's spool, as the fish may take violently and break the line or flip itself free from the hooks.

Some details of equipment can be excellent sources of information about the actual conditions, thereby improving the catch.

Left: A GPS navigator that allows simple, rapid storing of a position, for instance that of a shoal or other good fishing spot.

Centre: A depth and temperature gauge, showing the conditions at different levels – whether you fish from land or a boat.

Right: A topo-marker, for tracing out deep edges or shallows. The lead weight pulls the line to the bottom, and the H-shaped marker then floats over the given place.

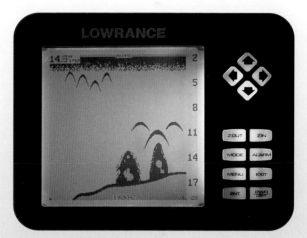

The echo-sounder is among the most important devices for a boat fisherman. Some call it fish-TV, naturally since it gives us the best picture of the underwater surroundings. But experience is needed to interpret the display correctly. Shown on this page are interpretations of three echo-sounder images.

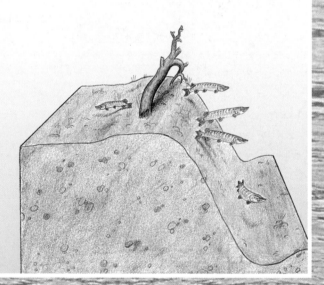

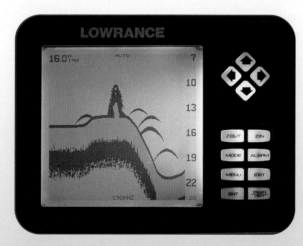

A primary use of the echo-sounder is to see where the fish lie in the water mass. It also provides information about the depth and the structure and type of bottom. This LCD screen shows fish at a clear deep edge. With regard to the type of water, the season, depth, and fish species in the area, these fish have been interpreted as pike, and the object above the deep edge as an old fallen tree stump.

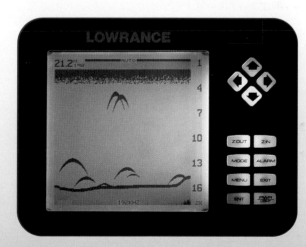

An echo-sounder does not show the bottom section directly below the boat, but those it has just passed. Only the information at far right on the screen is completely updated. One must also keep in mind that the emitted signals spread out sideways down through the water, usually in a cone of 18-22 degrees. As a result, fish near the surface look bigger on the screen than fish in deep water.

Casting Techniques

Being able to cast far and exactly is of enormous value to every enthusiast of spinning and baitcasting. Proper casts that enable the bait to be presented where you want it, together with the correct fishing technique for each occasion, are essential in order to have a good chance of hooking fish. This is true not least under difficult casting conditions and when the fish, for whatever reason, are shy or hard to attract.

■

The ways of casting in practice are about as numerous as the fishermen who perform them. All of us develop our own casting style according to body build and equipment. But the rod's action and length are primary determinants of the casting method. Even competition casters have a special style of casting.

A cast involves a rapid acceleration of the rod – no matter whether you use a rod with one or two handles, and cast underhand or sideways. The technique cannot be taught as a theory: it must be learned by training. A bad cast is usually due to an unrhythmical or jerky casting movement. Thus a comfortable posture before the cast is important, and other circumstances play a role too. The leading types of cast are the overhead (overhand) and the side-cast.

The overhead cast

This precise technique begins by sighting at the target with the rod, from whose tip the bait hangs down 20-50 centimetres. The rod is brought behind your back, normally over the right shoulder, although some prefer to raise it over the left shoulder. Then the rod is accelerated forward over the same shoulder, aiming toward the target. A rod with top action needs slightly greater "sting" in the cast than a rod with whole action, which is little more than pushed upward during the forward movement.

The line is released when the rod is most flexed and points somewhat over the target. If the rod is well enough tensed in the cast, and if you have aimed exactly and let the line go at the right moment, you will hit the target. But if you release the line too soon, the bait will fly up in a high arc and fall in front of you. If released too late, the bait will strike the water before you like a projectile.

The overhead cast is not very easy to learn for a beginner, who often lets the line go too early or late. Neither is this cast safe when fishing from a boat, where you have difficulty in controlling a bait that hangs behind you. Nor does an overhead cast reach as far as a side-cast, which flexes the rod more and makes it travel farther.

An overhead cast can be performed with both a one-handed and a two-handed rod. In the latter case, the greatest transfer of energy is produced with the right hand, which controls the line release at the moment of casting and, simultaneously, pushes the rod forward. The longer and more powerful a rod is, however, the more pressure is given by the left hand, which is stretched backward. In really strong surf-casting rods, the left hand pushes most, while the right hand serves mainly for guidance.

Overhand cast with one-handed rod

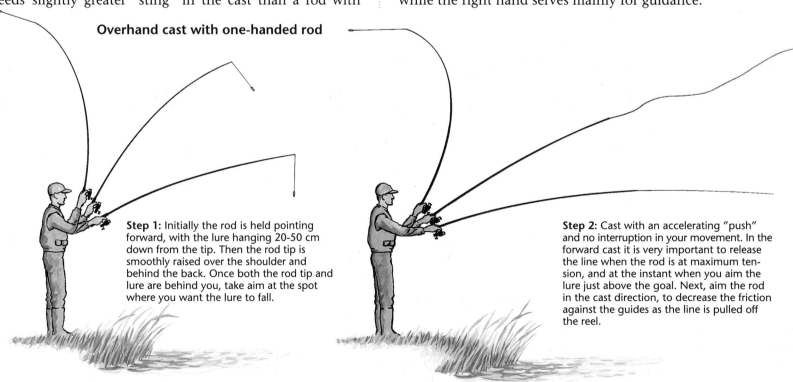

Step 1: Initially the rod is held pointing forward, with the lure hanging 20-50 cm down from the tip. Then the rod tip is smoothly raised over the shoulder and behind the back. Once both the rod tip and lure are behind you, take aim at the spot where you want the lure to fall.

Step 2: Cast with an accelerating "push" and no interruption in your movement. In the forward cast it is very important to release the line when the rod is at maximum tension, and at the instant when you aim the lure just above the goal. Next, aim the rod in the cast direction, to decrease the friction against the guides as the line is pulled off the reel.

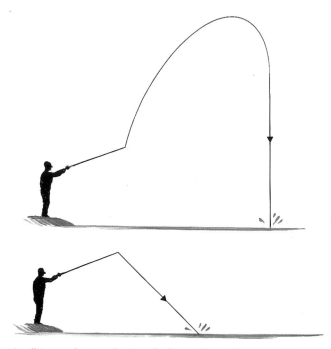

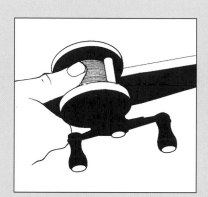

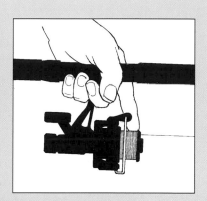

During the actual cast, the line must be able to shoot off the reel as easily and friction-free as possible. On a multiplier reel, the spool is released before starting the cast, and then your thumb is held against the spool until the line is to be let go. On a spinning reel, the bail arm is lowered with one hand while you lock the line with the other hand's forefinger or middle finger.

In all types of cast, releasing the line at the right moment is essential. If you release it too soon during an overhand cast, the lure will fly up in the air and fall a few metres away. If the release is delayed, the lure hits the water before your feet. In both cases the cast will be too short.

Overhand cast with two-handed rod

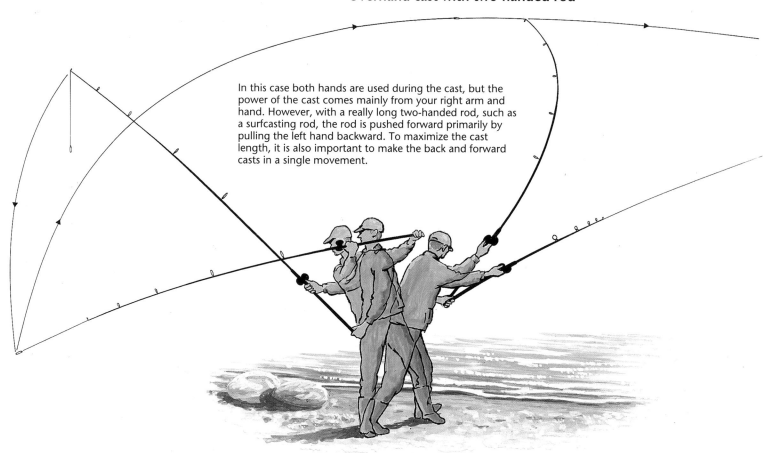

In this case both hands are used during the cast, but the power of the cast comes mainly from your right arm and hand. However, with a really long two-handed rod, such as a surfcasting rod, the rod is pushed forward primarily by pulling the left hand backward. To maximize the cast length, it is also important to make the back and forward casts in a single movement.

The side-cast

A side-cast is begun by bringing the rod horizontally backward. Depending on the rod's action, a forward acceleration is then made – still horizontally – and the rod is brought slightly upward, at which point the line is let out. Too early or late a release will send the bait flying to the right or left, respectively. You cannot aim with a side-cast, so it lacks precision, but it does yield greater force and a longer cast. In addition, the casting arc is longer than in an overhead cast, which means that the rod is flexed better. Even more flexing can be attained in the back cast, which continues in the forward cast, with a continuous movement that feels natural. This cast is excellent in a headwind, and the casting distance may be increased – if the rod's length and action permit – by having a little more line between the rod tip and the bait.

Side-casts are ideal for light spinning, where exact casting is not required. This cast is also often used from a boat, while sitting in the prow or stern to lay the casting arc outside the boat, without any danger for others aboard. Either a one-handed or a two-handed rod can be used to side-cast.

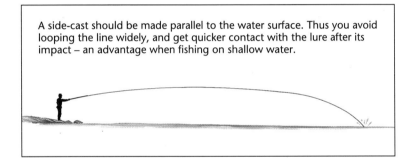

A side-cast should be made parallel to the water surface. Thus you avoid looping the line widely, and get quicker contact with the lure after its impact – an advantage when fishing on shallow water.

Right: In the side-cast, timing is significant. If you let the line go too early, the lure lands too far to the right – and too late means too far to the left. Only when your timing is correct will the lure go straight forward to the goal.

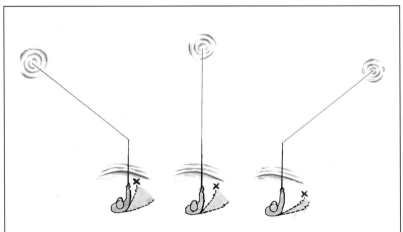

Side-cast

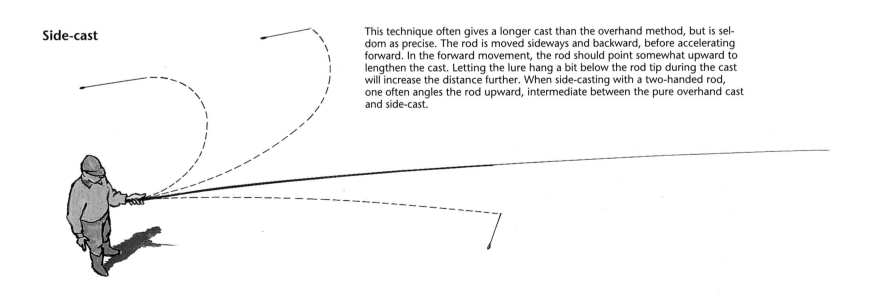

This technique often gives a longer cast than the overhand method, but is seldom as precise. The rod is moved sideways and backward, before accelerating forward. In the forward movement, the rod should point somewhat upward to lengthen the cast. Letting the lure hang a bit below the rod tip during the cast will increase the distance further. When side-casting with a two-handed rod, one often angles the rod upward, intermediate between the pure overhand cast and side-cast.

The pendulum cast

This is a short precision cast, and is best done with a spinning reel. The bait is started in a swinging movement with the free line, whose length may be from 30-50 centimetres to nearly the whole rod length. Once a fair swinging speed is reached, you aim at the target and release the line. Such a cast is used chiefly on confined waters surrounded by brushwood and branches, or wherever a cast of only a few metres is needed.

Right: The pendulum cast is very useful on minor waters with a high demand for precision. This photograph shows a typical situation: in the small deep holes are salmon, which have to get the lure presented properly with short but exact casts. Here the pendulum cast has the best chance of fishing the lure just where the fish are.

Below: Advantages of the pendulum cast become obvious in many circumstances, not least at places with branches and vegetation that render an overhand or side-cast difficult or impossible. The hanging lure is swung a few times back and forth below the rod tip to start the cast.

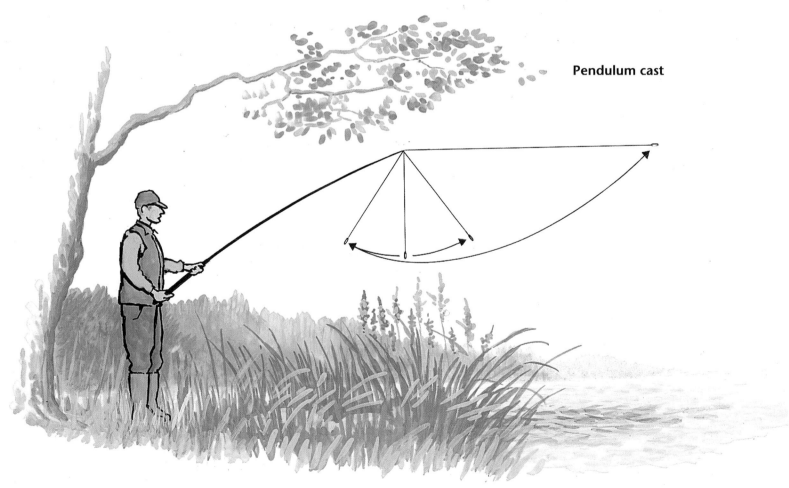

Pendulum cast

The catapult cast

This is another cast for small overgrown bodies of water that prevent casting overhead or sideways. It can only be performed with a spinning reel. You take hold of the hook bend, flex the rod, and release the bait just as the line is let go. However, this cast is not recommended when using graphite or composite rods, which are brittle and may be broken by it – unlike the much tougher fibreglass rods. More-over, you must be careful not to get a hook in your finger, or allow the bait to snap back on your clothes or face.

This cast is ever more rarely used today, but on small overgrown waters it can be the only way of getting the lure out to the fish. Hold the lure between your fingers, stretch the line and rod, then release and let the lure shoot out toward the quarry.

Catapult cast

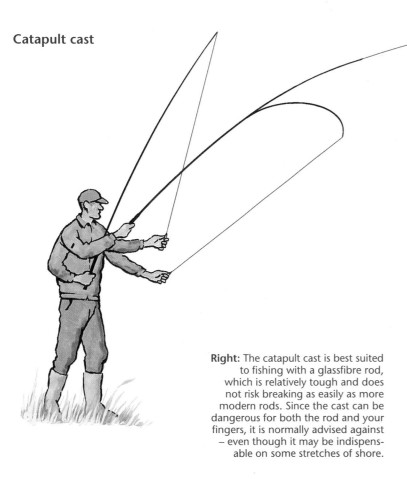

Right: The catapult cast is best suited to fishing with a glassfibre rod, which is relatively tough and does not risk breaking as easily as more modern rods. Since the cast can be dangerous for both the rod and your fingers, it is normally advised against – even though it may be indispensable on some stretches of shore.

Left: Overhanging branches can impede the cast, but an underhand cast can help to cope with the surroundings and reach the fish with the hook.

The underhand cast

Fishing from a boat is the main occasion for underhand casts. They are safe enough, but best done with a relatively short rod and an adequate distance between the deck and the water. The line hanging between the bait and the rod's top guide should be short. Commonly while leaning against the railing, you give the bait a short rotating motion, then move the rod upward and somewhat outward. This cast is easiest with a spinning reel, and calls for a bit more training if done with a multiplier reel.

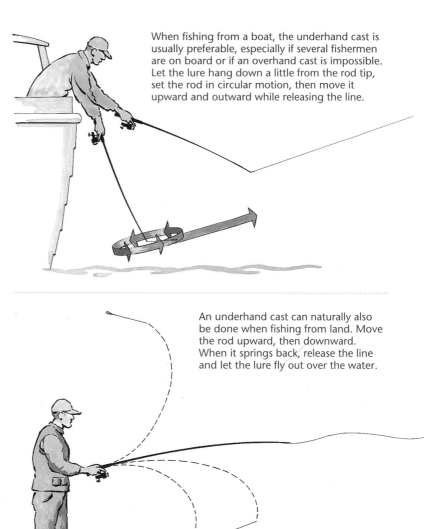

When fishing from a boat, the underhand cast is usually preferable, especially if several fishermen are on board or if an overhand cast is impossible. Let the lure hang down a little from the rod tip, set the rod in circular motion, then move it upward and outward while releasing the line.

An underhand cast can naturally also be done when fishing from land. Move the rod upward, then downward. When it springs back, release the line and let the lure fly out over the water.

Casting in practice

Precise casts are a key feature of spinning and baitcasting. Even if you aim at the target with your rod, this will not guarantee an exact cast. It is often better to aim well above the target and, instead, to brake the line's outrush, slowing down the bait. Thus, you can also place the bait at a suitable distance from the target, so as not to frighten the predatory fish. Then you need only retrieve the bait just over the fish. In effect, the cast's length can be controlled by braking the line. A thumb is laid on the spool when fishing with a baitcasting reel, but with a spinning reel the line is braked by laying an index finger on the spool or its edge.

By braking the cast, one also avoids the line arc that occurs when the bait hits the water. Avoided, too, are snags on the bottom, and one has direct contact with the bait already when starting to retrieve. If the water is shallow, it may be advantageous to begin retrieving even before the

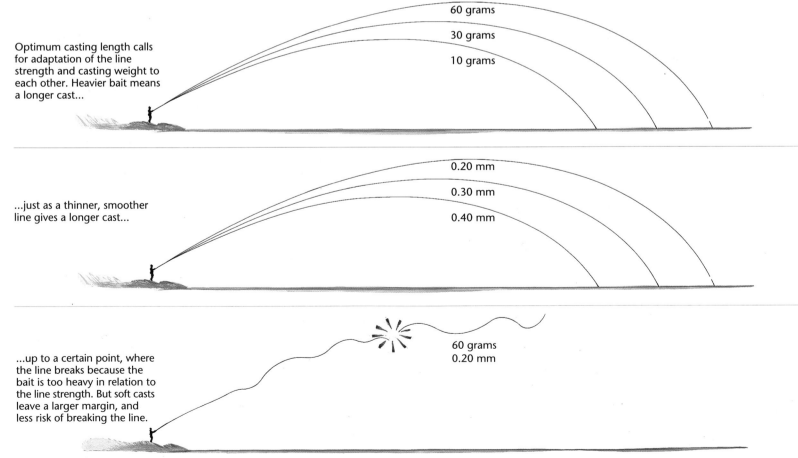

Optimum casting length calls for adaptation of the line strength and casting weight to each other. Heavier bait means a longer cast...

60 grams
30 grams
10 grams

...just as a thinner, smoother line gives a longer cast...

0.20 mm
0.30 mm
0.40 mm

...up to a certain point, where the line breaks because the bait is too heavy in relation to the line strength. But soft casts leave a larger margin, and less risk of breaking the line.

60 grams
0.20 mm

Poor line control during the cast may result in awful line tangles, especially on a multiplier reel. Tangles can take a long time to fix, and risk losing any fish that bite at the same time.

A good cast should be made with an even, connected movement. Here we see how the rod is energized during the backward cast – to be discharged in the forward sweep and give the lure a kinetic energy that is needed to shoot it across the water.

bait has reached the surface. In gusty weather, for example when a side-wind is blowing, one should cast low and be able to brake the line before the bait hits the water, so as to straighten out the large line arc.

Smooth casting movements

Exact casts are promoted by adapting the hangdown – the line length between the top guide and the bait – to the rod's action. If precision is desired, a fairly short piece of line should be used off the rod top. But the length must be increased if you cast with rods having fast action – that is, top action. Very fast rods, or those with a pronounced top action, can require this length to be almost as great as the distance from the top guide to the reel. With whole action, the hangdown should be short.

When casting, a uniform "gliding" motion is necessary to prevent an artificial lure from hovering in the forward cast, or starting to rotate. The lure should also hang still, with no rotation, as you begin a cast – otherwise it will easily go astray.

Precise casting is difficult in windy weather. Spinners tend to fly crosswise through the air, which shortens the cast – so they are best cast in a tailwind. Spoons and pirks, however, frequently cast far and exactly, thanks to their

compact form and weight. Thin spoons still have a habit of straying in the wind, but this can be corrected with a whole-action rod and a shorter hangdown.

Wobblers are notably hard to cast with, as they easily go crosswise in the air, and because their hooks often get caught in the main line. The reason is that a wobbler does not have its weight placed at the rear, like a pirk or spoon. Wobblers are best fished with a multiplier reel, since the spool's resistance guides them straight through the air during the cast. If they are cast with a spinning reel, you should put a light pressure on the line with your forefinger. This shortens the cast somewhat, but the wobbler flies straight and sure.

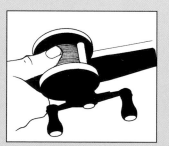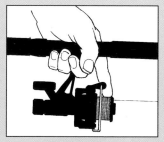

It is important to maintain good control of the line when casting out. This can prevent not only line tangles, but also an excessively long cast and a hard impact on the water. On a multiplier reel, control the line by pressing your thumb lightly against the rotating spool. On a spinning reel, keep your forefinger pressed lightly against the spool while casting.

Spinning technique

Correct presentation of baits is not only a question of long and exact casting, or of covering a body of water with a series of casts. To a great extent, it also involves fishing where the predatory fish are located, and retrieving the bait precisely enough in relation to the fish that they can see and take it. In most clear and shallow waters, presenting an artificial lure exactly is no problem: the challenge is to be quick at finding the right technique for retrieval, and the type of lure that the predators will take.

Except for predators that hunt pelagically – wandering in free water masses, alone or together, possibly in schools or groups – the majority of predatory fish hold at the bottom. In murky or deep water, we have to make the lure fish near the bottom throughout the length of the cast, and without snagging. A snag can result in lost lures, plants on the hook, frayed line, and bent or broken hooks, which lose time and efficiency in fishing.

The countdown method

Therefore, already in the introductory stage of spinning, one should learn the countdown method. This is used more or less consciously by all fishermen after a short period on the water, and when fishing with sinking lures such as spoons, pirks, jigs and sinking wobblers. It gives a built-in guarantee of fishing at the bottom, whether for salmon in a river, cod from a cliff or coast, pike in a lake, or pikeperch (zander, walleye) and perch on a lake's slopes and rocks.

Once their lures are cast out and begin to sink, many people are tempted to retrieve – without knowing if the lure is three metres above the bottom, or in the surface eight metres up, or far away from the fish. But the retrieval should start only when the lure reaches the bottom. So the depth must be estimated beforehand.

After the cast, the lure has to sink to the bottom. When it gets there, the line goes slack. This is the signal to start retrieving, with an adjustment to avoid bottom snags. Initially, make a silent count from the lure's impact on the water until the line slackens: 101...102... until, say, 107, each figure taking about a second. Then you retrieve. Next, count only to 106 and retrieve. The lure will fish just above the bottom with no risk of snagging.

Proceed to fish the place with, for example, a series of casts in a fan pattern, counting to 106 at each cast, until you can easily tell how long it takes for the lure to sink near the bottom. After a number of casts, you will have the right sense of timing and make good use of every cast at the same place – that is, with a given lure. If you choose a new lure there, its own sinking time must be found out by counting again.

The countdown method is an indirect means of measuring depth. It can thus also be used to search different fishing depths, such as 2-3 metres down or even deeper, since certain species – for example musky, bass and perch – often linger in free water.

This method is very helpful for all inexperienced beginners at spinning, and experienced practitioners always use it automatically. They let the lure sink to the bottom, and gauge the depth by counting mentally. Cast, retrieve – and get a bite!

Above: The fish normally stay at the bottom, so the lure must be presented there. Experienced sportfishermen often have an intuitive feeling for when the lure is fishing at the right depth – notably under difficult conditions, as in strongly flowing water.

Below: In the countdown method, after the first cast, count for example 101...102...103...104...105...106 until the lure has reached the bottom and the line slackens. After the next cast, count only to 105 and then wind in. Thus the retrieval begins just before the lure reaches the bottom.

Retrieval technique

Make it a rule to test the lure's movements before fishing, with a short cast followed by retrieval, so that you get an idea of the spinning speed which allows the lure to work best.

During retrieval, the lure will slowly rise ever farther from the bottom, unless you make regular spin-stops or brief pauses to let it sink again – down to, or preferably just above, the bottom. A spin-stop is not only a check on whether the lure fishes at the bottom, but can also release a predatory fish's striking instinct, because many species pursue artificial baits without taking them. A preyfish, if pursued, will swim away fast in a spasmodic manner. Such movement is imitated by the spin-stop. Hence, a rather jerky retrieval combined with spin-stops is a quite effective method.

In flowing water, a spin-stop often enables the lure to stand still amid the current. Good bottom contact is obtained by either lowering the rod, taking a step forward, or releasing a little line.

The use of many spin-stops is an obvious introduction to the "step-ladder method". This kind of retrieval combines good bottom contact with a lively, precise presentation of the lure. Spin-stops alternate with careful pulls of the rod, and the lure does not simply jerk over the bottom, but is retrieved at a varying tempo – slowly, then rapidly, and so on.

Longer spin-stops are needed in deep water than in shallows. Large baits also require longer spin-stops than do small ones. The combination of numerous spin-stops and short casts is a fine approach, although fewer and longer spin-stops are essential when casting far. A vital and attractive retrieval calls for more effort than winding the reel!

Together with good bottom contact, a varied retrieval works excellently on many different species of predatory fish: perch, pikeperch, pike, trout, salmon, garfish, cod and others. However, some species frequently demand a more even and speedy pace of retrieval with only occasional spin-stops – for instance, sea trout in marine waters.

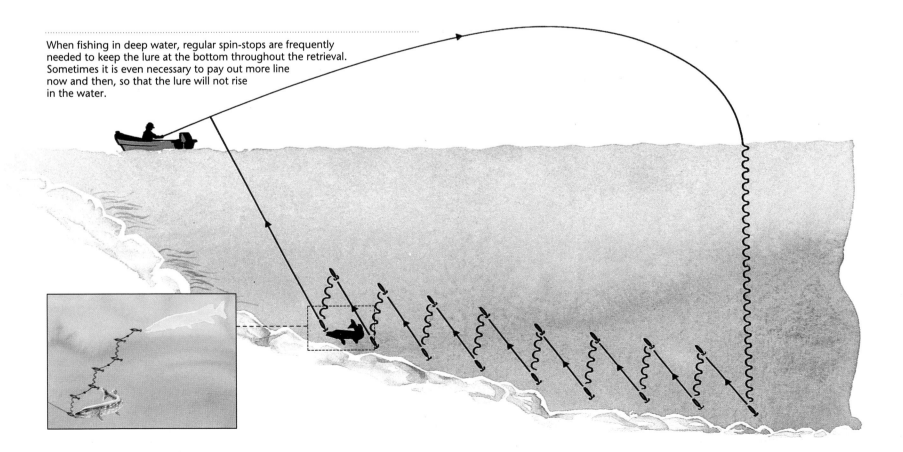

When fishing in deep water, regular spin-stops are frequently needed to keep the lure at the bottom throughout the retrieval. Sometimes it is even necessary to pay out more line now and then, so that the lure will not rise in the water.

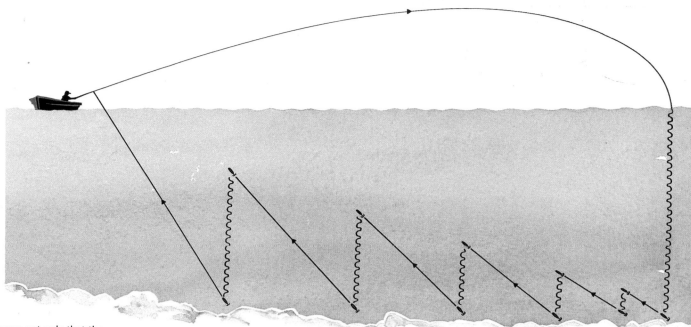

Above: The stepladder method ensures not only that the lure is at the right depth, but also that it is retrieved at a varying, irregular tempo. By changing the speed of your retrieval, the lure presentation becomes livelier and thus more attractive.

Whenever you see a predatory fish following the lure, or register cautious takes, you can get it to bite by speeding up the retrieval and making a short spin-stop, with full control over the lure. This is the normal behaviour of preyfish: they flee in terror, but stop when tired or disoriented in relation to the predator, or forced to find a hideout for protection. With a varied retrieval throughout the range of the cast, you increase the likelihood of a solid take.

Above: Fishing in different water levels is also benefited by the stepladder method. To work systematically through the levels, though, it is well worth trying the countdown method.

Right: When fishing in deep water for pelagic hunters – such as mackerel and pollack – a pirk is allowed to sink while you repeatedly raise and lower the rod tip. When the lure reaches the bottom, you wind in line and once again let the lure "stepladder-fish" through all the water layers.

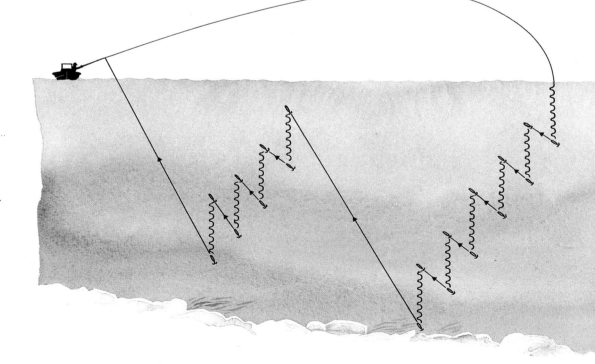

Searching a fishing area

There are no rules for how to find fish at a specific place – only guidelines. Casting in a fan pattern is a classic procedure, whether you cover 180 degrees from land, or 360 degrees from an anchored boat. Next you move to a new position, or anchor at another spot. A fairly uniform area can be fished from land by making a cast every 3-10 steps, depending on how still or clear the water is, and on how many holding places the area is suspected to contain. An area with many holding places, or obstacles such as stones, roots and the like, can be searched effectively by making series of parallel casts, first in one direction and then in the opposite.

When fishing from a drifting boat, its movement spaces out the parallel casts. One should always cast in the direction of drift – never onto spots the boat has already drifted over, where its shadow and presence may frighten the fish. During the search, attention must also be paid to the current, waves, sunshine and light, so that the fishing is adapted to these factors.

Searching in flowing waters

The right places are found with two techniques in flowing waters: by fishing either downstream and across the current, or else upstream.

Downstream fishing is done by casting obliquely down towards the opposite bank. The lure swings with the current toward your own bank, and is then retrieved. You can also begin retrieving early in the swinging phase, making the lure go against the current. Once a place has been searched, you go a few steps downstream and look for new places.

Cross-stream fishing is used in fast-flowing, deep waterways. A cast is laid over the current, or to some degree upstream, and the lure is given time to sink to the bottom. When the line has straightened out obliquely downstream, the lure is at the bottom, and then swings toward your own bank – or is retrieved as described above.

Upstream fishing is more demanding, but more effective as well. You can surprise the fish because they do not see you. The lure comes from an angle that is natural for predatory fish, and somewhat faster than the current, so its movement is lively and attractive. Often, too, the lure follows the current eddies and looks irresistibly natural.

Fishing in still waters from land

Above: By casting in a fan-shaped pattern, you can search the water from a promontory or other fixed position. To avoid scaring the fish, begin with a series of short casts – or initially cast from a place somewhat up on land. Then increase the casting length to reach as much of the water as possible.

Below: On a long and uniform shore, the water is fished with a series of parallel casts. Move along the shore and make one or two casts at intervals of a few metres.

Fishing in flowing waters

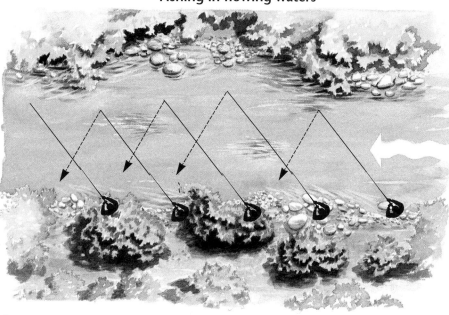

Above: Downstream fishing involves casting the lure obliquely downstream, and quickly retrieving any loose line. As soon as the lure begins to swing toward your own shore, begin retrieving so that the lure works against the current, until the place is fished out. Then walk a few steps downstream and make a new cast.

Below: Upstream fishing has the advantage that fish are easier to fool, as the fisherman is harder to notice. Moreover, the lure can be presented in a more lively and natural manner.

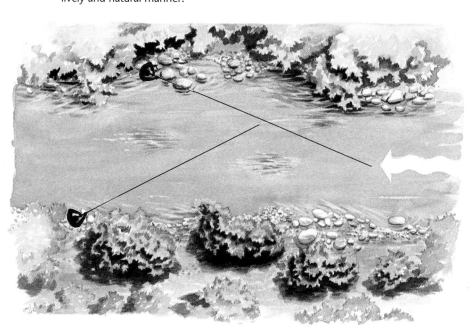

Fishing from a boat

Above: On open water during calm days in a boat, you can make a series of casts in a full circle. But often the boat drifts with the wind, making it better to fish the semicircle in the wind direction. Thus you will also keep meeting "new" fish that come within casting distance.

Below: When fishing from a drifting boat along a shore, the cast is parallel due to the boat's drift. Here too, remember to cast in the direction of drift – and ideally against the sun – so that the fish are not frightened by the boat and by possible shadows.

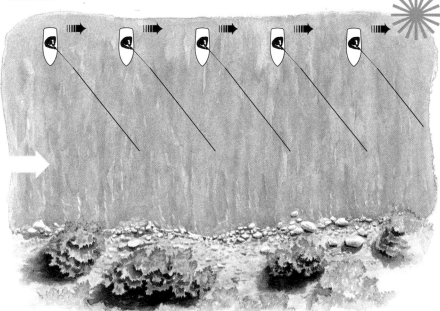

Artificial Lures

There is an almost unlimited range of artificial lures, mostly designed for particular fish species or fishing conditions. One must therefore know how different lures function and how they are to be used. Having learned about diverse types of lure, it can be enough to carry a dozen "killers" in the lure-box. Correct bait on the line will increase the chances of a catch, but the path to adeptness at spinning and baitcasting may be long and winding: its name is experience.

■

A rtificial lures can be divided into spoons, pirks, spinners, wobblers, jigs, and combinations of these, as well as plastic animals and flies. Each group includes thousands of variants. The types also differ in form, size, colour, weight and material. Spoons, pirks, spinners, and most jigs are sinking lures, but there are both sinking wobblers and floating ones. Within each group of lures, however, we can recognize the following main characteristics.

Spoons

Nearly all forms are found among spoons, but the majority have a real spoon- or S-shape. Their name is due to the fact that many of the first classic examples were spoon-like. Initially they were even fashioned from spoons – and few sportfishermen have avoided making a spoon out of just that utensil.

Both the spoon- and the S-shape hold these lures on course in the water. They should neither stray out to the sides, nor glide up to the surface when being retrieved. Their movement, besides the light, is also what enables the lures to send out reflections. Yet in principle only two types of spoon exist: broad, round and oval spoons – such as standard pike spoons – and long, thin spoons.

Broad spoons

A broad spoon moves slowly when it is retrieved at a normal rate. If the retrieval speed increases, the spoon begins to rotate and fishes ineffectively – a behaviour which is ever less pronounced for more slender spoons. The round and oval spoons imitate small fish, such as roach and crucian carp, while elongated spoons are imitations of smelt, bleak, sand lance, and small herring.

Generally, broad spoons are employed in still waters – for pike, perch and pikeperch – and have a calmly wobbling movement. Slender, elongated spoons are used in flowing waters and for coastal fishing. These do not wobble as much, and can be retrieved at high speed, or can stand quite motionless in the current and work. There are also spoons of thick sheet metal, which gives a longer cast, or of thin sheet that is more suitable for trolling.

Broad spoons.
(*From top, left to right:*)
Hammer, Ruggen, Pikko and Storauren, Crocodile Stubby, Atom, Moss Boss, Lillauren, Utö and Jurmo.

Weedguarded spoons. (*From top:*) Hobo, Atom Giller, Favorit Vass.

Weedless spoons

These spoons, usually of the broad type, are equipped with thin, stiff, single-strand wire that protects the hook. It is springy and thus exposes the hook to the fish when they bite. The hook shield prevents the hook from catching on weeds or other plants. Such spoons, therefore, are used only in areas with plenty of vegetation.

Their hooking abilities are, however, not the best, and this type of spoon involves a greater risk of losing the fish than do spoons without weedguards. Moreover, the hook is often fixed solidly to the spoon and cannot be replaced. Weedless spoons are designed mainly for pike fishing, and are to be retrieved in the same way as a broad spoon.

Broad spoons have a disadvantage: they do not cast as well as elongated ones. In addition, a cast against the wind is often ruined because the spoon tends to rotate at the beginning of the cast, although some spoons are less sensitive to wind than others. Further, a broad spoon takes a good time to sink to the bottom, though it does sink at a uniform speed. Hence, broad spoons are best in shallow waters of, say, 1-3 metres (3-10 ft).

Certain large spoons in the class of 18-35 grams (1/2-1 ounce) are provided with two or three treble hooks, on the theory that they hook the fish better since it bites the lure crosswise. Practice has shown, however, that the line often hangs itself in the first hook or the middle hook, and that the fish is hooked better with only one treble hook.

Broad, round and oval spoons perform best, as a rule, at depths of 1-1.5 metres if they weigh 5-10 grams, at 1.5-2.5 metres if 10-20 grams, and at 2.5-5 metres if 20-35 grams. Only in clear water with vigorously hunting fish can you expect to succeed with spoons when the depth exceeds 5 metres.

Fishing with broad spoons

A broad spoon is ideal for any kind of spinning in lakes and in the calmer parts of waterways – for perch, pike, musky and pikeperch. Use the countdown method, and let the spoon sink almost to the bottom before starting to retrieve. The spinning speed is correct when you notice the lure's movements in the rod tip. Vary the speed with spin-stops and a slow or rapid retrieval. Bear in mind that a predatory fish normally takes the lure during a spin-stop, and often when the line is slack.

As long as the spoon moves in deep water, it is retrieved with the rod tip lowered. When it enters shallow water, the rod tip should be lifted. Thus you keep closer contact with the spoon and can control its deep movements better. Some spoons have a built-in pattern of uneven movement: during retrieval, they lurch through the water but stray to one side at regular intervals. This unpredictable gait can make the spoon a true "killer".

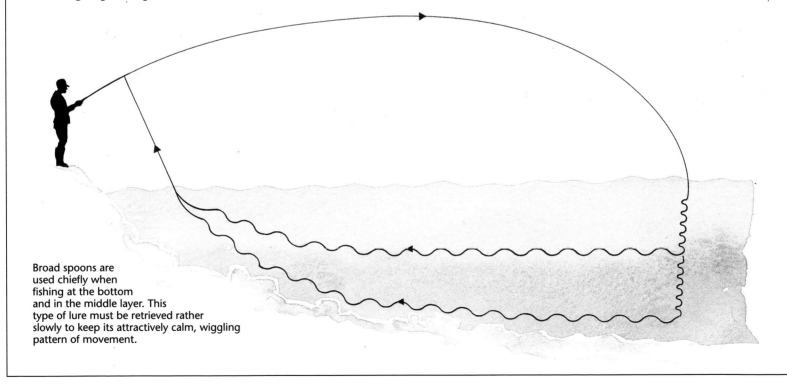

Broad spoons are used chiefly when fishing at the bottom and in the middle layer. This type of lure must be retrieved rather slowly to keep its attractively calm, wiggling pattern of movement.

Elongated spoons

Slender, thin and long spoons, with or without an S-bend, are imitations of fast-swimming fish. They are retrieved more rapidly than oval and round spoons, since a quick retrieval is just what they are intended for. Their primary use is in flowing waters, where retrieval is relatively slow and the current makes the spoon look alive. They are also used in coastal fishing for marine fish such as sea trout, cod and mackerel. The marine species that take elongated spoons are often fast swimmers with a slender body form.

This type of spoon was originally moulded in lead. But lead is a soft material, so the finish is not very durable on these spoons, or on pirks, whose painting and lacquer flake off when they hit rocks. Some lead-moulded pirks do have hard lacquer, yet it easily cracks if they hit rocks or snag on the bottom.

The drawback of lead-moulded pirks is that they are compact and heavy in comparison with their size. They cast well, but must be retrieved rapidly to avoid settling firmly on the bottom. The lead-moulded spoons and pirks that are produced today, though, have a larger bearing surface and less elongation than previously. For environmental reasons, lead-moulded lures will probably disappear from the market in time.

During recent decades, such small lead-moulded spoons and pirks have been gradually replaced by spoons made of iron or brass sheet. Some of these are straight and have a linear gait in the water. Others have a slight S-bend and are retrieved more slowly. This type of spoon combines the best properties of the earlier lead-moulded pirks with a more lively, attractive movement. Its elongated form also allows a fine cast. The spoon's rear part is often a little wider or heavier than its front part.

Elongated spoons do not twist the line as readily as the oval and round spoons. Their hooking abilities are excellent, too. Spoons of 5-15 grams are used at depths of 1-1.5 metres, 10-20 grams at 1.5-3 metres, and 20-35 grams at 3-5 metres.

Slender spoons. (*From top, left to right:*) Tobis, Hansen Fight, Flipper, Möre-silda, Crocodile, Sölvpilen, Toby, Trumf.

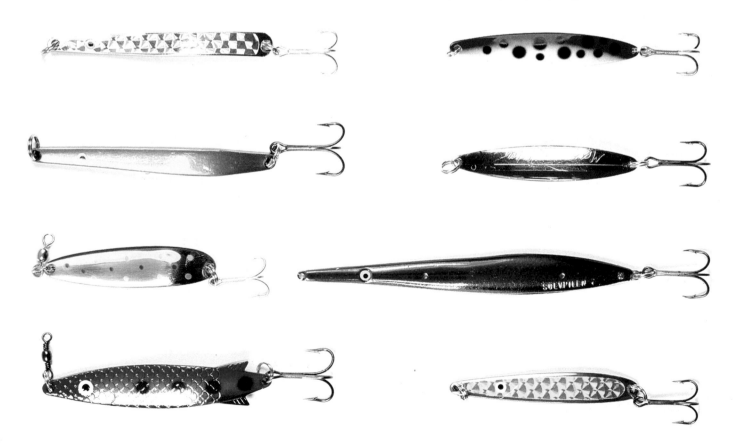

Fishing with elongated spoons

Elongated spoons are meant to catch fast-swimming fish in waters with wide surfaces – such as sea trout, cod, garfish and mackerel along coasts, or trout in lakes. Just as with broad spoons, the countdown method is employed when retrieving, if the predatory fish are holding on the bottom. Usually, however, they circulate in the middle layer or at the surface.

Its design makes this type of spoon best for rapid retrieval, when it imitates species like smelt, sand lance, and bleak that swim intermittently through the water. Repeated spin-stops and a varied speed of retrieval are also important when fishing with such lures. During spin-stops, a well-balanced spoon will sink horizontally and rotate around its own axle.

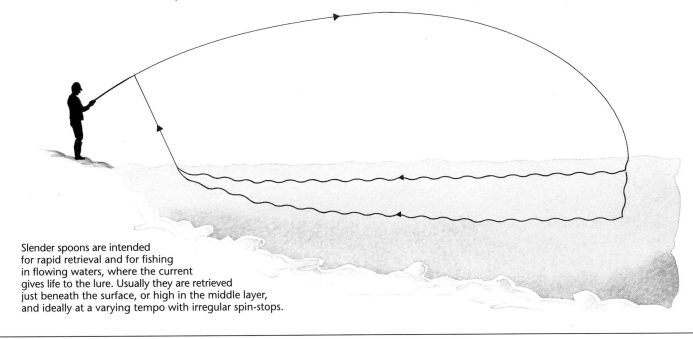

Slender spoons are intended for rapid retrieval and for fishing in flowing waters, where the current gives life to the lure. Usually they are retrieved just beneath the surface, or high in the middle layer, and ideally at a varying tempo with irregular spin-stops.

Pirks

A pirk (alternatively called a pilk, metal casting jig, diamond jig, or jigging spoon) may weigh from 40-50 up to 500 grams, when used in marine fishing for cod, pollack, cusk, mackerel and other predators. Pirks were originally a Scandinavian lure, employed by professional fishermen to catch cod. This group is very big, including hundreds of types and sizes, but generally they can be divided into light pirks for casting in shallow water (5-20 metres) and heavy pirks for casting in deeper water.

Some pirks are still made of lead and, being heavy and compact, serve very well in deep water, where the current is strong and the boat drifts fast. Other pirks, with a larger surface, are manufactured of brass or iron. These are livelier, for calm and less demanding conditions such as still or shallow water. The line thickness also influences the choice of pirk. So-called braided lines, based on spectra or kevlar, with a small diameter relative to their strength, enable one to use a lighter pirk.

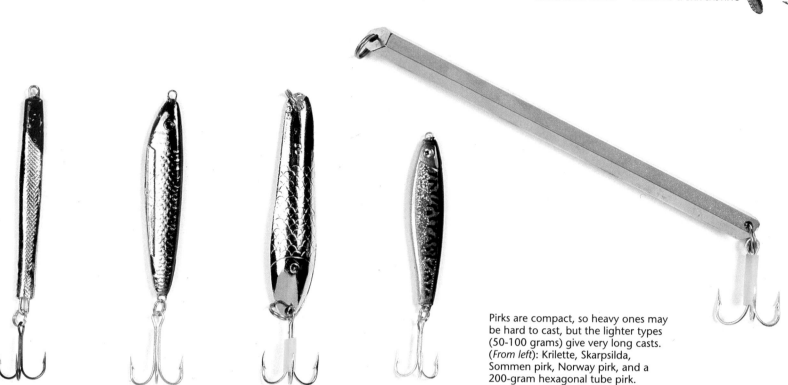

Pirks are compact, so heavy ones may be hard to cast, but the lighter types (50-100 grams) give very long casts. (*From left*): Krilette, Skarpsilda, Sommen pirk, Norway pirk, and a 200-gram hexagonal tube pirk.

Fishing with pirks

The lighter pirks are intended for casting on deeper water, often from a boat. They are retrieved in a jerky, varied manner – either on the bottom, where cod and cusk are found, or in the middle layer with its pollack and mackerel. During retrieval, one must also take account of the depth and the boat's drift, normally casting in the direction of drift.

Heavy pirks come into play for pirk fishing, or vertical fishing. Here the pirk is sunk to the bottom, and then the reel is coupled in. The rod's up-and-down movements give vitality to the otherwise compact pirk. In deep water and strong currents, pirk fishing requires you to have constant contact with the bottom, so that the pirk does not lift off it.

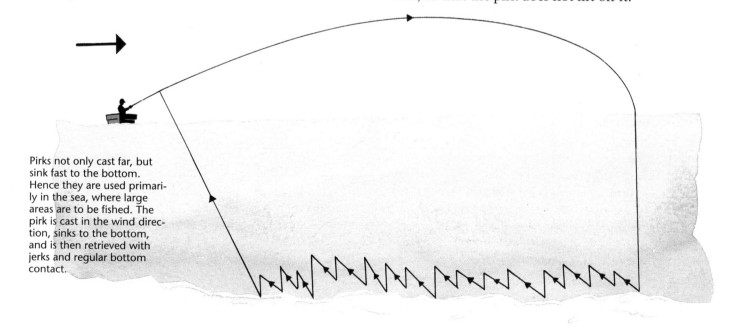

Pirks not only cast far, but sink fast to the bottom. Hence they are used primarily in the sea, where large areas are to be fished. The pirk is cast in the wind direction, sinks to the bottom, and is then retrieved with jerks and regular bottom contact.

Spinners

A spinner has the simple structure of a spoon that rotates around a wire or body, and moves straight in the water. It is actually amazing that so many predatory fish are tempted by spinners, which do not resemble any fish – as spoons and wobblers do. The spinner's body stays still while the spoon turns and gives it life. Moreover, the spinner continually sends out reflections, and the vibrations from the spoon attract fish. Numerous fish species that never take spoons or wobblers can be drawn to a spinner, such as various whitefish species.

Standard spinners

A standard spinner is made from a stiff, single-strand wire with a loop at each end, one for the hook and one to tie the line on. All spinners have a body, except some that are intended for very shallow water. In front of the body are a bead and a bend in which the spoon is mounted. The bead, made of plastic of metal, provides a light gait and minimizes friction between the body and the rotating spoon. Another design is employed by American spinners from Martin: the through-going wire passes through the spoon as well. There are also a few spinners with two rotating spoons.

It is essentially the spinner body's size and weight that, together with the spoon's form, determine which waters and depths the spinner is suitable for. A heavy body is able to spin in deep water and strong currents. A light body, for example on the classic Mepps spinner, gives a superficial gait that is most effective in shallow and slow waters.

The spoon's construction reveals how the spinner moves in the water. A short, broad spoon rotates slowly, so the spinner travels high, which is good for fishing in shallows. Such a spoon rotates more vertically in relation to the body, too. If you want to fish deeper with this type of spinner, it cannot be done with a bigger and heavier spinner of the same type, since the spoon creates a correspondingly greater lifting force and keeps the spinner at the same depth. Instead, you must choose a spinner with a relatively heavier body, or with a thinner and longer spoon, which will not only go deeper but can be retrieved faster.

A spinner works superbly on most predatory fish, but is

Standard spinners.
(*From above, left to right*): Lindy Big Fish, Musky Killer, Tee Spoon, Clearwater Flash, Killer Spinner, Bang Tail, Reflex, Mepps Aglia, Jig Flax, Tiger Tail, Panter, Droppen, Panther, Black Fury.

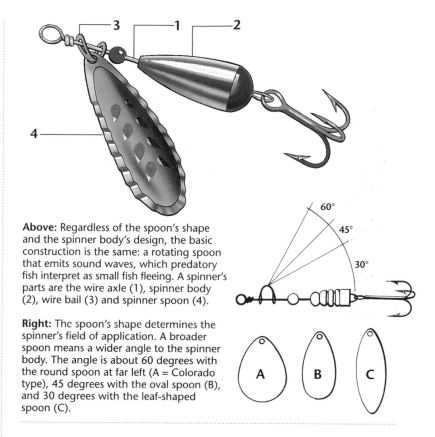

Above: Regardless of the spoon's shape and the spinner body's design, the basic construction is the same: a rotating spoon that emits sound waves, which predatory fish interpret as small fish fleeing. A spinner's parts are the wire axle (1), spinner body (2), wire bail (3) and spinner spoon (4).

Right: The spoon's shape determines the spinner's field of application. A broader spoon means a wider angle to the spinner body. The angle is about 60 degrees with the round spoon at far left (A = Colorado type), 45 degrees with the oval spoon (B), and 30 degrees with the leaf-shaped spoon (C).

less effective in cold water. For it must go at a certain speed if the spoon is to rotate, and thus often runs too high for fish in cold water.

Some spinners have a tendency to twist the line, because the rotating spoon pulls the body around with it. The line will then be destroyed, and may even wrap about the top guide during the cast – which will make you poorer by one spinner. However, on certain spinners, the through-going wire has a little bend in front, to prevent twisting. Classic spinners such as Mepps, Rooster, Vibrax, and Martin do not twist line, but many imitations are prone to cause a tangle.

A further variation is seen in spinners with a feather hackle around the treble hook. Large "bucktail" spinners, with a dense skirt of deer hair there, are used for musky fishing. Alternatively, an octopus skirt on the treble hook can obtain the same effect. This yields a long, billowy, enticing spinner with a total length of about 20 centimetres (8 inches). Standard spinners are meant for fishing in shallow or medium-depth waters, down to 3 metres.

Fishing with standard spinners

The majority of standard spinners are relatively light lures that sink slowly and do not cast very far. If you start the retrieval with a jerk on the rod tip, you can be sure that the spinner rotates, but you often feel it through the weight or resistance on the rod tip.

A standard spinner is fine for flowing waters, where it can even be made to stay at the same spot in the current, and to rotate and work at different tempos. If the current is too strong, though, the spinner will lift toward the surface. These spinners are most attractive if you avoid spin-stops but vary the retrieval speed and keep the spoon rotating.

Again, the spinner is excellent for retrieving near the bottom – in both still and flowing waters. But as soon as its resistance to the rod tip disappears, the spoon's rotation will have collapsed. By lifting the rod tip or retrieving a little faster, you can restart the rotation. Thus, the spinner's resistance on the rod allows you to check that it is working properly, and make it go just as slowly or as near the bottom as you want.

In flowing water, a spinner is usually considered best for fishing downstream. However, spinning upstream is a quite effective method, as the spinner approaches the fish like a natural prey. The fish can also see a spinner at a great distance. On the other hand, it is much harder to control the retrieval. You must retrieve the spinner a little faster than the current – barely enough to keep it rotating.

Heavy spinners with a compact body are ideal in deeper water, strong current, and upstream fishing. They need a relatively high initial speed and high retrieval tempo in order to rotate, while a low speed and tempo are sufficient for a light spinner.

There is a general belief that spinners are not very suitable in wide waters and windy weather. Yet the fact is that a spinner has a great advantage over spoons and wobblers: when it hits the water, it begins to rotate instantly. As a result, you avoid a line arc and can quickly reel in any loose line. Spoons and wobblers in a side-wind tend to create a large arc of line, as well as to drag in the surface and begin working only when the line is taut.

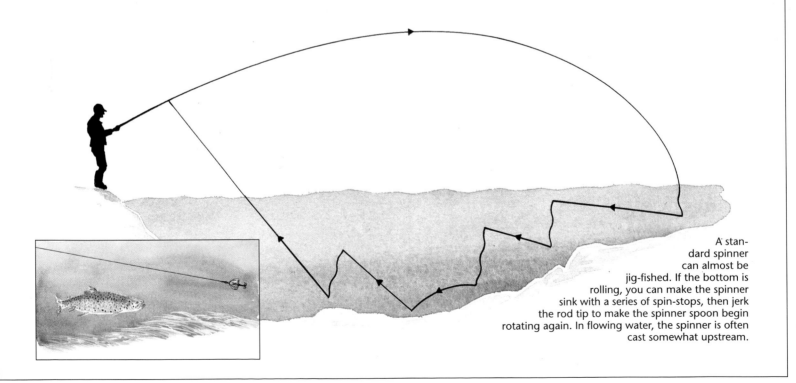

A standard spinner can almost be jig-fished. If the bottom is rolling, you can make the spinner sink with a series of spin-stops, then jerk the rod tip to make the spinner spoon begin rotating again. In flowing water, the spinner is often cast somewhat upstream.

Weight-forward (WF) spinners

This type of spinner, also called lead-headed, is perfect for fishing at greater depths, from about 4 to 7-8 metres, and moreover in a strong current. Its name is due to the head, or body, which sits in front of the spoon and is built like a keel. The head is nearly always made of lead. Such a design allows long, precise casts and the spinner never strays aside in a headwind cast.

The lead head is moulded solidly around the throughgoing wire, which – together with the keel shape – prevents the spinner from twisting the line. In contrast to other

The lead-headed spinner carries a lead head on the spinner's throughgoing wire in front of the spoon. Behind the spoon are often some little plastic beads, followed by a single or treble hook.

spinners, the spoon rotates even when you stop during the retrieval and the spinner sinks. Many predatory fish fall for this very manoeuvre.

All weight-forward spinners are built around a throughgoing wire. Consequently, some sportfishermen have concluded that no leader line is needed in, for example, pike fishing – but this is wrong.

The spoon on a WF spinner is small and slender, made of thin sheet metal, so the spinner works better in deep water. Some American WF spinners have a single hook, because fishing for walleye with jig tails – or with natural bait such as worms – is very popular.

Fishing with WF spinners

The WF spinner is phenomenal for "step-ladder fishing" in deep water and over deep edges. This is the only type of spinner that can be coaxed almost to "crawl" slowly up the slope and still keep working. It is therefore excellent at catching perch, pike and pikeperch. It sinks rapidly, and functions during both spin-stops and retrieval. The compact form also makes it ideal for upstream and cross-stream fishing in flowing waters.

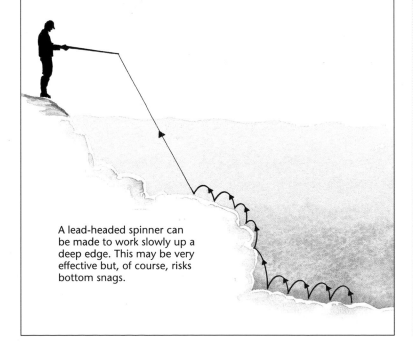

A lead-headed spinner can be made to work slowly up a deep edge. This may be very effective but, of course, risks bottom snags.

Spinnerbaits

Here is a type of artificial bait that was invented for bass fishing, but has quite successfully been used to catch perch, pike and musky in shallower waters with vegetation, roots or other obstacles. A spinnerbait is constructed around a V-shaped, single-strand wire. One arm bears a spoon, or a pair of spoons, not necessarily rotating, but strongly reflecting light. On the other arm is mounted a jig, with a plastic or hair skirt. The hook is either single, tandem-single, or treble.

In weedy, shallow water it is easy to catch on plants or the bottom, but this is hindered by the spinnerbait's design, where each hook is turned upward. The bait's hooking abilities are also good.

Spinnerbaits come in weights from 1 to 50-60 grams. The smallest are used for crappie, perch and minor bass, whereas the bigger ones are for pike and musky.

Spinnerbaits may be equipped with one or more spinner spoons. (*From above, left to right*): Mini Whacker, Bush Whacker, Limbernick, Fuzz-e-Grub, Lindy Big Fish Bait.

Fishing with spinnerbaits

It is possible to use spinnerbaits as attractors for rapidly searching through large water masses and persuading evasive predators to attack. Once the fish is located, other lures can be used that may be less colourful but are better at enticing and hooking it. Spinnerbaits can fish along the bottom, over vegetation, between fallen trees, and so forth. A varied retrieval with spin-stops will trigger the predator's strike, usually during a spin-stop itself.

Some spinnerbaits lack a skirt around the jig hook, and are meant for natural bait – worms, fish strips, or pork rind. Even though the spinnerbait originated to catch bass in reservoirs, this is a fine and unconventional lure for small pike, musky and crappie. However, if combined with a leader, it tends to snag on the main line, so it is often tied directly to the line.

Buzzbaits

A buzzbait is a type of spinner with a propeller on the through-going wire. The propeller may also sit on a wire arm, so that it resembles a classic spinnerbait. The hook and body are shaped as on a jig. Some models are constructed for natural bait, while others are made as a weedless spoon with a hook guard of single-strand wire. Certain buzzbaits also have two or three propellers.

Buzzbaits are intended to work in the surface water. The bait's propeller whirs and generates a gurgling sound. It can be used to advantage in murky water, since the sound is able to attract predators.

Typical of buzzbaits are the propeller-like spoons, or buzzblades. Some models resemble V-divided spinnerbaits (at right is shown a Buzzer'd). On other variants, the spoon spins round a straight wire axle, as on a standard spinner. The skirt often consists of thin strips of plastic or rubber, or of bucktail.

Fishing with buzzbaits

Originally, buzzbaits were created for bass fishing in shallow water. But as with so many other types of bass baits, this one came into use for further predatory species. Unlike spinnerbaits, a buzzbait is light and weighs from 7 to 30 grams. A typical warm-water lure, it works fine on bass and pike as soon as the water temperature goes over 12-13° C (55° F). The retrieval should be quick and begin just after the lure falls on the water, so that the propeller constantly operates in the surface.

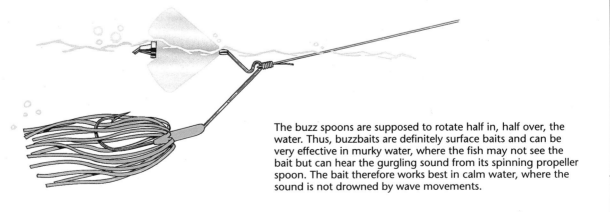

The buzz spoons are supposed to rotate half in, half over, the water. Thus, buzzbaits are definitely surface baits and can be very effective in murky water, where the fish may not see the bait but can hear the gurgling sound from its spinning propeller spoon. The bait therefore works best in calm water, where the sound is not drowned by wave movements.

Wobblers (plugs)

In contrast to spoons and spinners, which look like small fish only from particular angles, a wobbler is three-dimensional. Most plugs today are made of plastic, but balsa wood was once common. Plugs of balsa are still used to some extent, and many sportfishermen consider these more lively.

If you compare a balsa and a plastic plug with the same appearance and form, the balsa plug displays a lot more vitality. However, it is less durable and often suffers damage from fish teeth and impacts. Plugs are fantastic lures for pike, trout, salmon, musky, perch, and a long list of salt-water species. There are innumerable plugs which can float, sink, deep-dive, "hover" or serve for trolling. Some are also made for fishing right in the surface.

Floating plugs

Most plugs float, which means that they have a lower specific weight than water does. Thus, a plug floats because it is filled with air chambers or bubbles. The majority of wooden plugs, too, can float. A plug is provided with a "bill" or lip (or jaw-spoon) of metal or plastic, which makes it dive or cut down through the water when being retrieved. This bill is fixed on most plugs, but on a few it is adjustable so that the plug can descend to different depths. Some plugs are two-part constructions, and have a more lively slithering gait.

The plug's bill, in combination with the retrieval speed,

Floating wobblers.
(*From above, left to right:*)
Down Deep Rattlin' Rap,
Ukko Tipsy, Invincible,
Tobimaru, Windsheater,
Bomber Long A, Spoonbill
Minnow, Perch, Crystal
Minnow, Hot Shot, Ripplin'
Red Fin, Hi-Lo Shad, Wee-R,
Shad Rap.

Wobblers come in a variety of sizes. Their length and form must be chosen for the area in question – where you will fish and which species you are after. In natural size, the little wobbler is only 3 cm long, while the magnum wobbler is 22 cm long.

Deep-going wobblers have a long, powerful, nearly vertical spoon. With thin line and high retrieval speed, they can be made to dive down to 8-10 metres.

Suspending wobblers: Husky Jerk and Suspending Rattlin' Rouge.

Suspending wobblers

These wobblers have the same density as water, and thus neither sink nor float, so one can make them "hover" freely at any desired level. They maintain this depth even during long spin-stops and extremely slow retrieval. Fishing with such wobblers may be very effective when the fish are sluggish and hard to catch.

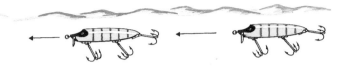

On certain wobblers (like this Hi-Lo) the spoon is adjustable in different positions. Thanks to this refinement, the wobbler can quickly be made to work at varying depths and adapted to diverse fishing situations.

The spoon's length and position are crucial for how the wobbler will move in the water. A wobbler with horizontally placed spoon cuts deep down in the water, while a more oblique spoon will make it go more superficially.

A vertical spoon forces the wobbler to run just below the surface, enabling you to fish in shallow water and over rich vegetation. An oblique spoon usually also calms the wobbler's movements.

determines how deeply it can dive and whether it wobbles little or much in the water. If the bill is small, the plug moves relatively little, but a large bill makes the plug livelier. If the bill lies almost horizontally, the plug will cut deep into the water, while a more transverse bill gives the plug a calmer gait. With a nearly vertical bill, the plug goes slowly and almost in the surface. In addition, some plugs have an adjustable metal bill that can be bent up or down to change the degree of diving.

Other forms of adjustment exist to influence the movement of a floating plug. For example, some plugs have two knot eyes, the upper one producing a deep gait and the lower one a more superficial gait. The plug may also be weighted with lead, a bit up on the line, so that it can go deeper. The Rapala or Duncan knot is common on small, finely balanced plugs. A fixed knot, tied high in the plug's eye, deepens its dive somewhat. If the fixed knot is slid down as far as possible in the eye, the plug will go more superficially. However, floating plugs are always limited as regards their fishing depths, due of course to their specific weight in comparison with water.

Many plugs are equipped with two or three treble hooks. By removing one or two of these – or substituting, for instance, thinner hooks – the plug acquires a lighter and livelier gait.

Swim Whizz (at left) has two knot eyes, allowing fast and simple selection of its depth. By attaching the line in the upper or lower eye, you can make the wobbler run deeper or shallower.

Fishing with floating plugs

The faster a plug is retrieved, the deeper it goes. But the rod tip must be kept low. In the last part the retrieval, the plug will wander up toward the surface, and then it is especially important to hold the rod tip down at the water.

Most floating plugs are intended to fish at depths of 1-6 metres. Since they float, numerous spin-stops will let them ascend toward the surface and – as the retrieval continues – dive again. This is a very effective technique for retrieving them. In cold water, though,

floating plugs are not so effective, since they demand a reasonable speed of movement in order to work at the bottom – and this speed is often too high, so a sinking plug or a lead-weighted floating plug is more effective.

In flowing waters, a floating plug has two advantages. It can be allowed to drift with the current down to an assumed holding place, and then be retrieved. Moreover, you can stop during the retrieval so that the plug soars over submerged obstacles such as plants and stones.

Floating, deep-diving plugs are recognizable by their frequently compact body, but also by the extra-long bill which makes the plug cut down to depths of 3-8 metres. On the other hand, a plug requires a certain retrieval speed if it is to reach maximum depth. Too slow a retrieval leads the plug to work inefficiently; and if you retrieve too fast, it will cut out in the water.

This type of plug is quite good at depths of 3-6 metres – and extremely effective for searching slopes at 3-7 metres, where it often hits the bottom and creates sounds that attract pikeperch, walleye and perch. The large versions of these plugs are mainly devoted to trolling for pike, musky and saltwater species.

A floating wobbler that is weighted can be fished just over the bottom, even in strong current and at relatively great depth. Too short a line between the three-way swivel and the lure, though, can worsen the wobbler's lively gait.

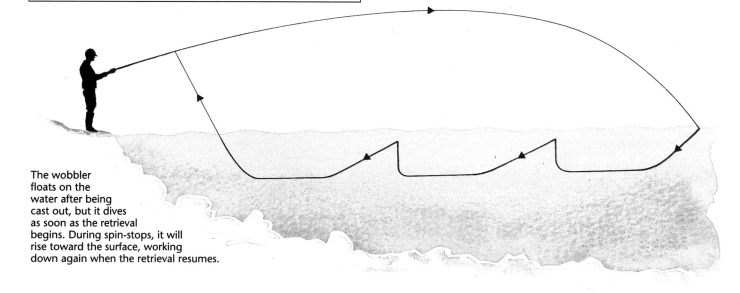

The wobbler floats on the water after being cast out, but it dives as soon as the retrieval begins. During spin-stops, it will rise toward the surface, working down again when the retrieval resumes.

Sinking plugs

A floating plug cannot, unless it is weighted, be used with the countdown method at great depths. Here the sinking plug is better suited. Such a plug is normally made of plastic, having no air chambers or bubbles. The plastic may either be denser than water or contain weighting. Wooden plugs also exist in sinking versions.

Usually the package shows whether the plug is sinking (S) or floating (F), but you can often tell the difference by feeling its weight in your hand. As with most floating plugs, the depth-going of a sinking plug depends on the bill's size, placement, and cleavage of the water, besides the location of the knot eyes. The plug can be adjusted, too, by changing the bill or replacing the hooks. A few deep-going plugs with a long bill can work down to 7 metres.

Fishing with sinking plugs

The speed of descent varies among sinking plugs. Small sizes are intended for depths of 2-3 metres, and the larger plugs can be used down to 8-10 metres, but it often takes at least half a minute for the plug to reach the bottom. You should thus use the count-down method for this type of plug.

When the retrieval is begun, the plug will slowly lift from the bottom. Hence, numerous spin-stops are important to make it stay at the bottom, where most predatory fish linger. You may then need to release a little line regularly, by switching over the bail on a spinning reel or disengaging the spool on a multiplier reel.

Sinking plugs are better than floating ones for fishing in cold water, since they can be retrieved slowly.

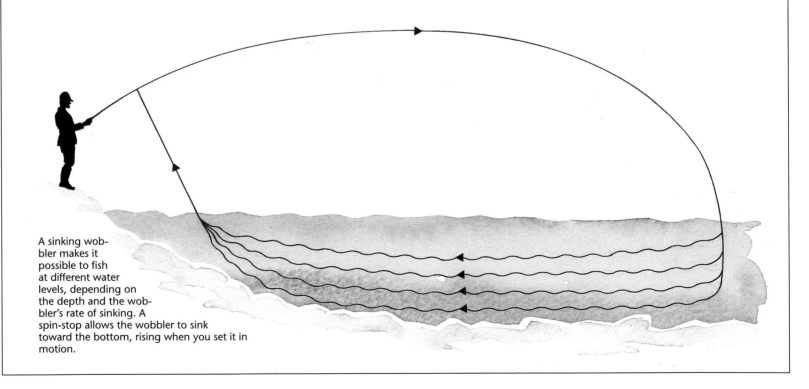

A sinking wobbler makes it possible to fish at different water levels, depending on the depth and the wobbler's rate of sinking. A spin-stop allows the wobbler to sink toward the bottom, rising when you set it in motion.

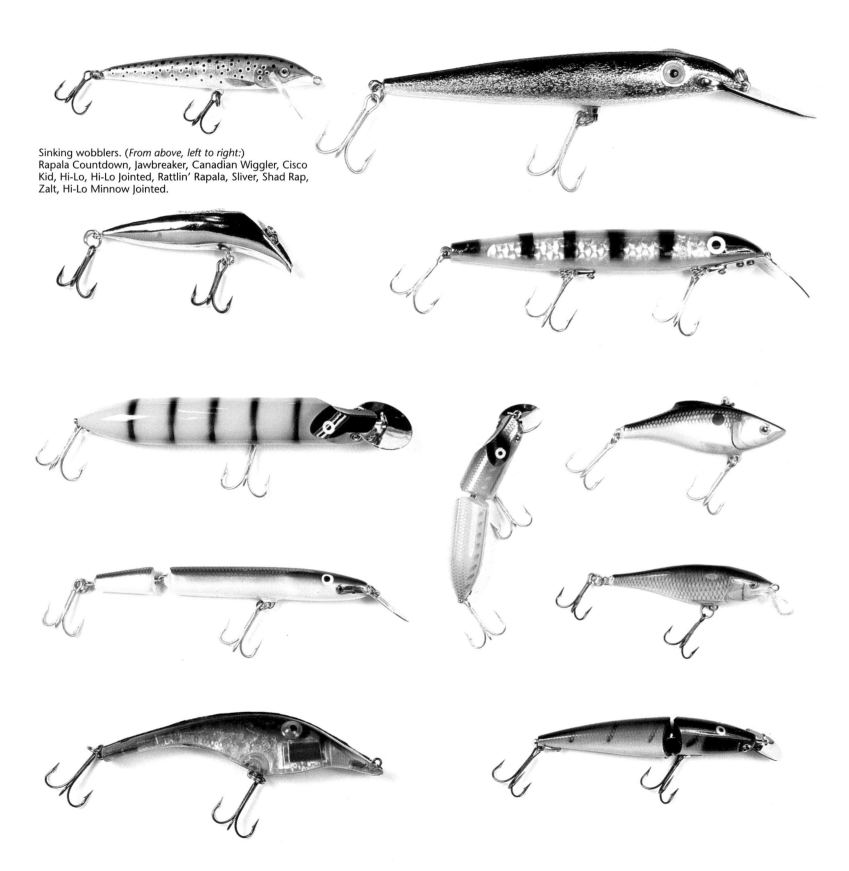

Sinking wobblers. (*From above, left to right:*) Rapala Countdown, Jawbreaker, Canadian Wiggler, Cisco Kid, Hi-Lo, Hi-Lo Jointed, Rattlin' Rapala, Sliver, Shad Rap, Zalt, Hi-Lo Minnow Jointed.

Surface plugs

The majority of small surface plugs are built for bass fishing in overgrown waters, and in shallow or vegetation-rich areas. This type of lure is not very widespread in Europe, but is used at times in light spinning for pike during the summer months – in shallow waters at temperatures over 14-16° C (60° F), when the pike are hunting in the surface. Yet the biggest types of surface plug, "jerkbaits", are for large pike and musky.

Surface plugs that resemble a cigar, called "stickbaits", are made for slow retrieval. The plug zigzags lazily from side to side and looks like an injured fish. Other surface plugs carry one or two propellers. Known as "propbaits", these are retrieved at an even speed, while the propellers whip up foam in the water. A further type of surface plug, the "crawler", has metal wings fixed across it. This lure is retrieved at a constant tempo and creates a special sound, rather like young birds fluttering over the surface.

The "chugger" can be described as an overdimensioned popper, and is used in flyfishing for bass and pike. Chuggers also occur in coastal fishing for stripers. This type of plug, however, is retrieved in jerks.

Left: Smaller variants of surface-going wobblers are mainly intended for bass fishing. In shallow or vegetated water, spinning within the surface itself is often quite effective, and can even be the only way of getting fish on the hook.

Surface-going wobblers.
(*From above, left to right:*) Zara Spook (stickbait), Mystic Pop R, Pop R, P.J. Pop (chuggers), Crazy Crawler (crawler), Big Game Wood Frog (surface-going when retrieved slowly), Crazy Shad, Dying Flutter, Jerk'n Sam, Nip-N-Diddee, Dalton Special, Tiny Torpedo, Big Game Woodchopper (propbaits).

Fishing with surface plugs

Surface plugs, discussed next, are used to catch bass, and some are also very good for small pike, pickerel and musky. The plugs are retrieved in the water surface or fished jerkily. They are best suited to minor lakes and overgrown water with small gaps in the vegetation. In addition, they work fine as attractors. Such plugs should imitate frogs, water rats, young birds, and sick or injured fish. All are fished with light equipment.

A bass has let itself be attracted by a crawler.

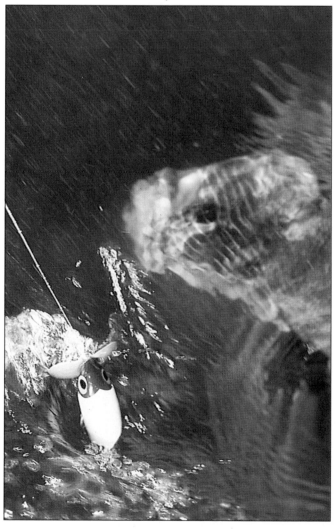

Coastal plugs

This Scandinavian type of plug is slender and long-casting, made of plastic or wood that contains lead weighting. Used in coastal fishing for sea trout, it imitates sand lance and small herring. A coastal plug is balanced with lead so that it casts nicely, can work slowly, sink gradually during spin-stops, and generally have the movements characteristic of a herring or sand lance. These plugs were previously regarded as cold-water lures, but in recent years they have proved to work well in all seasons and at all water temperatures.

Some coastal plugs run very superficially, now and then breaking the surface. They can therefore be used for spinning at night, when the sea trout in salt water are especially active. "Coastal" plugs have also been tried with success in river fishing for salmon and sea trout – perhaps not surprisingly, as certain coastal plugs, apart from the "wings", resemble the classic Devon spinners made of wood or plastic.

Coastal wobblers. (*From above, left to right:*) Sandgraevlingen, Slim, Tobis, Fynbo, Kutlingen, Minnow Spoon, Gladsax.

Coastal wobblers are common in Scandinavia, chiefly in coastal fishing for sea trout. These long-casting wobblers sink only slowly, and work in a very lively manner even with slow retrieval and repeated spin-stops, which are often necessary along shallow shores and at low water temperatures. Resembling Devon spinners, the coastal wobblers have also proved good at catching salmon and sea trout in flowing waters.

Jerkbaits are meant to imitate large, injured preyfish. This group of lures is represented here by a Suick Thriller, which is made of wood and measures 23 cm in natural size. The wobbler's rear has a metal spoon for easier diving.

Jerkbaits

A jerkbait is a big plug for pike and musky, made of wood and often 15-25 centimetres long. Some are floating and can descend to depths of 1-2 metres; others are sinking and may be used down to 2 metres; a few are distinctive magnum-size surface plugs. Jerkbaits are the only plugs that should not be retrieved, but jerked through the water. Models with a bill are able to cut down through the water, while models with no bill run entirely in the surface.

Jerkbaits are fantastic fish attractors, and will remain a natural part of the equipment among American pike and musky fishermen. In Europe, they are less known but definitely one of the most interesting artificial lures, since they manage to tempt even large pike up from 5-8 metres to the surface.

Jerkbaits are used with relatively strong, very stiff, spinning rods and with baitcasting reels filled by spun line, either dacron or kevlar-based braided line. Certainly they can also be used from land, but they are primarily "boat lures".

Fishing with jerkbaits

Once cast out toward a pike's presumed holding place, a jerkbait is pulled in by holding the rod down toward the water and "chopping" the plug through the surface, so that it sucks along plenty of air beneath the surface – and pops up again a moment later, whereupon the retrieval continues in the same way. Another manner of taking in the plug is to jerk the rod alternately to the left and right.

This method of fishing demands an extremely stiff, short rod of 6.5-8 feet, also because the hook does not catch easily when the pike takes. Often the fish attacks from one side, or leaps over the plug repeatedly until hooked. Due to the difficulty of hooking the fish, spun line of 30-50 pounds is frequently used. After the fish is hooked, it must be tired out carefully, since it can soon shake itself free as a result of the stiff rod, the inflexible line and the robust hook.

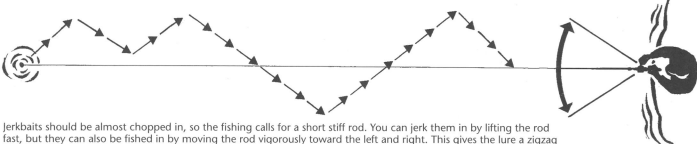

Jerkbaits should be almost chopped in, so the fishing calls for a short stiff rod. You can jerk them in by lifting the rod fast, but they can also be fished in by moving the rod vigorously toward the left and right. This gives the lure a zigzag gait both horizontally and vertically. The fishing-in technique is reminiscent of the classic method with stickbaits, illustrated here: Walking the Dog.

Jigs

The jig belongs to the classic artificial baits in American bass fishing. Although occasional jigs appeared on the European fishing scene during the 1960s, only in the 1970s did they really enjoy a breakthrough for pike and pikeperch fishing. Then they became an increasingly common option to other lures in, for example, trout fishing at rivers and lakes – and next for fishing in shallow marine waters. This is strange, as there can hardly be any cheaper or better artificial bait than a jig, which long ago was included in the survival gear of various fleets together with hooks, lines and other emergency accessories.

Normal lures, such as spoons and plugs, have built-in patterns of movement. The jig is different. At first sight, it looks most like a lump of lead with a tuft of feathers or plastic and an upturned single hook. In spite of that, there are diverse designs of American jigs – and some forms go back to the 1920s and 1930s. The keel and projectile types are intended for flowing waters, where the jig's shape makes it cut downward. The ball types are meant for spinning in still waters, while the banana and mushroom types apply to light jig fishing from a boat and to fishing in deep water.

Some jigs also carry a long bill. In this respect they resemble a plug, but the jig lacks the plug's ability to cut down into the water. Other jigs are provided with propellers or small rotor blades. The knot eye – which is the hook eye as well – may have a forward orientation to keep plants off the hook. But most jigs have the eye on top of the lead head, which is moulded around the hook. The latter is nearly always of Aberdeen type and browned, gilded or nickel-plated.

Jigs come in weights from 0.25-0.50 grams up to 40-50 grams or more. The largest are used for marine fishing. Hair, feathers or plastic make up the body, a so-called silicone body. The smallest jigs should have the lightest bodies, which thus usually consist of hair or feathers. Hair jigs are notably light and lively. Bucktail hair is air-filled and gives the jig a breezy gait. Feathers – especially from marabou – are virtually charged with life and vitalize the jig at the least movement. Hen-hackle feathers were also once common, being tied around the jig to sprout from the sides, and pulsing when moved even slightly.

Silicone bodies are the most widespread variant today. The first rubber jig bodies appeared as early as the 1860s,

The jig was originally the typical bass lure, but many people now consider jigs effective for diverse species in both fresh and marine waters. A jig's lively plastic tail enables it to be fished in very slowly without losing its attractiveness. Despite its simple design, it works fine in most fishing situations.

and now occur in countless forms that imitate, for instance, fish, worms and larvae.

The majority of sportfishermen use tight knots on jigs, but a Duncan or Rapala knot creates a loose knot loop that enables the jig to work more vitally. A jig can also be attached to the line with a snap, but this may dampen the fine movements of a small jig.

Jigs with a rubber body are cheap to work with, since you can buy replaceable bodies for them. However, some toothed predatory fish can destroy a rubber body in no time. If you get a bad bite or the fish is difficult to hook, it may be because the jig body is too long – but a body made of hair, feathers or rubber can be shortened with a knife or scissors to facilitate hooking. Rubber jigs are best stored in tackle boxes marked "Wormproof", which prevent certain chemicals in the rubber bodies from smearing off, or melting both the bodies and the box's plastic. Bodies of each colour should be kept in a separate plastic bag. This will also keep them from drying out.

Perch is among the numerous species that are readily tempted by a colourful rubber jig.

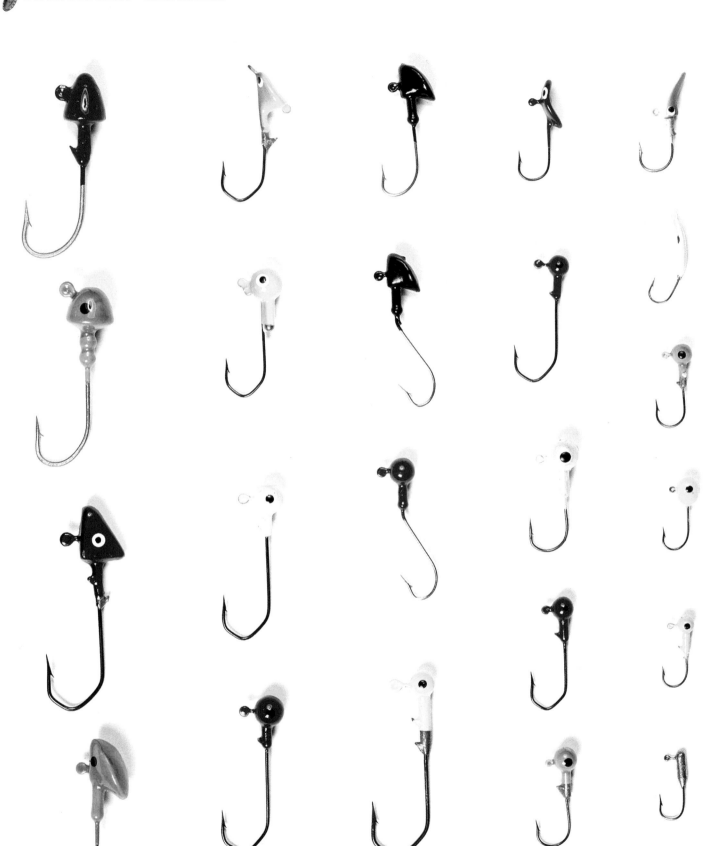

Jig heads come in a range of colours, forms, sizes and weights. Some common variants of jig heads are round, oval, tubular, banana-shaped, keel-shaped and conical. The hook's appearance may also differ according to the area, and to the type of jig body it is intended for.

Fishing with jigs

All of the lures discussed previously are retrieved. But a jig has to be both "worked" and retrieved. The jig itself is dead, and the fisherman must bring it alive with rod and wrist movements during the retrieval. Vigorous jerks along the bottom are needed – whether long tempting jerks, or short chopping jerks, depending on the kind of fish you are after. Correct use of a jig is certainly a craft, but it can yield great satisfaction in the right hands.

Maintain continuous contact with the jig, but do not stretch the line so much as to affect the jig's gait. Make a strike at the least suggestion of a take. In contrast to spoons, plugs and other lures, it is quite common that a jig's construction attracts cautious nibbles without hooking the fish. Apart from flies, almost no other type of artificial bait is in such close touch with the fish at the taking stage. Many people believe that a jig is suited only to fishing on hard bottoms without vegetation; but if there is any vegetation, you should use an ultra-light jig that bounces off the plants. The hook does not snag, since it is turned upward.

Due to the highly varied and jerky retrieval, extreme concentration is required of the fisherman – in all phases of jig fishing. The fish often takes when the jig is not moving. Small jigs of 1-5 grams work best with a one-handed rod, while large jigs call for a stronger one-handed rod or a light two-handed rod. Jigs of 20-50 grams, intended for marine fishing, are fished just like a pirk, although with less powerful movements.

There are also weightless jigs, to be weighted individually so that they fish at a desired depth – in both still and flowing waters. These are most appropriate for bass and trout in small waters.

Jigs have many practical advantages. Their aerodynamic shape gives long casts even in a headwind, and the compact head allows exact casts as well as good bottom contact. Moreover, a jig cuts down into the current better, so it is easier to keep in contact with the bottom than are other types of lure. The upturned hook not only minimizes bottom snags, but ensures penetration of the fish's upper jaw. The hook tip does not get dulled against stones, and thus stays sharp.

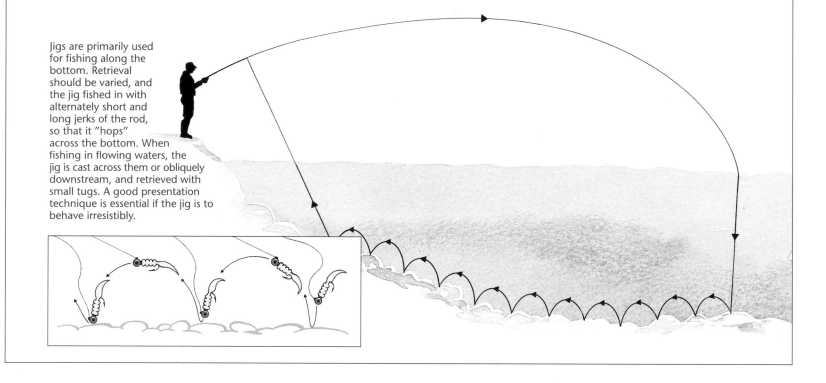

Jigs are primarily used for fishing along the bottom. Retrieval should be varied, and the jig fished in with alternately short and long jerks of the rod, so that it "hops" across the bottom. When fishing in flowing waters, the jig is cast across them or obliquely downstream, and retrieved with small tugs. A good presentation technique is essential if the jig is to behave irresistibly.

Plastic animals

The first animals or artificial lures made of plastic were patented in 1860. Around the period of World War I, they began to grow popular, mainly for American bass fishing. In those days, their plastic was hard by comparison with very soft modern imitations of diverse animals and worms. During the late 1940s, soft plastic worms were developed, and soon yielded record catches of bass. Europeans, though, considered plastic animals or worms to be worthless, thinking that they were to be used instead of natural worms.

Today, there is a wide range of very naturalistic copies of, for example, salamanders, frogs, worms, crustaceans, crabs, snakes, lizards and salmon eggs. The lifelike soft plastic imitations are almost perfect and have eyes, legs, scales, wings and so on.

On some plastic animals, the hook must go through the body, so that the fish does not notice it until hooked. This also prevents bottom snags and plant clogging. Some plastic bodies are impregnated with taste and scent substances – a development started by Berkley among others. The plastic may have varying consistency, from relative hardness to extreme softness. Most plastic animals sink, but several types must be weighted and a few, such as frog imitations, are meant to float.

While plastic animals are specially developed for bass fishing, they have also become popular in fishing for pike, pickerel, small musky, perch and even saltwater fish. Plastic worms, too, have been created particularly to catch bass. These are very soft, often 20-30 cm (8-12 inches) long, either already provided with hooks or intended to be given one or two single hooks – carefully inserted in the worm so that their tips are not visible. Such worms can be put on ordinary light jig hooks as well.

Salmon eggs are made as both individual eggs and small clumps of roe. They are used as a substitute for natural salmon eggs or roe, and fished with bottom tackle or sometimes with a float in flowing water – for trout, rainbow, steelhead, sea trout, or various species of Pacific salmon.

Colour and form are the key attributes of a rubber animal. Just as with jigs, the fisherman has to give them life through a natural presentation. There is a vast range of rubber imitations and some of the commonest types are shown here: worms, crabs, lizards, leeches and small fish.

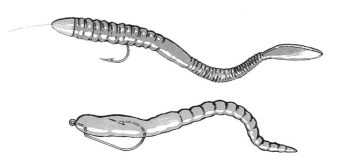

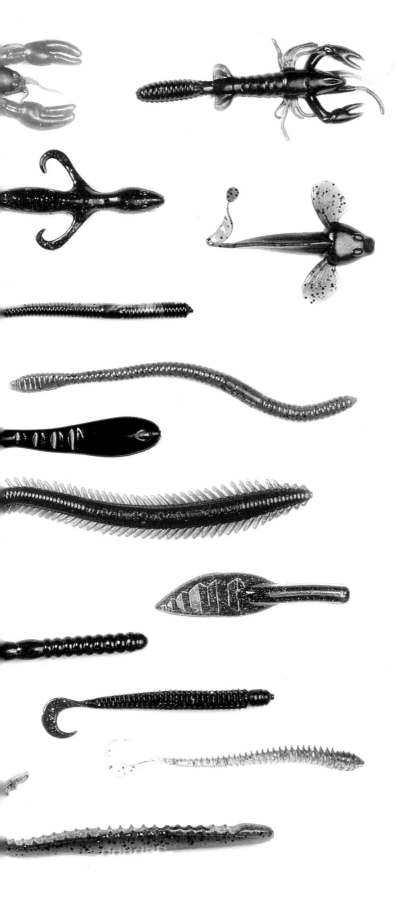

Above is a so-called Carolina rig, with a floating rubber worm and bare hook tip, as well as a lead head in front – best suited for fishing in open water. Below we see a Texas rig, with the barb placed in the rubber worm body, used mainly for fishing in waters that contain much vegetation.

Large rubber insect imitations in flowing waters can, for example, catch big sea trout and salmon.

Casting floats

There are occasions in spinning when a spoon, plug or spinner is too large a lure for the predatory fish and, for example, a fly is much more suitable. Especially salmon in many waters can be so shy and cautious that big lures do not work. The diminished appetite for large bait may be due to the water temperature or level, insect hatchings, the season, spawning or other conditions.

An alternative is then to spin with flies in the surface, aided by a casting float. This device comes in two basic versions. One, the Bonnand type, is shaped like a cigar, with a red top, and contains lead as a weight. It is filled with air and can also be used as an ordinary float. At each end is a hole to tie the main line or the leader in.

The other version is the classic plastic "bubble", or Buldo. A transparent or colourful ball with two knot eyes, it can be opened via two small rubber valves and filled with water – the casting weight – so that it floats exactly in the surface. Also available are oval variants to be filled with water.

The fly should be on the end of a leader 1.0-4.5 metres long. Many sportfishermen use a permanently fixed leader, which is tied to a casting bubble. There are two kinds of sliding leader. The first is a 50-cm length of 0.40-mm line, inserted through the bubble and provided with a swivel at each end for the leader or main line. When the fish takes the fly during retrieval, you thus have 50 cm of "loose line" which the fish can pull out together with the fly. The second kind, used when you want to give more "loose line", is made by ending the leader with a swivel, to which the main line is tied after being inserted through the casting bubble. This swivel serves as a stopper.

Casting floats essentially function as casting weights. In recent years, however, different sorts of casting weights have been introduced. These are normally made of plastic or wood, with casting weights built or moulded into them. They are used in the same way as casting floats – with both a fixed and a sliding leader.

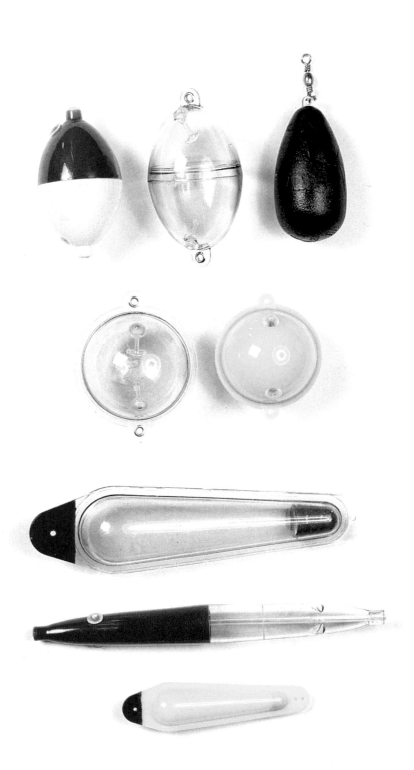

There are both transparent and coloured variants of casting balls and casting floats. A round or oval casting ball must be filled with water in order to be cast. In the cigar-shaped, air-filled casting floats, by contrast, the casting weight consists of lead, so they serve as ordinary floats too. At the top, far right, is shown a casting dub made of wood, with moulded-in lead as the casting weight.

Fishing with casting floats

To fish with a long leader and an often heavy casting weight, you need a relatively long, strong rod and a line of 0.25-0.35 mm. The cast is carried out when the leader lies in front of the fisherman in the water – never behind. Retrieval should be slow with many pauses, depending on which species of fish you are after. A lot of sportfishermen dislike this method, since the fishing is monotonous and may even be boring. But there is no doubt of its effectiveness.

Plastic bubbles can be weighted so much that they sink. In some put-and-take fishing, weighted "neutral" and "sinking" bubbles are frequently used at depths as great as 5-8 metres.

If you want to fish deep with a fly, you can weight the leader with lead shot, or perhaps tie a piece of fast-sinking flyline into the leader.

The strike should be delivered with a smooth, controlled movement, because the plastic bubble gives quite a resistance in the water. Beginners have a habit of making too hard a strike, which results in the line breaking at the bubble.

Casting floats are useful in both still waters and rivers, where they enable a fly to fish just as well as the flyfisherman's floating line with a fly.

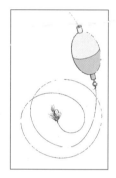

Fishing with a sliding leader means that the fish is given a little loose line when it takes. The two swivels function as stops, both when retrieving (*left*) and when the fish has taken the lure (*right*). Many think that a permanently mounted leader gives better hooking, but that the contact with lure and fish is improved by a sliding leader.

Right: Shown here are three methods of mounting a casting float on the line. Above is a permanent mounting, and below it are two variants with a sliding line.

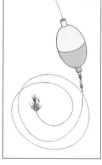

Below: In Scandinavia, fishing with long-casting balls has become a frequent – and rewarding – way to present traditional flies for coastal sea trout.

Spinning with flies

Spinning does not by any means rule out the possibility of using flies in deep water. If the fly is weighted slightly up on the line, it can be fished at depth in both still and flowing water. In Scandinavia the so-called "spinning-fly" method is thus applied to trout, salmon and seagoing trout in streams and rivers. However, this has angered flyfishermen and been forbidden in many places due to its effectiveness.

The leader is 1-1.5 metres long, of 0.20-0.40 mm line, depending on whether trout in small rivers or salmon and sea trout in large rivers are fished. It is tied in a three-way swivel, the distance to the sinker being 20-30 cm long. The choice of fly is not very difficult. Ordinary trout flies serve for all forms of trout fishing, while double-hooked flies or tube flies are used for salmon and sea trout.

Lagging flies

It often happens that a predatory fish pursues a plug, spoon or spinner without biting – no matter what type of bait or retrieval technique is used. In this case, a "lagging" fly offers both an alternative and a surprising arrangement that can trick the fish. You simply knot a fly in a short or long leader on a spoon, plug or spinner, after removing the hook(s).

Char is a typical fish species that gladly takes a lagging fly. Perch, pike, trout, and garfish in salt water, too, respond positively to it. But the fly tends to get hung up in the main line when casting against the wind, so a lagging – or perhaps "persistent" – fly should be used only in calm weather or with the wind at your back.

Droppers

Droppers are flies, plastic animals, or micro-jigs that are tied to the line above the lure. They markedly increase the chances of catching fish, since many predators are curious and often become "envious" when they see a little fish being chased by a bigger one. Perch, trout and bass, as well as marine species like sea trout, mackerel and cod, readily take droppers. The droppers are tied in a leader 30-50 cm over the main lure, and it is frequently only to them that the fish reacts.

Spinning with a fly can yield fine catches in rivers with salmon and sea trout. This salmon could not resist a weighted tube fly, fished at the bottom.

Fishing with spinning flies

Spinning with a fly in flowing water can be done exactly as with a spoon. All the fishing is oriented directly or obliquely downstream, so that the fly swings in toward your own bank. By paying out line or lifting the rod, you can make the fly work deeper or higher. During this process, you regularly raise and lower the rod to "pump" the fly in: it more or less zigzags against the current as it approaches your bank.

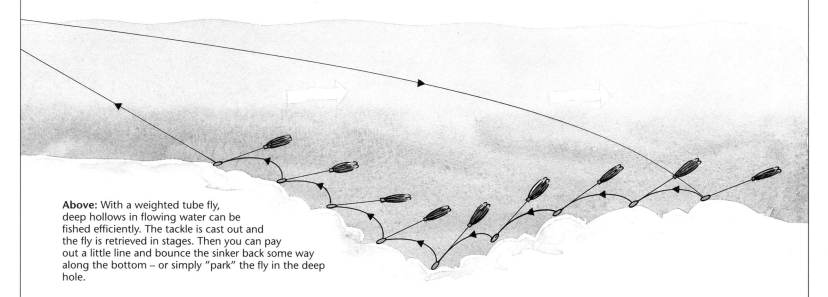

Above: With a weighted tube fly, deep hollows in flowing water can be fished efficiently. The tackle is cast out and the fly is retrieved in stages. Then you can pay out a little line and bounce the sinker back some way along the bottom – or simply "park" the fly in the deep hole.

The spinning fly can be weighted by attaching the sinker to the main line, either directly or via a leader. The leader, which should be thinner than the main line, is then fastened in a swivel or three-way snap. But the line between the swivel and fly must have the same breaking strength as the main line.

It is not unusual for predatory fish to become "envious" when they see a smaller fish hunted by bigger ones, and this reaction is what makes the dropper an effective attractor. A dropper is normally attached to a leader 30-50 cm above the lure. Likewise, a fly dragged after the lure can attract a bite, but the leader should then be only about 10 cm long.

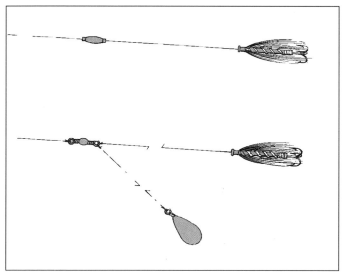

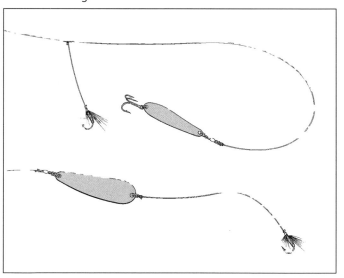

91

Choosing the bait's colour

Many factors determine the effect of colour in artificial baits, so the rules for selecting colours cannot be strict. Besides, when the fish are on the take, colour often has no importance at all. But you should base a colour on the fish's natural prey. Some fresh waters are dominated by prey-fish such as crucian carp and rudd, which are imitated with gold and copper colours – while roach, bleak and smelt can be imitated with silvery colours. In clear flowing waters with trout and salmon, natural colours commonly do best.

Even the water's colour can influence the choice of colour. Frequently good in brownish waters are silver, copper and nickel, or strong and fluorescent colours. In dark, murky water, silvery and fluorescent colours are notably effective, and this applies equally to the cold months when the fish are much less active. Provocation is another key ingredient in selecting colours: you can choose one that provokes the fish to bite, such as a fluorescent colour.

The significance of colours is best understood by knowing which colours of light are absorbed in the water. In clear water, nearly all colours penetrate to a depth of 5 metres; below this, the red colours are absorbed while yellow, green and blue prevail. Spinning, however, is done mainly in shallower waters where all colours are visible.

Predatory fish in shallow waters often have bright colours. For example, a perch in clear shallow water has red fins and a yellowish body, whereas in murky deep water it has yellow or grey-white fins and light-grey scales. Thus, in shallow waters the choice of colour is important, but in deep water the challenge is rather to use lures that the fish can see and to present them in the right way.

The value of lure colours is often exaggerated, but in many waters the colour can be as influential as the lure's shape, size and movements. As a rule, in brownish and murky water (*upper photo*) strong colours should be used – such as silver, copper, gold, flash and fluorescents. In clear water (*lower photo*) natural and dark colours are recommended instead, such as silver – alone or combined with blue or black – and zebra or "nature colours". One must also, of course, take account of which preyfish occur in the given water, at what depth the lure will work, and whether the sky is bright or dark.

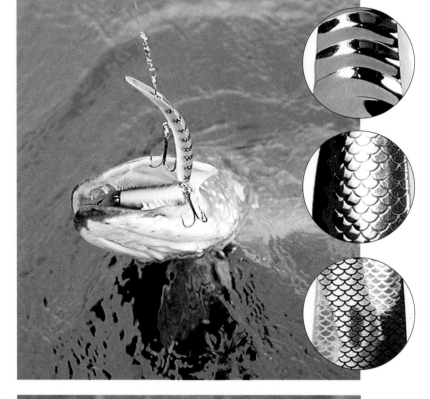

Size and gait

Many fishermen are insecure when spinning, and arm themselves with numerous types of lures, until they find good ones. Then they gradually limit themselves to a handful of lures, whose gait and catching qualities they have confidence in. They know how their "favourites" fish at different depths, and the retrieval speeds and techniques – as well as colours – which are best in the water at hand.

Some general rules, though, exist for choosing the correct lure. First, a lure's weight should make it possible to fish effectively in the given water. If the fish are far out, the lure must be heavy enough for casting to them. If they are standing deep, the weight of the lure should enable it to fish along the bottom, throughout the retrieval distance.

Big fish are normally attracted by large lures, since they prefer taking a single mouthful to many small bites. Likewise, if the water becomes murky or disturbed by wind and weather, you should choose a larger lure with more flash or colour. The worse the water gets, the less shy the predatory fish are.

The movements of artificial baits point to a further rule. Salmon and trout, as well as bass and perch, are most tempted by lures that have a quick, enticing gait. On the other hand, relatively slow movements draw predators such as pike, pikeperch and musky.

Finally, one should keep in mind all the external factors that affect the choice of lure: the wind, weather, season, air pressure, the water's level and colour, its temperature and clarity, and the type of bottom – sandy or muddy, vegetated or bare, flat or rolling. Lakes or waterways, and the times of day you fish at – such as morning, evening, or in bright sunshine – are further variables. In addition, of course, the choice will depend on the fish's spawning, migrations, feeding habits, and the preyfish in your water. These are factors you cannot do much about, but must adapt to.

When spinning, however, a fisherman has full control over certain essentials: how the lure is presented – at what depth and retrieval speed – and its colour, gait and size. In sum, adeptness at spinning does call for a fair share of experience!

The right lure in the right situation

Experienced fishermen know that faith in a particular lure can be more important than the lure itself. This is undoubtedly because a believer in the lure's superiority fishes with greater self-confidence and presents it more attractively. Greater experience also brings a better ability to choose baits that attract fish in given situations, and to present them in a manner realistic for the fish. However, this depends on the fish being willing to bite. Presenting the right bait correctly is thus not enough: one has to fish at the right place and time as well. Coaxing a scared, sluggish or sated fish onto the hook is much harder than tricking an active and hungry one...

Natural Baits

There is little profit in going to good fishing waters, at the right place and time, with the right technique ready for action, unless your bait is also optimum and the presentation is correct. Since the age-old invention of fishing hooks, people have tested every possible sort of natural bait, and modern sportfishermen are still at it. When artificial lures yield no results, a clever sportfisherman tries to combine them with natural baits, or to fish only with the latter. Not just the fish's sight and lateral line system, but all of its senses, should be stimulated. In many predatory fish species, smell and taste are at least as important.

Worms

Worms are probably the most widespread type of natural bait. In freshwater fishing, all kinds and sizes of earthworms are used – while the main distinction in saltwater fishing is between lugworms and ragworms.

Large earthworms live in nutritious soil, and can be either dug up or "lighted" out. They are storable for long periods, in a refrigerator or a compost box. Worms are used not only by float and bottom anglers, but also when spinning with a casting bubble to catch trout. In the United States, worms are a very effective bait for small-mouthed bass, being fished alone or on a jig hook – as opposed to a spinner for walleye, or a drag leader for char. Again, worms are excellent on droppers to catch perch, for example, and they are quite popular when ice-fishing for this and other species. By contrast, many smaller worms such as caterpillars and compost worms are best suited to angling.

In marine waters we find lugworms and large ragworms (sand leeches), which dig their dwellings in the bottom. A lugworm is identified by its wiggling pattern on the bottom. Ragworms do not reveal themselves, but often occur beneath mussel beds, eel grass and seaweed on soft muddy bottoms. These saltwater species of worm are doubtless the best baits in all bottom angling for cod, bass, flatfish and others. However, lugworms are difficult to preserve for any length of time – unlike ragworms, which are more firm and sit better on the hook. Ragworms can also be used for spinning with a casting bubble.

A pinch of earthworms can be a very good bait when fishing for salmon and sea trout in flowing waters. Helped to the bottom by a sinker, it bounces along somewhat more slowly than the current.

Five examples of tackling with different kinds of worms for spinning and baitcasting. Shown at left are three ways to put lugworms and ragworms on the hook (their tails have been clipped off at the hook tip to prevent bad bites), and at right are two variants with one or more earthworms. Normally the hook should go at least partly through the worm's firmer white "belt", but this obviously does not apply if the worm is rigged as shown at far right.

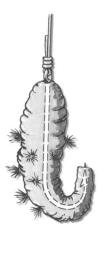
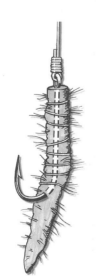
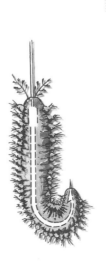

Larvae and insects

Innumerable larvae and pupae exist that are generally called "worms". Many of them serve to improve the attracting qualities of artificial lures, but are also useful in ordinary angling. Larvae and casters must be the commonest baits in modern angling, and play a widespread role in ice-fishing as well as fishing for perch, crappie and bluegill. The same is true of mealworms, while various larvae of large insects are popular on droppers or small jig bodies.

Diverse types of insects, too, can be used as baits. The best known are mayflies and grasshoppers for trout – and in some places for grayling. Grasshoppers also provide bait for small-mouthed bass.

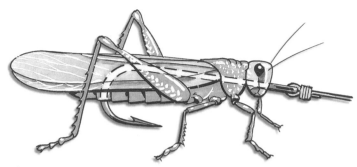

Grasshoppers are sometimes used for spinning and baitcasting – as when catching trout in a stream, where this bait may be fished either floating or weighted.

Soft, loose larvae – which may be ruined if you try to thread a hook through them – are tied carefully onto a bigger hook...

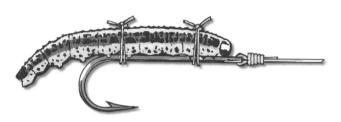

...whereas firmer larvae can take the hook tip through their thicker parts. The less deeply the hook is set, the longer the larva will stay alive.

In an individual pupa, the hook should be completely hidden, stuck into its thick part. A hook size of 14-16 is best for spinning and baitcasting.

Shy fish can be fooled with pupae and larvae – either weighted with a sinker, or fished on a leader dragging several inches after an artificial lure. When fishing with two or more such baits, the hook is inserted through their thicker parts.

Crustaceans and mollusks

Through the ages, crayfish have been a superb bait for many predatory fish. In whatever size, they work wonders on species such as bass. You can fish with a single or treble hook in a whole crayfish, or use only crayfish tails.

Shrimp can be fished either raw – as a lot of fishermen prefer – or cooked to give them an attractive red colour. They are also very good bait for trout in fresh or marine waters, and their uses range from striped bass, bonefish and snook to cod, flatfish and sea trout. There are numerous ways to tackle shrimp, but usually a single hook is stuck in through the head or tail, and out at the breast.

Crabs are employed primarily as a bait in salt water for striped bass, sea bass, cod and other bottom fish. Small "peeler crabs", which have just shed their shells, are especially popular for bass.

Snail meat, regardless of whether it comes from small fresh-water snails or large kong snails, has always proved its worth as bait – in bottom and float angling as well as with droppers. The meat is often tough and sits firmly on the hook.

Mussel meat is an excellent bait for cod, flatfish and bass. In freshwater fishing, one can also use the meat from fresh-water mussels to catch, for instance, catfish and bass.

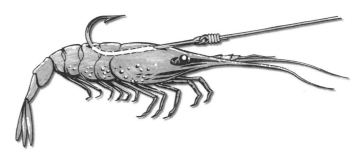

Shrimp are a popular bait for many species, notably in salt water. A shrimp can be fished with a single hook inserted either in the top of the head...

...or in the tail, so that the tip emerges at the bottom. To make the shrimp sit better, clip off the outer part of its tail.

Large unshelled shrimp can be effective for salmon fishing in rivers and streams. Frequently, conserved and coloured shrimp are then used, with a hook tackle tied to their undersides.

As crabs grow, they shed their shells regularly. The new shell is then relatively soft, leaving the crab vulnerable to predators. Crabs are thus often used, in part or whole, as bait for coastal fishing in both Europe and North America.

Above: Little crayfish occasionally serve as bait when, for example, spinning to catch trout and smallmouth bass. In dead crayfish, the hook can be inserted as shown above...

...but live crayfish should be tackled up with the help of rubberbands, as shown below.

Amphibians and cephalopods

Many countries ban the use of live bait animals such as frogs. But in the United States, amphibians such as frogs and salamanders are popular baits for bass, pike and musky. In several East European and Atlantic states, frogs are considered the best baits for catfish.

Squid

Squid meat has the great advantage of being pale and tough, so that it attracts both marine and freshwater species. Small deep-frozen squid are used to fish for pike, instead of herring or other dead bait – and very successfully for catfish. The consistency of such squid makes them quite suitable to catch a broad variety of fish species in both fresh and salt waters.

In the USA, salamanders are a common bait when fishing for pike and especially bass. Nearly all kinds of salamander catch bass, but small and young ones are usually best. The hook is often placed in the front of the head.

Small cephalopods are frequently fished whole. This bait sits well on the hook, which should be fairly big – inserted through the body and out at the head.

On a large cephalopod, the arms are worth using for spinning and baitcasting. They can be quite effective if retrieved slowly and given life with attractive movements of the rod tip.

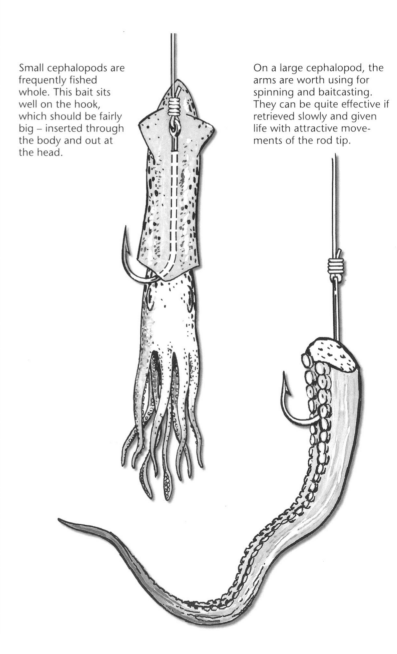

Frogs have long been considered very effective in pike and bass fishing. This, of course, is why an American tackle-box may contain plenty of artificial frog imitations when spinning and flyfishing.

Eggs and roe

Salmon eggs are hard to beat when fishing for salmon, steelhead and trout, whether in natural waters or in put-and-take areas.

The most refined method is to set one, two or three big salmon eggs on a little single hook. This is allowed to drift with the current and tempt steelhead or rainbow trout. Certainly these fish also take clumps of roe, but large clumps are used chiefly to catch king salmon. A cluster of roe can then be drifted over the bottom, or fixed to a treble hook on the well-known spinner Spin-N-Glo. Sea trout in flowing waters are effectively fished with a roe cluster on a single or treble hook.

Furthermore, conserved salmon eggs and salmon roe are obtainable as a substitute for the fresh goods. Conserved roe may contain added flavourings. Even bottled pasta dough may be flavoured with salmon roe, fish oil and worms. The pasta is rolled into balls of desired size, and can be set on a single hook or squeezed around a treble hook. The dough is meant especially to catch salmon and trout, in both natural waters and put-and-take areas. Some kinds of this dough have become amazingly popular, in fluorescent colours and with glitter.

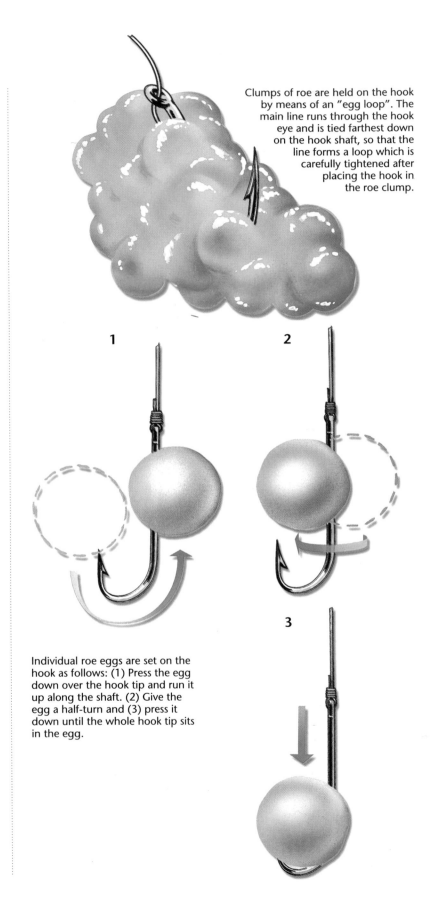

Clumps of roe are held on the hook by means of an "egg loop". The main line runs through the hook eye and is tied farthest down on the hook shaft, so that the line forms a loop which is carefully tightened after placing the hook in the roe clump.

1 **2**

3

Individual roe eggs are set on the hook as follows: (1) Press the egg down over the hook tip and run it up along the shaft. (2) Give the egg a half-turn and (3) press it down until the whole hook tip sits in the egg.

Roe – presented with light equipment – may be extremely useful in catching, for example, elusive trout and salmon.

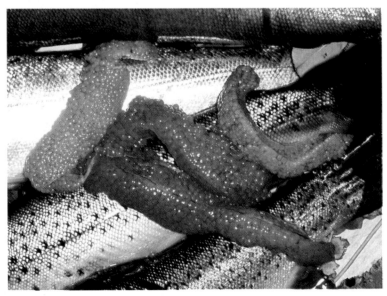

Conserved bait

Natural baits of many types are conserved – including lugworms, fish and shrimp. Conserved and salted baits are seldom as good as fresh baits, but sportfishermen commonly use conserved baits as a reserve – until they catch a fish that can be used as bait. An advantage of most conserved fish species is that the treatment makes them tougher, giving a better grip on the hook.

Pork rind

This type of bait has long existed in America, but never been widely accepted in Europe. Pork rind is meat from a pig's cheek – cut, prepared, and conserved in different ways to become soft, tough and elastic. It is not worth the trouble of producing by yourself, since it costs little and can be bought in a vast range of colours and shapes. Pork rind is mainly placed on jigs, feather hooks, spinners and spoons, when fishing for bass, pike and musky.

Conserved small fish are seldom as good as fresh fish, but they may be a necessary alternative when the quarry is hard to catch.

Pork rind comes in numerous forms and colours. A soft and lively bait, it is used together with, for example, spoons and spinners or jigs when fishing for pike and bass.

The hook sits in the head of a conserved fish, which is then weighted with a sinker somewhat up on the main line, or is retrieved hanging on a short leader after an artificial lure.

It is also attractive to mount conserved small fish on a little jig. This combined bait is jig-fished in the traditional way.

Fish

Fish are the ultimate bait for a great number of predatory fish species. Both live and dead baitfish may be used, as may pieces or strips of fish. In fresh waters, small whole bleak, roach and smelt are placed on single or treble hooks – primarily to catch bass and perch, but also crappie and bluegill among others. Larger baitfish are used mainly for pike and catfish.

There are various ways to put a baitfish on the hook. If it is a live fish for stationary use, the hook is inserted between its dorsal and tail fins – or in the tail. If you want to spin with the fish, or drift with only one hook, the hook is placed in its upper or lower jaw. But dead baitfish, when used without moving to catch pike or pikeperch (zander and walleye), are usually provided with two treble hooks, in the side and in the tail, with the hook tips pointing backward.

Small baitfish can be mounted on jig hooks and offered to pikeperch, perch and pike. Countless tackles have been developed for spinning with baitfish that are either whole or beheaded. These ready-

made tackles consist basically of a leaded head and an arm or body, perhaps equipped with barbs, which is stuck into the baitfish. One, two or three small treble hooks, mounted on an extra-strong and thin wire, are stuck into the bait's sides. Then the bait is ready for serving to the predator. Such a bait is retrieved in the same manner as an artificial lure. However, during the cold season, you should often pause so that it lies on the bottom.

Fish strips are fine for certain species in fresh water, examples being pikeperch and perch. They can be fished on a single hook, or mounted on jigs or feather hooks – which

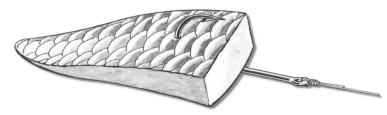

Strips of skin from perch and herring, for instance, have a natural colour and scent, but must be cut properly to look alive.

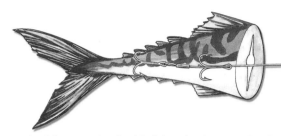

A piece of tail from mackerel, whitefish or herring can give the impression of a bigger bait. The tail fin is attractive, although this bait has a weak scent.

Eel can be good bait in certain waters. Small eels are fished whole, but large ones are cut in pieces and mounted on the hook so that only its bend and tip are visible.

The front, obliquely cut part of a small baitfish is a good substitute for a bigger specimen. It can take a long cast and has a strong scent.

If sewn together, belly parts from perch or whitefish, mounted on spinning tackle, are a good substitute for baitfish, but they easily tear apart when attacked.

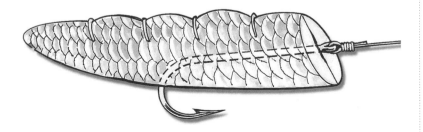

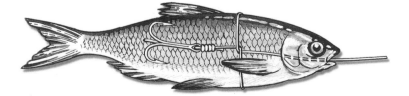

This way of tackling up bait works well for both live and dead fish, which sit securely and can thus be cast far. The treble hook is exchangeable for a single hook.

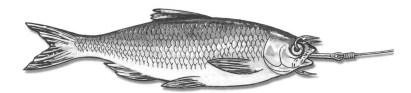

By placing a treble hook in the dead baitfish's mouth as shown here, a durable tackle results. The weighting is done with a sinker, either somewhat up on the main line or on a separate leader.

On this spinning tackle – sometimes called the Drakovitch tackle – the treble hooks sit on the dead baitfish's outside. The bent steel wire in the fish's abdomen holds the bait in place.

With the help of a bait needle, the steel leader has been inserted through the anal opening and out through the mouth. But one must take care that the hook tips are not buried in the flesh.

Here too, the leader has been run through the fish's mouth with a bait needle. This variant with only a single hook is best suited to small baitfish.

On this spinning tackle, the wire leader has been run through the whole fish body with a bait needle. The treble hook, placed through the eye and lower jaw, holds the bait in place even during a powerful cast.

are used as droppers for perch. Moreover, pieces and strips of fish are employed in stationary bottom fishing for pike-perch, large perch, catfish and pike.

In salt water, whole fish as well as pieces, strips or fillets are an easily accessible kind of bait that can tempt nearly all marine fish. They may be fished stationary on the bottom, drifted or spun, depending on the species you want to catch. Fish strips combined with droppers, or fished with a pirk, are excellent baits for cod, ling, and even halibut.

Attractor oils

Scents, flavourings, and attractor oils are used chiefly to prepare artificial baits – but also to drench, spray, or inject natural baits. Some lures are actually designed to be treated, wet, or filled with these substances.

In addition, there are diverse types of dough for use as the only bait on a hook, or together with an artificial bait. In extensively fished waters and under special conditions, when the predatory fish are not tempted by the stimuli that a bait normally sends out, one can benefit by preparing artificial baits with attractive substances. One should not, however, take for granted that they will work on all predatory species.

There is a wide range of oils, pastes, and dough preparations which give out scented substances. For spinning and baitcasting, they are used almost solely in combination with natural or artificial lures, so as to add attractive smells and/or tastes.

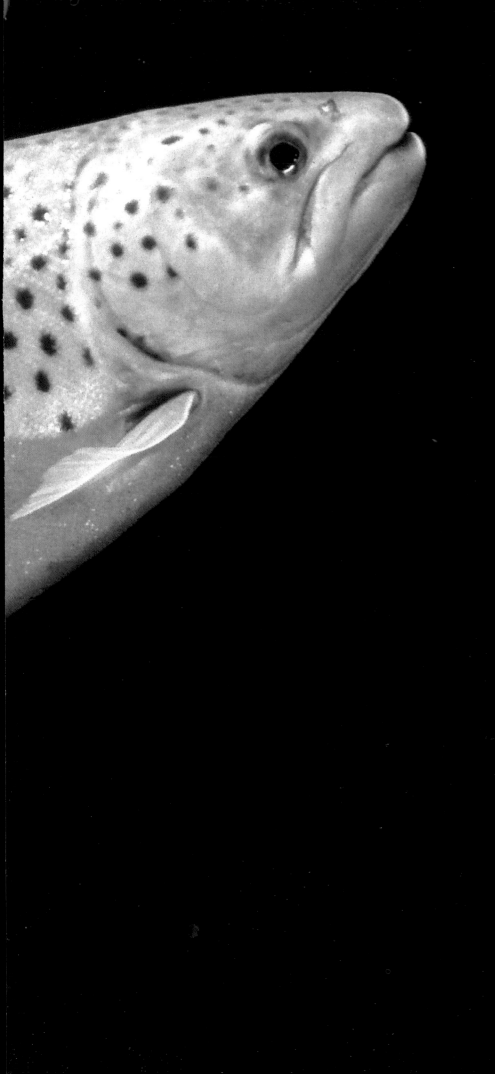

The Environ- ments of Fish

Spinning and baitcasting with success owes a great deal to knowledge about the fish, their surroundings and prey, not only about your own methods and equipment. How fish will react to baits, how their environment determines factors such as the choice of bait and fishing technique, and how their prey indicate the right bait as well as its presentation, are keys to winning on the water.

■

Many of us think that the sciences of fish and water are needless for making a good catch, but nothing can be more wrong. Such lessons give us a much better grasp of the fish's situation, and lay the basis for finer enjoyment, not to mention rewards, when fishing. They may even prove to be essential for having any chance to hook the fish under difficult conditions. So they deserve a place in our baggage as much as do our equipment, tackle and baits.

To keep things simple enough, however, the next pages will take up only what is relevant for sportfishing in general, and for spinning and baitcasting in particular. Around the world we encounter a huge number of fish species, each adapted to its surroundings – and the variations in types of fishing water are so wide that we have to concentrate on their fundamental patterns.

It is certainly true that one can spend a lifetime at the same fishing water without entirely figuring out what makes the fish take a special bait in given circumstances. But here lies much of the mystery and excitement in fishing. Being constantly sure about the fish's location and appetite would indeed lead to boredom, if not to overfishing. Nature's apparent capriciousness may, in fact, be the driving force behind our enthusiasm at the sport.

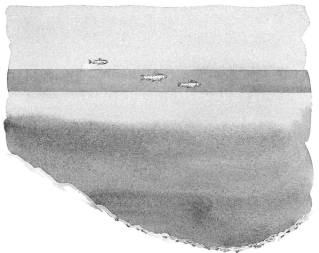

The fish

Virtually all fish are cold-blooded creatures with fins and a spine, living in water and breathing through gills. Few other similarities between them exist, though. Nearly 20,000 species of fish occur on Earth, and their adaptation to varying environments has resulted in amazing diversity. Body structure, colouring, surrounding water temperature and depth and salinity, possibilities of spawning – these and further factors combine in maximizing every species' ability to feed, protect, and multiply itself.

Their cold-bloodedness (poikilothermy) means that, unlike mammals, fish have a metabolism and other body functions adjusted to the water temperature. When it gets cold, they become sluggish and lower their food intake. The colder it is, the less they eat – even if food is abundant nearby. This is the main reason why, in ever colder waters, the fish are increasingly hard to tempt with bait.

Every fish has its optimum temperature: it is most active within a narrow range, such as 10-15° C (50-59° F). With extreme activity, its metabolism and appetite are vigorous,

Most of the fish species in lakes follow a seasonal migration pattern. In spring, the fish move from bottoms to warmer shallow water (*above*). When the surface water in summer becomes too warm, they descend 5-10 metres to the thermocline (*middle*). In autumn as the water cools, the fish can be found in both deep and shallow areas, but go ever deeper with the fall in temperature.

also making it eager to take bait. If the water becomes colder, the opposite happens, depressing both the fish's activity and its urge to satisfy either hunger or fishermen. In a word, negative impact on the fishing arises when the water is colder or warmer than the optimum temperature.

The fish tries to find areas or layers or water where the temperature feels more comfortable. For example, in autumn or winter, the colder water forces it to seek the warmest places – usually near the bottom. During the spring, when the water warms up fast in the surface and in shallow coves, the fish prefers to circulate there. But in summertime, the surface water is so warm that the fish descends to a suitably cool level. Consequently, our chances of catching it are improved by fishing in the areas or levels with temperatures as close as possible to the optimum temperature of that fish species.

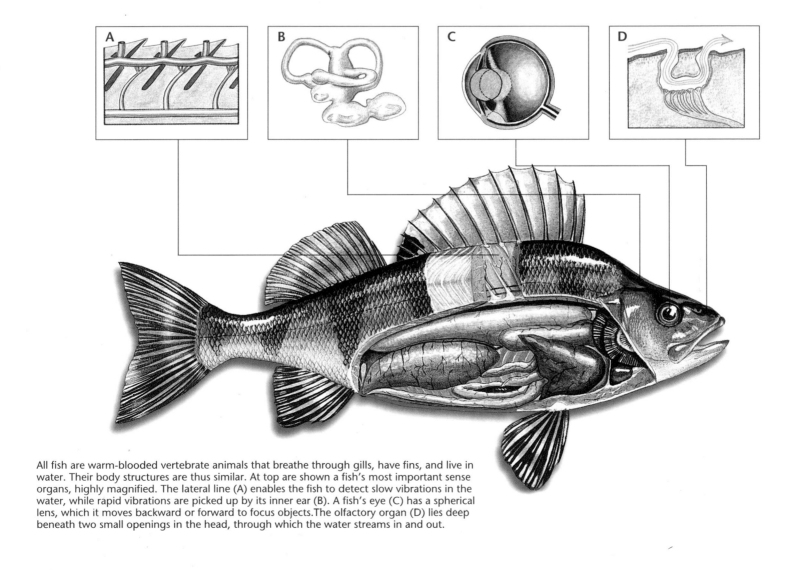

All fish are warm-blooded vertebrate animals that breathe through gills, have fins, and live in water. Their body structures are thus similar. At top are shown a fish's most important sense organs, highly magnified. The lateral line (A) enables the fish to detect slow vibrations in the water, while rapid vibrations are picked up by its inner ear (B). A fish's eye (C) has a spherical lens, which it moves backward or forward to focus objects. The olfactory organ (D) lies deep beneath two small openings in the head, through which the water streams in and out.

A fish's senses

To orient itself in the surroundings, a fish uses its senses just as we do. It can see, hear, smell and taste – but it also has a lateral line, comparable to a hearing organ, extending from the head to the tail. This allows the fish to feel pressure waves in the water, and to determine their direction. It can thus locate objects in either light or darkness. Here is a valuable aid to its search for food during the night, at great depths, or in murky water.

Yet most of the fish species that interest us, when spinning and baitcasting, hunt primarily by sight. A fish's eyes are "designed" with the power of seeing in two directions at the same time. It can focus on an object with both eyes, too, when judging exact distances. This field of vision, or "window", lies straight in front of it and is rather narrow, however, being adapted only to relatively short distances.

The eyes of predatory fish are, as a rule, most suited to feeding in daylight. Still, there are exceptional species with a highly developed ability to see in the dark. Among the best examples is the pikeperch (zander and walleye) – a distinctive night and dusk hunter. Its habit is to sneak up on prey under cover of darkness and attack them quickly. This strategy, of course, requires it to see better in the dark than its prey do.

Considering a fish's limited talent for seeing far away, your bait must be moved – or otherwise made attractive – if the fish is to notice it at all. The bait should send out pressure waves that can be detected by the fish's lateral line, but strong reflections of light or trails of scent also draw attention. A typical instance of lures that generate pressure waves is the spinner, whose rotating spoon produces waves a fish can hear at long distances. Similarly, a plug may contain rattles whose sounds attract fish. This enables you to search a larger area, or entice a less gullible fish onto the hook. However, there is scarcely any artificial bait which can perfectly imitate its natural model. For the same reason, fish that are difficult to trick can seldom resist a correctly presented natural bait, whose smell and taste are genuine.

The fish's senses of smell and taste contribute much to its capacity for orientation and finding food. Some species, like eels, have superb smelling powers, and most fish can detect smells from far away. This has led to increasing experiments with combinations of artificial bait and fragrant substances – as well as to the fact that natural baits are often superior when the fish inhabit a relatively limited area.

Besides locating food, the fish's smell organ – which lies around its nose – helps it to recognize an approaching danger. For example, the smell of a seal can make fish dissolve their school instantly and flee in panic toward all directions. Even during long migrations, smell plays a great role. Thus salmon show phenomenal precision in finding their way back to the river where, much earlier, they were spawned and spent their first years.

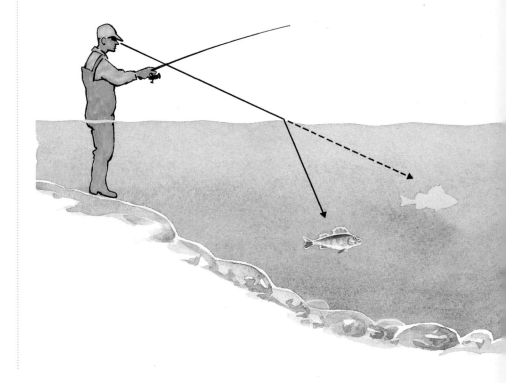

Refraction of light in the water makes it hard for the fisherman to tell exactly where an object is in the water. For example, a fish seems to lie more shallow and far away than it actually does. This illusion applies also to bottom structures and other surroundings under the surface.

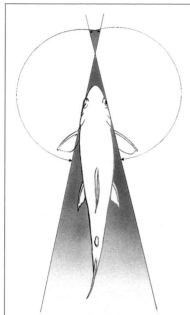

Thanks to its spherical lenses, a fish has a very wide field of vision. Yet only in a narrow frontal region can it see with both eyes at the same time, with "binocular" vision. To each side, it sees with only one eye – and in the "blind zone" behind it, nothing can draw its attention.

A fish can see out of the water through its "window", shaped like an upside-down cone with an angle of about 97.5°. This is formed by the directions in which refraction allows light to reach the fish from above the water surface. As a result, the closer a fish is to the surface, the smaller its field of vision upward.

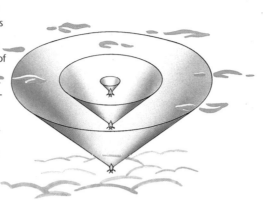

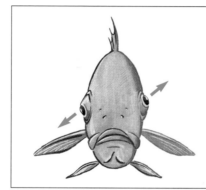

Unlike humans, a fish can move its eyes independently of each other. As shown here, it is thus able to look down (or forward) with one eye and up (or backward) with the other. Still, it can focus on objects with both eyes only inside its binocular field – directly ahead, up or down.

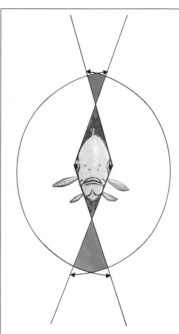

The eyes' way of working also gives the fish an extensive vertical range of vision. Despite seeing with only one eye to each side, it has binocular focusing power in the upward and downward directions as well as in front.

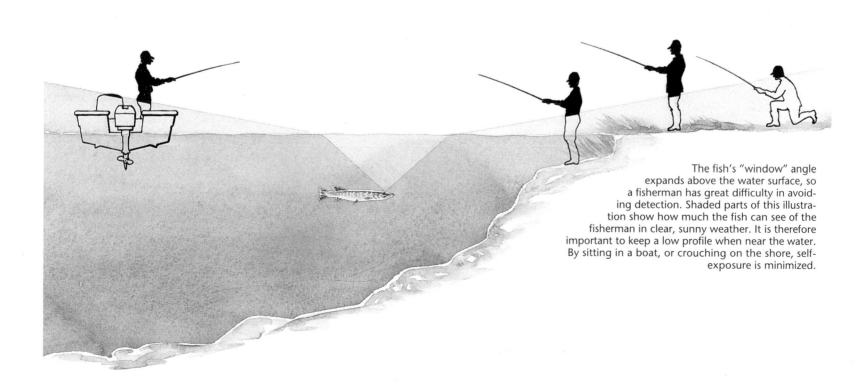

The fish's "window" angle expands above the water surface, so a fisherman has great difficulty in avoiding detection. Shaded parts of this illustration show how much the fish can see of the fisherman in clear, sunny weather. It is therefore important to keep a low profile when near the water. By sitting in a boat, or crouching on the shore, self-exposure is minimized.

Instinctive behaviour

But the biggest difference between us and fish is that they cannot think rationally. A fish does not choose when it bites, nor does it think before it takes or rejects a given bait. Whether fish think at all is doubtful, though we may like to say they do. Their actions are best termed instinctive: special stimuli, or signals, make them respond automatically in some way. A question that has continually intrigued sportfishermen throughout the world is why fish prefer one particular bait and seem completely uninterested in another. Equally baffling is why a fish repeatedly swims after a bait without taking it, and then may suddenly gobble it with violent force.

The short answer is that a certain stimulus, in a certain situation, can release a certain pattern of action. Usually the bait's colour and shape are what trigger the fish's response, but additional factors may influence the "decision" to bite. The more "key stimuli", or main bite-triggering features, are built into a bait, the greater are its chances of being taken. Also typical of an attractive bait is its exaggeration of some key stimuli. These may be its shape, colour, manner of moving, or generation of sound waves. Again, a good example is the spinner, with a rotating spoon that sends out strong pressure waves able to release the fish's strike-reflex.

Hunger and territory

The commonest cause of a bite, obviously, is that the fish feels hungry. A famished fish hunts food, and can therefore be tempted rather easily to take bait. The bait's characteristics somehow signal "food", and thus release the bite. It is a matter of stimuli that activate the fish's instinctive reflex when anything edible appears nearby.

As mentioned, there are situations when the fish shows a

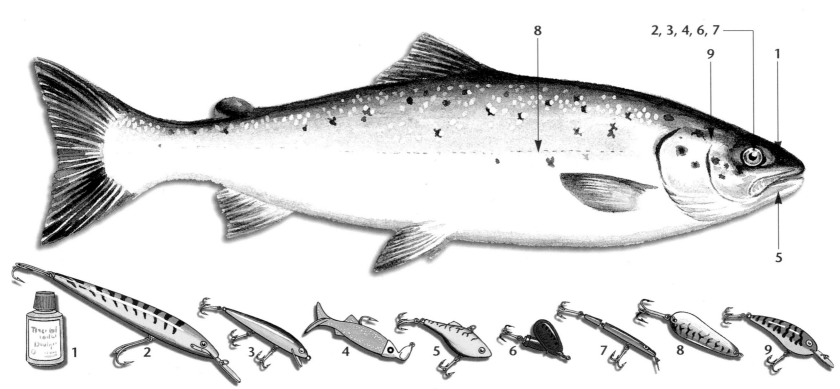

Different types of lure affect the fish in diverse ways – and the more of the fish's sense organs are stimulated, the greater the chances of catching it. Properties that mainly release the fish's instinctive striking reflex are (1) smell, (2-3) shape, (4) size, (5) consistency, (6) action, (7) colour, (8) vibrations and (9) sound. Most lures, of course, are made "irresistible" by exaggerating these typical stimuli.

clear interest in the bait but still does not take it. Such passiveness is explained chiefly by a low level of activity, due for instance to the water temperature, the air pressure, or the fish having just eaten something else. In any case, a hungry fish eats best – and an actively hunting predator needs fewer stimuli to be tempted than does a recently fed, sluggish one.

Another reason why the fish bites may be territorial behaviour. This involves, not an active hunt for food, but aggressive acts to defend, for example, a spawning or holding place. Perhaps most typical are salmon, which stop eating before they migrate up a river, yet continue to take baits – preferably in strong colours – that cross their path. Food has nothing to do with their reflex, which is a lingering urge to bite and/or a defence against invaders of their territory. Frequently the fish become a little more aggressive when the bait's colour agrees with the species' spawning hues, such as red. A key stimulus is then the bait's red colour.

Rainbow trout have many of the traits that characterize a good sportfish. They are usually eager to bite, and thus relatively easy to catch, besides being pugnacious – and excellent to eat. Here is a well-fed specimen entering the net to be landed.

The water

Water environments are almost as diverse as fishing waters. But they share many characteristics too, and can be divided into categories that occur in every part of the world. The roughest distinction is between fresh, marine and brackish waters, followed by that between still and flowing waters. What makes such types of water different, and how does it influence the fish? This is extremely important for the choice of fishing method, technique and tactics.

All water on Earth comes from the sea. The sun's heat produces steam and clouds, which the winds blow over land. There the clouds drop water in the form of rain or snow, to collect in brooks that merge into streams and then rivers. These empty into the sea, where the same hydrological

cycle begins anew. But the water carries other substances, in amounts that are not the same throughout the cycle. They give rise to several properties which determine the various living conditions of fish. Examples are the salt content, oxygen content, and acidity or pH value.

Salt, oxygen, and acidity

Almost any fish is able to change its environment from fresh to salty water and vice versa. This is because a salt-water species has a lower salt content than the surrounding water, while a fish in fresh water has a higher salt content than that water. In other words, the two kinds of fish differ less in salinity than the water types do. This necessary balance is regulated largely by the fish's urine quantity and gill functions. Although regulation of salt is

vital for fish – as for human beings – there are only a few species which can maintain the regulation in both fresh and salty waters. Familiar instances are salmon, sea trout and eels, but it can also be done to some extent by pike, pike-perch, perch and cod. Hence, these species occur rather commonly in brackish waters.

Living organisms need oxygen as well. The water receives oxygen mainly from the air – due to rain, currents, waves, and storms that stir up the surface. Likewise, the rapids and falls in a river add oxygen to it, a primary reason why the areas just below them are often good fishing places, since the fish there have a better supply of oxygen. Yet the leading source of oxygen in water is photosynthesis: submerged algae and green plants use energy from sunlight to generate oxygen.

Another crucial aspect of the water's quality is its pH value. Water with a value of 7 is called neutral. A lower pH value makes the water acidic, whereas a higher one makes it alkaline. Elements such as calcium are alkaline, so waterways through areas with plenty of these (for example in limestone) are naturally alkaline. But when the pH value is below 6, the water is said to be acidified – and at values below 4.5, nearly all life in the water is extinguished. Today, acidification of waters in the industrialized parts of the world is increasing constantly, because ever more nitrogen and sulphur are being released in the air to fall upon land and water with precipitation. To "restore" (neutralize) acidified waters inland, large quantities of calcium must be added continually.

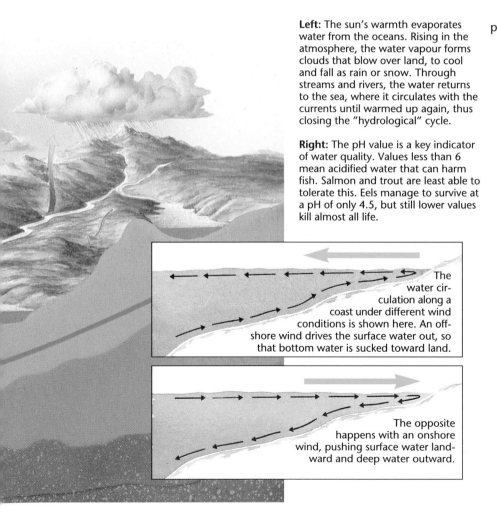

Left: The sun's warmth evaporates water from the oceans. Rising in the atmosphere, the water vapour forms clouds that blow over land, to cool and fall as rain or snow. Through streams and rivers, the water returns to the sea, where it circulates with the currents until warmed up again, thus closing the "hydrological" cycle.

Right: The pH value is a key indicator of water quality. Values less than 6 mean acidified water that can harm fish. Salmon and trout are least able to tolerate this. Eels manage to survive at a pH of only 4.5, but still lower values kill almost all life.

The water circulation along a coast under different wind conditions is shown here. An off-shore wind drives the surface water out, so that bottom water is sucked toward land.

The opposite happens with an onshore wind, pushing surface water landward and deep water outward.

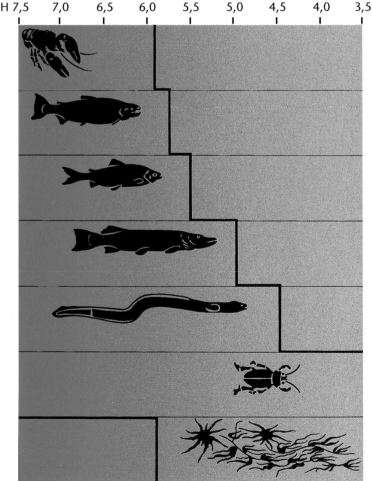

Light and sound

The conditions for light and sound in water are quite different from those in air. Sound actually travels much faster in water, at about 1,500 metres per second, compared to 330-340 in air. Thus, water is by no means a silent realm, something we sportfishermen are rarely aware of. The sharp acoustics in water are a good reason for us to be as quiet as possible when fishing. This applies especially to fishing from a boat, but even on land it is advisable to "sneak" toward the shore and avoid scaring the fish.

Fish do have ears – internal and filled with fluid, allowing them to register high-frequency vibrations in the environment. However, the principal organ enabling them to "listen" is the lateral line. This fluid-filled channel can detect low-frequency sound waves, and is so sensitive that the faintest pressure waves are felt. Since water is an excellent conductor of sound and the fish have such well-developed hearing organs, our fishing must be adapted accordingly. As noted above, the best rule for oneself is to move noiselessly at the water – although one may benefit by using "noisy" baits, which draw the fish's attention and hopefully trigger a strike-reflex.

As for illumination, we find the opposite relationship: light waves are absorbed far more quickly in water than in air. Even in very clear water, only about 1% of the sunlight is left at a depth of 150 metres. The conditions for light in murky water are still worse, and this may be important when fishing, as the fish's ability to notice the bait with its sight is seriously impaired.

To hunt effectively, the majority of fish species depend on light. Pike, for instance, live mainly in rather shallow waters at 1-12 metres. Hence they see poorly in darkness, and need good illumination to make use of abilities such as distinguishing colours.

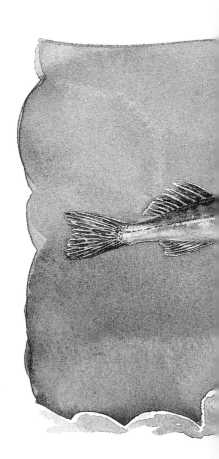

The role of colour

In the spectrum of visible light, blue colours have the most energy, and red colours the least. The practical result is that blue – and next green – are the colours which penetrate deepest in water, while red is absorbed first. When spinning in deep water, the fisherman should thus select baits of blue and green, which are most visible, and avoid the red ones. But silver is the "colour" that best reflects light in deep water, so this is the obvious choice for fishing at depth and/or in murky water with poor visibility.

Some fish species can see colours better than others do.

Among the leaders in this respect are pelagic fish – those which live in the middle layer or the surface water, and hunt chiefly in daylight. Species that live at the bottom in deep water, where the light is so weak that colours hardly exist, are endowed by nature with much worse colour vision, doubtless since it would be wasted on them. In recent years, lures with fluorescent colours have become increasingly common. These hues are strengthened if hit by the ultraviolet rays in sunlight, and can then be seen at long distances. As the UV rays are relatively intense in weak light, fluorescent baits work best under bad light conditions.

The perch is a typical night hunter. It lives in deeper water that is comparatively dark, where an ability to notice different colours is not important. Not only good at seeing in very murky conditions, this fish has also evolved a special strategy for hunting food in darkness.

Right: Light is absorbed much more strongly in water than in air. Its different wavelengths are absorbed at varying rates as it penetrates water. First the red component disappears, next the yellow, then the green and finally the blue. Thus, what illuminate deepest are the blue-green parts of the spectrum. But at depths of 100 metres, the light is too weak even for plant photosynthesis, giving life little chance.

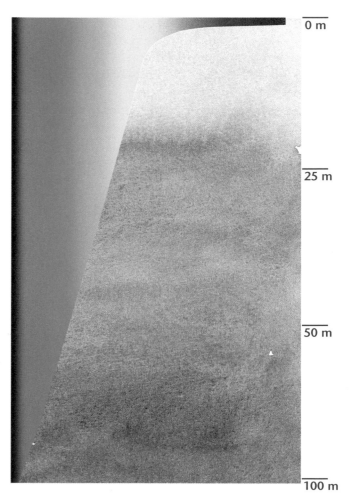

0 m

25 m

50 m

100 m

Currents and temperature

A continuous circulation process goes on in lakes, the sea and, not least, waterways. It greatly influences not only the supply of nutrients and oxygen, but also the variations in water temperature. Currents in turn are affected by the winds, changes in the air's pressure and temperature, and phases of the moon. Tidal currents are due mainly to the moon's and, in some degree, the sun's pull on sea water. These enormous swings of the world's water masses appear most clearly in the ebb and flow of tides, which can alter the water level by up to 15 metres at, for example, the coasts of northwestern France and of Newfoundland.

The interval between ebb and flow is about 12 hours and 25 minutes, or half a "lunar day". Since a solar day is only 24 hours, the time of every ebb or flow is therefore advanced by 50 minutes every day – a shift that will persist as long as the oceans do. Moreover, when the earth, moon and sun are in line with each other, at the new and full moons, a "spring tide" occurs. The difference in water level is then largest, as the ebb water is lowest and the flow highest.

Fish in coastal marine waters tend to move in search of food with the same rhythm as the tides, so the periods before and after an ebb or flow are comparatively good for fishing. Thus, many sportfishermen around the world rely on "bite tables" which are derived from the moon's movements and their tidal effects. Such tables, of course, are more relevant to fishing in the sea than in lakes and other inland waters.

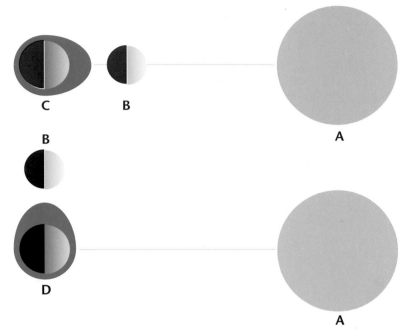

Above: The fishing along coasts is often greatly influenced by tides, which sweep marine food – and therefore also preyfish – toward the land. Tides and their effects on the water level are caused by the pull of the sun and moon on the seas. Spring tides (C), the strongest kind, occur at the time of a new or full moon, when the sun and moon are in a straight line with the earth. Neap tides (D) are much weaker and occur at the half-moon, when the three bodies form a right angle.

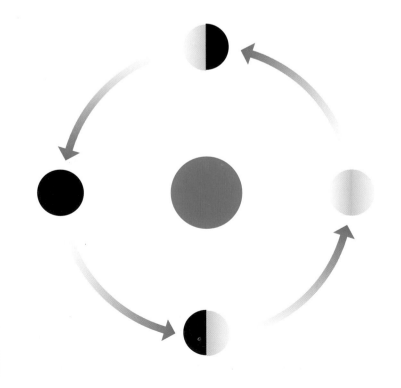

Right: For coastal fishermen, it is essential in many parts of the world to know when the tides will occur. Strike tables are calculated on the basis of the tidal cycle and the moon's position relative to the sun and earth. Here the moon's phases are shown throughout a month. A neap tide occurs at each half-moon; the spring tide is highest and lowest at the new and full moons respectively. But a "moon day" is 24 hours and 50 minutes long, so the tides shift in time by 50 minutes every day.

There is much truth in the saying that 90% of the fish are in 10% of the lake. Since fish migrate regularly according to factors such as the wind, temperature and food supply, they are sometimes very hard to find – a particular surprise to the beginner. But some places are fairly sure bets for fishing: inflows and outflows, underwater banks, deep edges, coves, headlands, isles, straits, and overgrown shores.

During winter, the water masses are relatively stable. As water is heaviest at +4°C, this is the bottom temperature. When the spring sun warms up the surface, the masses begin to move and mix...

until the temperature in the surface is so high that the water separates into layers. These often result in a thermocline, between warm, oxygen-rich surface water and cold bottom water. Across it, the temperature may fall by up to a degree per metre...

but when the water cools in autumn, and all the water approaches the same temperature, the layers mix again. This restratification goes on until the heaviest water is once more at the bottom.

Water circulation

Primarily in the world's temperate zones of climate, the temperature differences in lakes influence the water's density and weight. This creates a regular circulation, with horizontal layers of water, which are most distinct in deep lakes. During summer, the warm water is lighter than cold water, and forms the surface layer. But since water is most dense at 4° C (39° F), the opposite relationship can occur in winter, with the warmest water at the bottom. Consequently, during spring and autumn when the water warms up or cools down, these layers exchange places, the temperature at one time being equal throughout the water mass. It is mainly in summer that the movements of layers produce great contrasts in temperature.

Between the surface layer (epilimnion) and the bottom layer (hypolimnion) lies the thermocline (metalimnion). This zone may be only a few metres deep, yet within it the temperature difference is largest, varying by as much as 10°C (18° F) from its upper to its lower boundary. Often we find species such as pikeperch, pike, bass and perch in the surface layer, and others like trout and salmon in or just above the thermocline, because the former have a higher optimum temperature than the latter.

In lakes, too, the wind may influence the water temperature and the currents. A gale can drive water toward one part of the lake, so that powerful undercurrents return this water when the wind dies or changes direction. Both the gale and the following circulation increase the supply of oxygen in the water, which can stimulate the willingness of fish to take bait.

Hunters and their prey

Where the predatory fish are located in different seasons and types of water is determined by several factors. In addition to the water temperature, currents, depth, salinity and bottom structure, we have to know where the fish can most easily feed.

The shore zone of a lake is normally richest in species of fish. Hence, the competition for food is also greatest there. Species that are highest in the "food chain", namely predators, often need – at least temporarily – to enter the shallow waters in search of food. A predator that commonly occurs very near shores is the trout. So, at times, do other species such as pike, bass and perch.

While pike enjoy somewhat cooler water, and approach the land chiefly during spring and autumn, bass and perch love warm water and are frequently quite active in shallow coves when these have warmed up well. Perch always strive toward the warmest water and are thus found both at the surface layer during summer, and in the least cold bottom layer during winter.

Flowing waters are an environment to which some species are better suited than others. The streamlined body shapes of, for instance, trout and grayling enable them to live even in strong currents. Bottom-dwelling species, such as catfish, can also endure fast currents in spite of their less smooth forms, because they are very good at taking shelter behind stones and in holes on the bottom. However, pike are among the species that do not thrive in strong currents, and therefore inhabit deep holes or backwaters, as well as the calmly flowing parts of streams.

In the sea, for obvious reasons, spinning and baitcasting is usually confined to the shallows and to areas near land. Here the supply of food, and the locations of predatory fish, depend mainly on the bottom's depth and character, and on the water's salinity, currents and tides. Spool-shaped species such as mackerel and pollack live in the middle layer, but can easily rush from one level to another during their tire-

Many predatory fish species, such as trout, have a diurnal rhythm that is largely controlled by the light. In daytime, these fish stay in comparatively deep water without eating much (*below*). At dusk, they rise to shallow waters and hunt with the help of darkness. Frequently they do not return to deep water until dawn. This is why the "golden hours", from just after sunset to just before sunrise, are widely considered the best fishing times.

less quest for prey. Distinctive bottom-dwellers like flatfish stay as far down as possible – and between these extremes are many more species with their own ways of adapting to local marine conditions.

Right: Some fish species, including pike, become cannibalistic in certain situations – notably when other preyfish are scarce. A pike can also take amazingly big prey, up to half its own body weight. This greedy behaviour occurs in both lakes and flowing waters, and creates conditions for stocks of few but huge pike.

Fish and nutrients

Food chains of diverse kinds exist in all water environments. These sequences of hunter, prey, prey's prey, and so on, differ primarily between fresh and salty waters, but also within each of the two realms. Rather than surveying how such chains are built up, we need only note that the fish of interest in spinning and baitcasting – predatory species – are almost always at the top of their chains. Perhaps the best example is the pike, a so-called top predator which heads the chain everywhere it lives.

Predators eat other fish, or insects, that are lower down in the chain. Where, when, and how they do so is important for us to know, since we try to catch predators by presenting natural or artificial bait as though it were edible. In general, a predator hunts more or less actively by pursuing schools of small fish, such as vendace, smelt and herring. If you come upon a school, its predators are likely to be close behind.

Small fish also have their optimum temperatures, seasonal migrations, and places that provide food or shelter – and their predators must follow in order to eat them. With this in mind, one can usually find relatively good fishing spots. Preyfish often linger in shallows, on underwater ridges, and at deep edges. Equally rewarding may be deep holes,

The food chains in lakes and seas are elaborately interconnected. Such a complex food web has a great number of organisms, each stage serving as food for the next. The primary consumers are usually the phytoplankton. These nourish plant-eating plankton, which are consumed by planktonic predators. The latter become food for fish fry that, in turn, nourish top consumers like the pike, perch and trout.

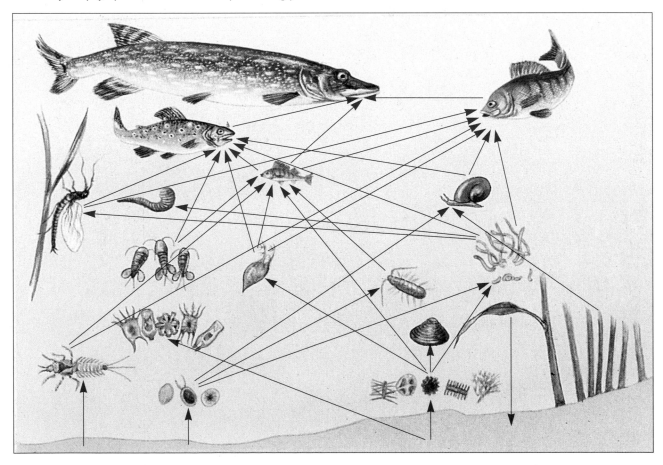

fast-flowing parts of the water, and areas with submerged springs. Worth searching, too, are inflows and outflows, whose oxygen supplies and temperature variations are appreciated by numerous species of fish.

Migrations and meals

Apart from certain fish that migrate far in the sea, predators in lakes and other still waters frequently undertake regular journeys to follow their prey. These travels may depend on the time of day or the season, and are most influenced by the food supply, water temperature, and spawning period.

Right: A largemouth bass heads for the surface to take a well-presented lure. In an instant, it's on the hook...

Below: As a rule, large predatory fish try to maximize their food intake with a minimum of effort. This means gaining as much as energy as possible while losing as little as possible. One result of the energy-saving principle is that a fish prefers a single big mouthful over several small ones.

Such migrations also occur in streams, rivers and other waterways, but to a lesser extent. The predators in flowing waters have a much stronger habit of waiting for the food to arrive, rather than actively seeking it. Lying in a current lee to "ambush" passing prey is characteristic of species ranging from trout to pike.

In conclusion, old hands at spinning and baitcasting commonly catch fish where a newcomer fails, and not just due to luck or chance. The basic reason is knowledge and experience, gathered during a long time of practical fishing. Despite adverse odds, a clever fisherman can get a big one on the hook precisely through awareness of where the fish is holding, when it is hungry, and how – with which methods and baits – it can best be tricked into taking. There are no shortcuts into the record book: you have to keep fishing and go on learning from whatever you catch, as well as from whatever gets away!

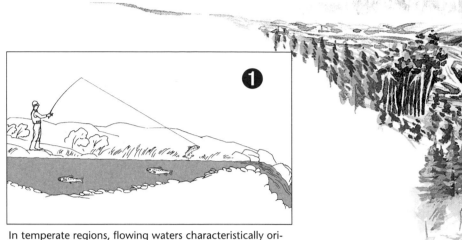

In temperate regions, flowing waters characteristically originate in high mountains, where their sources are cold and well-oxygenated. The strong, fast current is ideal for fish such as trout.

Typical of some fish species, in both fresh and marine waters, is that they hunt through the bottom or middle layers during the day...

...and chase their prey to the surface when the light fades. Certain species stop hunting at sundown, while others continue all night.

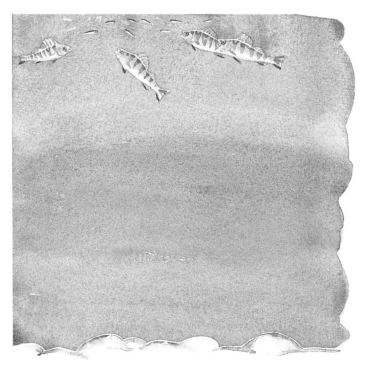

The upper parts of a river's middle section are comparatively deep, with a slower current. The water's oxygen content is still quite high, and there is a greater diversity of species.

Farther downstream, the current is still slower and the river becomes shallower and wider. Typical here are eel, perch, and possibly anadromous (seagoing) species.

In the lowest section, the water tends to be sluggish and murky. The bottom is often muddy, with abundant reeds and other rooted plants. Prominent species are pike and various whitefish.

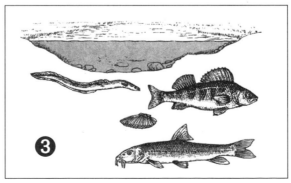

Fishing in Fresh Waters

It is well known that most catches of fish tend to be made by only a small share of the world's sportfishermen. These adepts are distinguished partly by their knowledge of how fish live and behave, which leads them to the best fishing places. Moreover, they try to be either specialists – mastering a single area, species or technique – or else generalists who can easily choose the best method and bait in any circumstances. In both cases the freshwater fisherman has a lot to learn about this relatively peaceful, often fish-full environment.

Pike

The pike (*Esox lucius*) is one of the biggest predators in fresh water, and a more popular quarry today than ever before. It inhabits lakes, pools, rivers and streams, ranging from northern Norway to Italy and far into Asia, as well as in much of the eastern and northeastern United States, Canada and Alaska. However, pike are not happy in Arctic, deep, cold lakes or high mountain waters. Like numerous other freshwater species, they tolerate a certain salt content. They can live in seas with salinity up to 0.7% and are therefore also common in, for example, large parts of the Baltic.

Pike have all the hallmarks of a good sportfish. Their way of life, appearance, and ability to grow heavy are fascinating to many sportfishermen. In Europe their weights exceed those in America. Pike of around 20 kilograms (44 pounds) are landed every year by Europeans, while the limits are 15-18 kg (33-40 lbs) in North America, although most places yield pike of up to 6-7 kg (13-15 lbs). This species also has some close relatives. The chain pickerel, weighing up to 1.5 kg (3.3 lbs), and two even smaller species, occur only in North America. Another instance is the muskellunge, and Asia boasts the Amur pike.

Spinning for pike

A hungry pike is not hard to get on the hook, but as a rule the fishing calls for an awareness of spinning methods and baits, and of the pike's holding places. In early spring, late autumn and winter, the water is cold and you have to retrieve slowly. Artificial lures should be worked across the bottom with many spin-stops, alternating slow and rapid retrieval. Between late spring and early autumn, the warmer water increases the fish's activity, so the retrieval must be livelier and still more varied.

Spinning for pike can be categorized by the depth of water involved. In shallow water, light spoons of thin sheet metal are used. Small spinners of 7-12 grams are classic lures for pike, but light spinners with large spoons and a high gait are also very effective. Floating plugs are superb

Pike are a popular species of sportfish in numerous countries, mainly because this gluttonous predator can grow very large and is common in many waters. It can also offer exciting and spectacular fishing.

Vital facts

When the water warms up in spring, the pike prepare to spawn. A female pike grows larger than males, and is followed by one or more of them during the mating. Her eggs hatch after 10-15 days and the fry live on food such as small insects and larvae. Once a few centimetres long, the young pike begins to eat fish fry. It grows fastest in water with plenty of preyfish whose sizes suit its successive years of growth. The pike has a vigorous appetite and prefers preyfish weighing 10-15% as much as it does. If the preyfish are abundant, it usually eats a big meal 1-2 times weekly, instead of constantly chasing little fish. This manner of hunting characterizes stocks of large pike, while small pike are in a continuous state of growth and therefore feed more often. Probably as a result, the pike is famous for rising to bite in particular periods. It is also cannibalistic, and it eats a great deal besides fish – including frogs, water voles, and young birds.

Pike hunt chiefly by using their sight, but have well-developed senses of taste and smell – as is shown by the ease of catching them with dead baitfish. They are most active in daylight, and studies have revealed that they become almost totally inactive in darkness.

Though normally staying at the bottom, pike are sometimes found much higher up. Thus, it is not quite true that pike are typical bottom-fish dwelling among reeds and tree roots. They are especially active in autumn and just after spawning. During these periods, too, they often occur in the shallows. Summer brings them into deeper water, for example at submerged edges and shoals. But in cold climates, as in Scandinavia and Canada, you can fish for big pike in shallow water throughout the summer.

When a pike is on the take, it seldom proves hard to tempt with a spinner, spoon or wobbler. Often, though, one must know where the pike are holding, and adapt one's spinning method accordingly.

Right: Among the most effective lures when spinning for pike is a wobbler (plug), whose movements and shape imitate the fish's natural prey quite well. A wobbler can also be fished at nearly all depths, and is thus able to trick deeply dwelling big pike onto the hook.

when spinning in shallow water. As soon as the water temperature rises, surface plugs start to pay off among reeds, water-lilies and other vegetation. Even the biggest surface plugs, such as the Suick, do excellently in shallows.

In wider lakes, pike move to deep water during the late spring. Once they go below 3-4 metres, however, heavier equipment is needed. Before the retrieval begins, the lures should be given time to sink to the bottom, since that is where the pike are lurking.

Heavy drags of 25-35 and sinking plugs are fine in deep water. As you retrieve, many pauses should be made, enabling the lure to stay at the bottom all the time. Fishing with weighted, floating plugs may also be effective. The line or leader is weighted according to the depth, the retrieval speed, and the plug's size and weight. Small plugs, of course, require less weighting than big ones.

Weight-forward spinners are the only type of spinner that works well for pike in deep water. This type is used down to 8-10 metres.

A pike's jaws are endowed with hundreds of teeth that can quickly shred the line, so it is always essential to use a steel leader when spinning. A leader 20-35 cm (8-14 in) long is perfect, but you can tie your own leaders with, for example, nylon line of 0.65-0.75 mm.

Natural baits can be extremely rewarding in some types of water. But this fishing requires much greater knowledge of the fish's locations than does spinning with artificial lures. Perch and roach are common baitfish, and other small fish can also appeal to pike.

Pike fishing with natural bait

The practice of fishing with dead or live baitfish is widespread primarily in Great Britain and Central Europe, where this tradition has existed for ages. It is most effective in coloured and hard-fished waters, especially during the cold months and when the holding places of pike tend to be well-defined and familiar. Compared to the mobility of spinning, every form of fishing with natural bait has a limited degree of water coverage – yet experience shows that large pike are often caught with baitfish.

The majority of live baitfish with lengths of 10-20 cm (4-8 in) can be used, such as roach, bleak and other whitefish. However, it is forbidden to use live baitfish in several countries, including Norway, Holland and Germany. Fishing with dead baitfish is usually done with roach and herring, but pieces of eel have also proved their worth.

There are two main ways of fishing with baitfish. One is float-fishing, with a fixed or sliding float, depending on the water depth. The baits can be presented either at the bottom or in free water. The other method is bottom-fishing with a fixed or sliding tackle, possibly combined with a sliding float.

Both live and dead baitfish are mounted with a treble hook in the tail. Many pike fishermen use two treble hooks for dead bait – one in the tail and one in the side. The hooks are placed with their tips pointing backward, since the pike normally take the prey crosswise and turn it in their jaws, then swallow it with the head forward. This fishing employs a steel leader 35-40 cm (14-16 in) long. In the case of dead baitfish, one often uses a bite indicator, and usually fishes with two rods at the same time. Treble hooks of sizes 4-10, depending on how big the preyfish are, serve ideally here. The best size for baitfish is 15-20 cm (6-8 in).

Spinning with dead baitfish is also enjoyed in some countries. Most simply, the baitfish is mounted with a treble hook in the upper and lower jaws, and another in the side. Then the baitfish is weighted with lead on the leader, and retrieved slowly or in jerks. Floats may also be used for simple spinning.

Ready-made tackle for spinning with baitfish is available as well. Such a tackle consists of two or three small treble hooks, a leaded head, and a loop which is run into the baitfish. In recent years an East European tackle, the Drakovitch, has won notable popularity for spinning with dead baitfish. It simplifies a type of tackle that has existed for decades in Central Europe. The retrieval is done in jerks near the bottom with repeated spin-stops.

Fighting and landing the fish

During the fight, an even and strong pressure is kept on the pike, and in shallow waters it does its best to leap. In many countries, fish are traditionally released to the water. For this purpose, a pike can be either beached or else landed with a large hand-net. But a net is unsuitable when you fish with big plugs, since the hooks easily catch in its meshes. A gaff is also commonly used in some countries, being carefully drawn into the lower jaw corner. Alternatively, the pike can be gripped beneath the gill with a leather or working glove. Small pike may be landed by taking a firm grip over the neck.

Small pike can be landed easily with a steady grip over the neck, but for larger ones a net or gaff should be used. An important point is to tire the pike out thoroughly before landing it, since otherwise it may shake itself off the hook. Once it is weary, it can be led into the net – which should then be in the water – and lifted.

Muskellunge

The musky (*Esox masquinongy*) is a relative of the pike that occurs in the northeastern United States and in southeastern Canada from Lake Abitibi down to Lake of the Woods. Farther south, it lives in the upper Mississippi and Ohio Rivers, in New York, Pennsylvania and Tennessee, North Carolina and Georgia, as well as in the St. Lawrence River and the Great Lakes. It can grow larger than pike – up to 25 kg (55 lbs). Excessive sportfishing for decades has decimated its stocks, and examples over 10 kg (22 lbs) are now rare. Yet specimens of 10-15 kg (22-33 lbs) are still caught every year in, for example, the St. Lawrence and its tributaries. While even so-called professional sportfishermen must devote several days to hooking a musky, it is considered by many to be the ultimate "pikefish".

Among other terms for this fish are muskalonge, lunge, blue pike and muskallunge. It is long and slender, some-

what paler than a pike, and has distinct wide vertical stripes. There are three subspecies within the musky's region of distribution. It is thought to have originally lived in salt water and migrated up the Mississippi – where the stocks were isolated due to the Ice Age, and from where it later spread out. Fossils show that it also existed in southern Europe during the Tertiary period.

Spinning for musky

Musky can be caught both by spinning and with natural bait on tackle, but spinning is the usual method. In general,

Vital facts

The musky spawns in shallow water, preferably on a smooth bottom with tree roots and branches, at about the same temperature as for pike – but the spawning occurs at night. Afterward, the musky stays in shallow clear water, around vegetation banks, seldom at depths of more than 4-5 metres.

Occasionally these fish wander out to deeper water, where they are nearly impossible to catch. In rivers, they prefer the deep calm parts, and their most typical holding places are at inflows. They stay in the same areas during most of the summer, although the warmth in rivers often makes them migrate higher up.

Musky grow fast, and eat like gluttons in springtime. Late summer and especially autumn are regarded as best for musky fishing. The females become larger than the males, and the growth is most rapid in the northern latitudes of distribution. One musky of 69.7 lbs (31.6 kg) has been age-determined to 30 years. The fish's menu is identical to the pike's, as is its way of hunting.

rapid retrieval gives the best results. Large "bucktail" spinners, spinnerbaits and buzzbaits are designed for musky. This was originally also true of many of the surface plugs which are now used for pike.

Most big muskellunge are females, and are normally caught in September and October – often during the afternoon. Musky fishing demands a lot of patience. The fish is a loner and frequently needs a great number of casts to be tempted into taking. Pike may follow the bait once or twice before taking, but this behaviour is more typical of musky.

Left: The musky, a close relative of the pike, occurs only in North America. It normally weighs 11-22 lbs (5-10 kg) and is caught chiefly in autumn, with artificial or natural baits.

Above: A "freshwater crocodile" has taken the bait and tries desperately to get free of it during the fight's last phase.

Zander

The European pikeperch, or zander (*Stizostedion lucioperca*), is naturally distributed across Eastern Europe, Russia and southern Siberia. From there it has spread to western Europe and occurs from southern Scandinavia down to the northern parts of Italy and Spain. It has even been implanted in Great Britain, though not appreciated by English anglers. Zander also live in brackish water, and can be found throughout the Baltic.

A close relative is the Volga zander, in southeastern Europe as well as much of Russia and Siberia. In the United States and Canada are two others – the walleye and sauger.

This fish enjoys murky water, where it faces no competition from pike. It hunts smaller fish such as roach, bleak and perch. Wide waters are its preferred habitat, to depths of at least 4-5 metres.

Spinning for zander

Sight, smell and hearing are all used by zander when they hunt. But the spinning technique used for pike has no impact on these fish, since they cannot swim as fast or see as well. The key to zander fishing is slow retrieval with good bottom contact and, ideally, bait that "jabs" the bottom – thus relying on the fish's hearing and sight.

Probably one of the best types of artificial lures for zander is the jig. Its special body and upturned hook also make it easy to fish just over the bottom.

A jerky retrieval creates sounds that attract pikeperch. Jigs with silicone bodies are extremely effective. The combination of a jig with fish strips is arousing, too, as it activates the zander's sense of smell. Many scent-impregnated rubber bodies work superbly on zander. In all seasons and water temperatures, you should retrieve slowly and jerkily, though a bit faster during the hot months. A jig performs as spectacularly in still waters as in flowing waters, where the zander prefer deep channels with stones and considerable current.

Pikeperch are active in darkness, and spend most of their time at the bottom in deep water. They should be fished by retrieving slowly and trying to keep in contact with the bottom.

Vital facts

Zander spawn from late March until the beginning or middle of April, at a higher temperature than for pike. The sticky eggs are laid on branches and stones in shallow water. River mouths, too, are favourite spawning places. After a few weeks the spawning ends, when the temperature reaches 15-16° C (59-61° F). But windy weather can quickly silt up the eggs and the spawning bottoms. This is one reason why zander stocks are classified according to good and bad years.

Soon after hatching, young zander eat water-fleas and plankton. Next they adopt a menu of fish fry and small fish. Similarly to pike, they are also cannibalistic.

The zander has a special way of hunting, which is shown by its shape and body structure. Being less slender than the pike, it cannot swim fast. Yet its night vision is excellent, and it has large eyes that shine like reflectors in a lamp's light. It is built to live on the bottom, where it can follow prey for long distances. The prey is attacked from behind. Zander in general are active fish in cloudy weather and at night.

During the summer, zander move out to the shoals and edges in deep water. At evening and night, they return to hunt in shallow water or higher levels. Towards morning when it gets light, they swim back to the depths. These daily migrations also occur in autumn. During that season and in winter, they often run up rivers and streams. Zander always prefer hard bottoms – stone, sand, cliffs and banks. Small ones are quite sociable and frequently form little schools to stay in limited areas. Large zander are usually solitary.

It is typical for a stock of zander that the fishing is good for some years but then deteriorates. Such variations are presumably due to the supply of prey-fish. Many waters contain zander of 1-3 kg (2.2-6.6 lbs) and bigger ones only exceptionally. In other waters, there can be a few years of fine fishing for medium or large zander, whereupon the fish die out – to revive a few years later. Examples of 1-2.5 kg are the rule, while weights of 5-8 kg (11-18 lbs) are rare and the maximum is 12-14 kg (26-31 lbs).

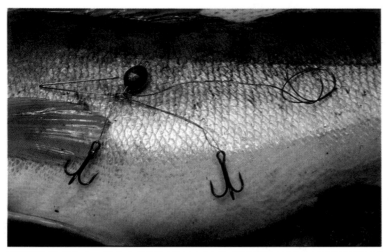

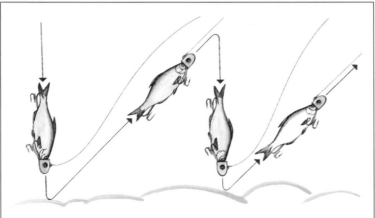

When fishing with natural bait, the weighted baitfish is fished in with repeated spin-stops and good bottom contact. The upper picture shows a so-called Drakovitch rig, with a shackle that is run into the baitfish's belly.

The pikeperch is not famous for being a great fighter, but it is an excellent foodfish. Since it can be difficult to hook, sharp and slender hooks are often necessary.

Weight-forward spinners are well suited to spinning for zander. They not only give better bottom contact, but can be retrieved in jerks and continue to rotate as they sink. Moreover, the spinner head generates clear sounds when it hits the bottom.

Spinning with a plug – which may be a "deep-going" type with a rattle and a long bill – is unbeatable for zander. The rattle makes sounds that attract the fish while the deep-diving plug's spoon jabs the bottom. It was once commonly believed that zander are partial to small preyfish, and thus also small baits, but with experience they are found to gobble even big plugs of up to 20 cm (8 in).

No matter what type of artificial bait you use, false bites are frequent, and time alone can teach you to distinguish "bottom contact" from a zander's cautious nibble. Hence it is important to use needle-sharp hooks and, if possible, replace the treble hook with a thinner one – especially in water with lots of little zander.

Keep in mind that zander are most active by dark – whether in the morning, evening, night, or during cloudy and windy days. On the whole, low-pressure weather is best. On bright days the fish must be sought in deep water. Particularly during winter and just before it ices up, shallow water can yield zander. What the species may lack in fighting spirit – compared for example to pike and trout – it definitely outweighs with its unpredictable behaviour, which has thrilled sportfishermen down the centuries. Besides, it is a marvelous food fish.

Being relatively shy, a pikeperch frequently takes the bait with careful hesitation. Gliding tackle is thus usually best for catching it, either at the bottom or some metres up.

Zander fishing with natural bait

The zander's manner of using its senses make it a true challenge to catch with natural baitfish. It bites somewhat hesitantly and may be shy. A sliding tackle is therefore best used. This allows the fish to swim away with the bait and feel no resistance from the sinker. You can also combine sliding tackle with a sliding float.

An electronic bite indicator is employed when you have fish strips, fillets, or dead baitfish on the hook. A steel leader is not necessary, but this or some other strong leader material is worth using, since the fishing often takes place in waters that also contain pike. A nylon leader of 0.35-0.40 mm is

quite adequate, unless you fish in areas with roots, stones and other obstacles that the fish can exploit.

When fishing with live baitfish, the treble hook is inserted in the back or tail, or between the dorsal and tail fins. With dead baitfish or fish strips, though, it is stuck in the tail root or the thin part of the strip. Use hooks of size 6-10 according to the bait's size. Baitfish of 12-16 cm (4.5-6.5 in) are fine for zander.

All fishing with natural bait is done on, or just over, the bottom. During the night, zander move upward in the water, so at a lake's shoals and edges it is occasionally best to fish a couple of metres above the bottom.

Walleye

The American pikeperch, or walleye (*Stizostedion vitreum*), is common in the northeastern United States, notably around the Great Lakes, from where it has spread to many other states and to Canadian provinces. However, it has an affinity with large lakes and rivers. Walleye are found in both clear and murky lakes, more or less resembling the European zander. They can weigh nearly 10 kg (22 lbs), but 1-1.5 kg (2.2-3.3 lbs) is most usual.

Spinning for walleye

This sport is basically no different from spinning for zander, as both species have the same way of life and behaviour. Familiar methods are fishing with a jig, lead-headed spinners, plugs with rattles, and deep-going plugs.

Vital facts

This fish spawns in shallow water at a higher temperature than pike. The fry live briefly on insects, larvae and crustaceans, but soon begin to eat small fish. Just like the zander, walleye are typical bottom-dwellers. Deep edges, shoals, stony areas and rocky banks are their favourite lairs. At evening and night, they enter shallow water or higher levels, and are then most active. But they can also be caught in daytime, and the best season is spring.

Walleye move in groups, seldom at depths of more than 4-5 metres. Towards summer, they seek deep water, but rarely go down over 10 metres. During this season they may – like the zander – stay a few metres above the bottom, particularly at dusk and night. Thus it can be hard to catch them with artificial lures, yet not with live bait. In the autumn, they return to shallow water and remain there all day and night.

Another option is the spinner rig, an American tackle that has also been tried with great success on zander, especially in Central Europe. It consists of a spinner blade on a nylon leader of 0.40-0.45 mm. The spinner's "body" is a row of beads, and the leader is tied to a single hook. The distance between body and hook can vary by up to 5-6 cm (2-2.3 in). On the hook is set a natural bait such as earthworm, fish strips, salamander, young frog, or leech. This is a sliding tackle with a sinker of suitable size. The length of leader before the spinner is 60-80 cm (23-31 in), and the retrieval should be slowly "crawling". You can simplify the rig by removing the spinner blade, so that in practice you are fishing only with a through-going sinker, leader, and bait on a single hook – but the spinner produces sound waves that attract the fish. With a spinner rig, your strike must be rapid, although you should wait a few seconds if fishing with the simplified rig. Both types of tackle can be used for regular spinning – and for fishing from a boat, when the tackle should be virtually dragged over the bottom.

Also appropriate for spinning with natural bait are lead-headed spinners with a single hook. Earthworms, fish strips, leeches and other natural bait are all used here.

Fishing with whole baitfish is a very unusual method of catching walleye – unlike the zander fishing in Europe.

Far left: Wobblers are a well-known aid to spinning. Both deep-going wobblers and those with rattles can attract fish, especially in daytime when they are holding in deep water near the bottom.

Left: Under cover of darkness, a walleye moves up to shallower water in order to hunt. Then it can be tempted with various kinds of spinner rigs – whether simple ones or elaborate versions baited with, for example, earthworms or imitation worms.

Perch

The perch (*Perca fluviatilis*) occurs all over Europe, Asia and North America, except in the Arctic regions and in clear, cold mountain lakes. It also enjoys brackish water and is common along the Baltic coasts. There are perch in the smallest meres as well as the biggest lakes and rivers. This fish is easily recognized by the black stripes over its back, and its red or yellow fins. Its colours tend to be strongest in clear water. It weighs from a few tenths of a kilogram up to 2-3 kg (4.4-6.6 lbs).

Spinning for perch

Because of their capricious inclination to take bait, perch provide exciting experiences for sportfishermen. One day they may attack whatever moves, and the next day you may try everything in the bait-box with no results. If a perch follows a spoon, spinner, jig or plug without biting, this is a sign of unwillingness. A varied retrieval with many

Vital facts

Perch spawn in shallow water during early spring, and then move to deeper water. While the perch in shallow lakes and rivers pursue a vagabond life, big lakes contain both pelagic perch that hunt in deep water, and typical shallow-water perch that occur near the shores almost all year round.

Being a distinctively predatory fish, the perch prefers clear water – but in murky water its spawning opportunities are often better, and neither its eggs nor young are as easily noticed by other fish. Thus coloured waters tend to have abundant stocks of small perch.

This is a sociable fish and usually lives in schools of varying size. They gather at deep edges, shoals, in deep parts of streams, at boat piers or bridge pillars. A school also gives good protection against higher predators.

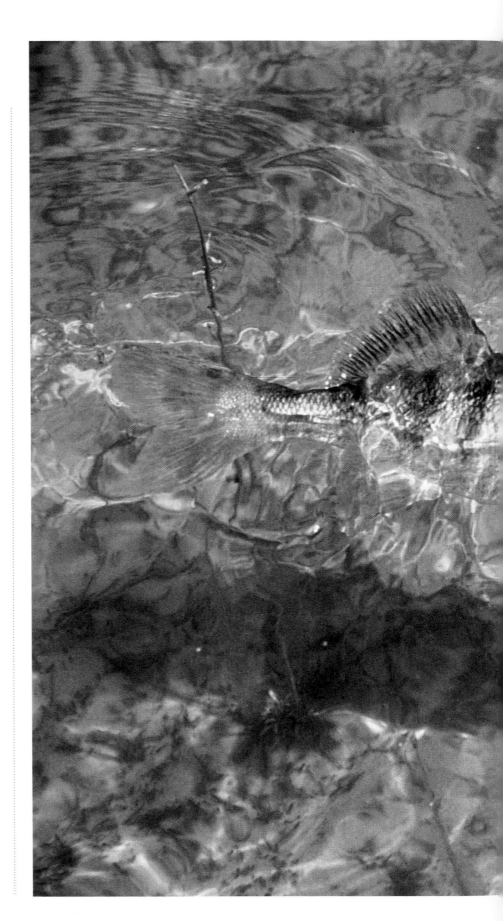

Characteristic of a perch are its black transverse stripes from the back down toward the abdomen, and red or orange-yellow fins. The clearer the water is, the stronger the colours tend to be.

spin-stops and tugs is then important. Impulsive and unusual methods of retrieval are frequently essential to attract such perch. Even a particular movement may be what triggers their reflex – or a certain colour of bait, since perch have excellent colour vision. Once the first perch has taken bait, it commonly starts a chain reaction and others do so as well.

Perch are not confined to the bottom: often they occur 2-3 metres up. During the summer, they may hunt small fish in the surface, and their presence in big lakes is often revealed by diving gulls. It is therefore wise to search a body of water in different ways, for example at the bottom, just above it, in the middle layer and at the surface.

However wild and greedy the perch is when biting, it can be sly and unreachable when, for instance, the weather makes it unwilling. There are many indications that its mood is influenced by the air pressure. A stable low or high pressure is normally good for the fishing, yet a rapidly falling or rising pressure may lead perch virtually to stop hunting. Still, some sportfishermen have quite the opposite impression about how air pressure affects the fishing.

Spinning for perch can be pursued with almost all types of artificial lures, but certain types do work better than others. Spinners and small spoons are traditionally used in shallow waters, although fishing with a jig is usually best. In deep waters, great success is often achieved with a heavier jig, a lead-headed spinner, or deep-going sinking plugs.

Using a dropper, a little fly or micro-jig, above the lure is a fine trick to play on perch. Their innate curiosity, together with envy of the little prize, can provoke a bite. Slow, jerky retrieval is especially worthwhile with dropper flies, which can also be baited with worms, larvae, or a piece of fish skin. Moreover, perch love strong or contrasting colours such as red/black, orange/yellow and white/red. Marked "eyes" on a jig may yield further attraction.

Perch fishing with natural bait

It is equally possible to catch perch with natural bait, and many sportfishermen have begun their pastime by doing this with worms. A float or a bottom tackle for angling is effective throughout the year, and best of all in the winter

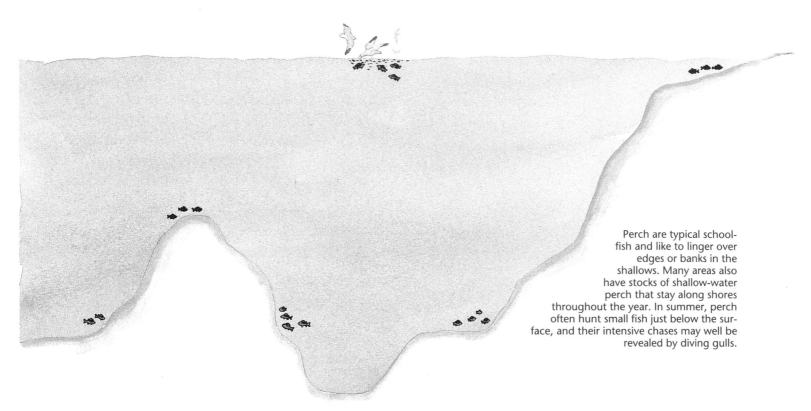

Perch are typical school-fish and like to linger over edges or banks in the shallows. Many areas also have stocks of shallow-water perch that stay along shores throughout the year. In summer, perch often hunt small fish just below the surface, and their intensive chases may well be revealed by diving gulls.

While jig fishing is widely regarded as the best way to catch perch, sinking wobblers can also succeed, particularly with large specimens in deep water.

The perch's temperamental biting behaviour may call for refined tricks to get it on the hook.
A reluctant perch can often be made to bite by using repeated spin-stops and a varied retrieval.

when perch are less active. In general, fishing with a float is most suitable in shallow waters, and bottom tackle in deep water – specifically a paternoster tackle with, or without, dropper traces. If you fish from a drifting boat, such tackle is very rewarding and the hooks can be baited with worms.

Large perch are often caught with live baitfish, on a bottom tackle or in combination with a float. Baitfish are a selective way of fooling big perch in waters that have abundant stocks of whitefish and smaller perch.

Just as one fishes for pike with dead baitfish, selective bottom-fishing for big perch is done with cut, bloody strips of various whitefish species. Here a sliding tackle is used. Since perch are predatory, they eagerly take these strips – a superb method in waters full of whitefish, eel, and small

perch that attack other types of bait and would thus sabotage directed fishing for big perch.

Fighting and landing the fish

A perch's mouth is soft and cannot always be hooked securely. So it must be tired out with uniform, but not excessive, pressure. Small perch can be slid up on land where the shore allows. If fishing from a boat, you can grip the line and pull perch on board with a calm, careful movement. But landing with a net is safest. A big exhausted perch can be landed smoothly and gently by taking the lower jaw with your thumb in its mouth, and holding your forefinger under the jaw for support – a grip that is also used in bass fishing.

Bass

The American bass may well be the most popular sportfish in the world. There are six species and four subspecies of American black bass, but in practice they are divided into smallmouth bass (*Micropterus dolomieu*), weighing up to 4 kg (8.8 lbs), and largemouth bass (*Micropterus salmoides*) which can weigh nearly 10 kg (22 lbs). These have different distributions. Smallmouth bass originally lived in the northeastern United States and southeastern Canada, and have not spread as far as largemouth bass. The latter first inhabited the eastern USA, from the Great Lakes to Florida and the prairies, but has spread by implantation and now occurs in all the western states. It has also been quite successfully implanted in Mexico and Central America, as in Guatemala and Costa Rica. The same was done in Cuba as early as 1915, and it exists in Hawaii. Largemouth bass even reached Brazil in 1926, and can be found in 16 African countries such as Morocco and South Africa.

In 1879 an English biologist brought the bass to Europe, and it was implanted in many countries – including Hungary, Austria, Switzerland and Russia – but died out. Today there are small stocks in the southern parts of Germany and France, although it is more widespread in Italy and Spain. At most places in Europe it weighs hardly over 2 kg (4.4 lbs), but Spain has the best bass waters and yields specimens up to 5 kg (11 lbs).

In the USA, bass have spread along with people, being regarded as a good "reserve fish" to keep on farms. All canals, lakes, rivers, reservoirs and small ponds now contain bass. These fish tolerate high temperature, multiply easily and grow fast. Their inability to live in many countries is due to their need of warm water at 20° C (68° F) during May and June, when they spawn. On the other hand, they survive in water up to 30° C (86° F). Yet they cannot take murky or muddy waters, and have thus done poorly in many African countries, whose rivers are often turbid.

Spinning for bass

Bass fishing is not easy in deep water, and the finest experiences are obtained in shallows that help you to hook the fish. A bass can see extremely well, which makes the bait's colour important, but it is still more essential to retrieve slowly at depth along the bottom. However, even if this applies to

Bass are extremely popular sportfish, notably in the USA. They occur in both deep and shallow waters, but are typical warm-water fish, so one usually finds them in the water areas with highest temperature.

Vital facts

After the spawning, which takes place in shallow water, fishermen begin to spin for bass. However, the fishing depends on the weather and improves as it gets warmer. Bass have a broad diet – from small worms and insects to fish fry, small fish, mice and frogs. They often behave sociably and may move in little schools, groups or "packs", but are also found individually.

As a rule, bass alternate between deep and shallow water but do not go very far. They presumably maintain territories and spend most of the time there at the bottom. When encountered in shallow water, they stay near vegetation – reeds, lilies, trees, and whatever else can provide shade or protection, as well as edible small fish.

Bass fishing is not difficult once you find the quarry. This is the real problem, besides deciding the right type of artificial bait. At the start of the season, the bass are in shallow water where the temperature is highest, and as it approaches 20-21° C (68-70° F) your chances improve. Later in the season, when the water gets too warm, the bass move to deeper water and must be sought at the bottom – very seldom in the middle layer. While they linger among plants and stones in shallow water, deep water finds them at reefs, edges and shoals, as preyfish gather there too. In the morning and evening, the bass return to shallow water along the shores – and notably in vegetated waters, fishing in the morning is best of all. Towards autumn and winter, the bass are again wherever the temperature is highest.

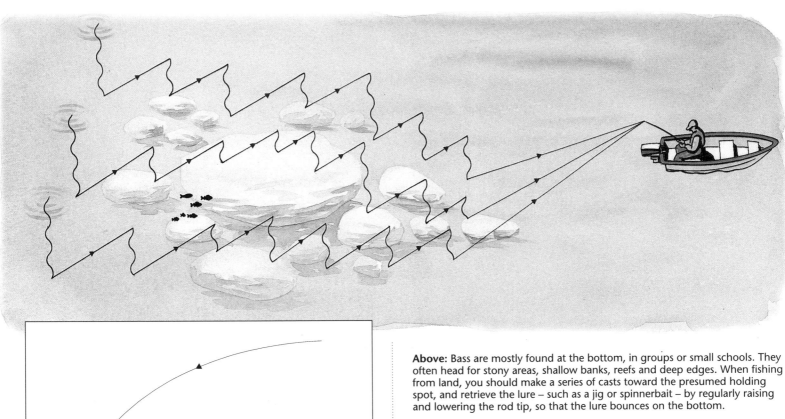

Above: Bass are mostly found at the bottom, in groups or small schools. They often head for stony areas, shallow banks, reefs and deep edges. When fishing from land, you should make a series of casts toward the presumed holding spot, and retrieve the lure – such as a jig or spinnerbait – by regularly raising and lowering the rod tip, so that the lure bounces on the bottom.

Right: The commonest means of landing a bass is to lift it with a firm thumb-grip in its mouth.

four out of five fishing trips, the fifth may show that a rapid retrieval is better. Generally, you should retrieve near the bottom, although there are rare occasions when bass can actually be caught at the surface – for example during the morning and evening. Of course, surface fishing for bass is more common in shallow clear lakes, ponds and rivers.

Fishing with a jig is the oldest and most widespread method of spinning for bass. But it requires the fisherman to have control over the bait's movements, since the jig itself shows little life during a uniform retrieval with no variations. Proper jig fishing involves casting out, letting the jig sink,

and then spinning it in with short tugs – slowly or with rapid changes of movement.

The fishing is easy over smooth bottoms, but it becomes much harder in areas that are rolling, vegetated, or full of trees and roots. Particularly for smallmouth bass, it is necessary to fish at the bottom, because this species tends to stay on bottoms with stones and cliffs. Largemouth bass are more readily caught somewhat above the bottom, as they are drawn to plants and other sources of shade.

When fishing from a boat in shallow water, you can benefit by using spinnerbait. This is retrieved in the surface

at first and then allowed to sink, so as to attract the attention of bass.

Spoons, spinners, and all sorts of plugs – surface types, sinking and floating – are excellent both in shallow water and out to several metres of depth. In deeper water, deep-diving plugs and weight-forward spinners are recommended. There is no doubt, however, that most sportfishermen find greater excitement in fishing the shallows with surface plugs, as well as with plastic worms. These long silicone creatures are mounted on a hook, forming a so-called Texas rig, which comes in different versions.

As in so many other kinds of sportfishing, one should fish for bass with thin lines and small baits on a bright day in clear water. Warm days and periods call for concentration on the morning hours, starting to fish before it gets light. A rippled surface is often more advantageous than mirror-smooth water. You should also keep quiet and avoid making noise in a boat or with its engine.

Bass fishing with natural bait

If the fishing is slack, natural baits are frequently best – such as small live fish, lampreys, bee larvae, grasshoppers, salamander, crustaceans, leeches and worms. All kinds of natural bait for bass should be set on a single hook, so that they look more lively. Use as little weighting as possible – and as small a float as possible, if you prefer to fish with a float. Once the bait sinks after the cast, be sure that the bass can easily pull out line when it bites, and then make your strike.

Many sportfishermen consider plastic worms to be a thrilling way of catching bass. No matter whether you use a Texas or Carolina rig, the fish can hardly resist the long silicon worm on it – as this largemouth bass learned.

Far right: Just as for many other species, the "golden hours" of morning and evening are generally best for bass.

Bluegill

The bluegill (*Lepomis macrochirus*) is a popular "public fish" in the United States. Its colours differ widely between waters, but it often has 6-8 stripes across its back and sides, which may be yellowish or dark blue. It seldom weighs more than 1 kg (2.2 lbs), although some are nearly twice as heavy. Bluegill were originally distributed from Minnesota down to the Great Lakes, southward to Georgia and westward to Arkansas. Today the species is implanted in numerous small ponds in almost every state.

Spinning for bluegill

Catching a bluegill is commonly the first fishing experience for a child, and the pleasure of it may last a lifetime. This is an entertaining, wild and bite-crazy fish, taking the tiniest of artificial lures – spinners, spoons, and primarily jigs. As a rule, one succeeds best with a slow, varied retrieval. But you may well have to try different types of bait before you find just the one that triggers the fish's reflex. At times, the very first cast attracts a bite – and next a whole school can dissolve as soon as the bait hits the water. In any case, wherever the first bluegill is caught, more of them are likely to be available. An imaginative retrieval with light equipment can yield many fine rewards.

Vital facts

Bluegill live in clear, small ponds and lakes with vegetation, overhanging and fallen trees, but can also be found in city environments such as parks. The fish spawn in May and, for a few days, the fry are protected by the male. They grow slowly, often resulting in overpopulation of the water. Their diet consists of larvae, water insects, crustaceans, and occasionally small fish or fry. Bluegill tend to occur in rather shallow water, although big ones are sometimes caught in deeper areas. They swim in dispersed schools of no great size.

Panfish is a collective name for bluegill, crappie, perch and "white perch". Here we see a bluegill, which not only tastes fine but is also an enjoyable sportfish, taking either artificial or natural baits.

Bluegill fishing with natural bait

Perhaps the most familiar way of catching bluegill today is with a float, a single leader, a couple of lead shot, and a worm on a small hook. Yet combinations of artificial and natural baits are frequently better, such as small jigs baited with mealworm, earthworm or larvae.

the record exceeds 2 kg. Both species are just as generous and willing to bite as the bluefish.

Spinning for crappies

Crappies also resemble bluegill in being a great challenge to catch with ultra-light spinning gear. The smallest spinners, spoons and plugs are very effective, but jigs are probably the best choice, since the fish often circulate in overgrown waters and in places with vegetation, branches and rough bottoms. The fish stay at the bottom regardless of whether it is in a sunny, shallow cove or in deep water.

Crappie fishing with natural bait

These fish eagerly take natural bait. A single float with a leader, and a hook baited with a worm or a small fish, are convenient and profitable. As in fishing for bluegill, you can also use artificial lures – chiefly jigs that are baited with a fish strip, a whole little fish, worms, larvae or some other accessible bait. Normally baited jigs are used, but the fish then needs a bit more time to swallow the bait before you strike. Crappies have a large mouth and are tired out by keeping an even pressure on the line with no jerks.

Crappie

Here is another extremely popular fish, which – along with bluegill, perch and "white perch" – is known as panfish, since all of them are wonderful to eat. The two species are black crappie (*Pomoxis nigromaculatus*), which has black patches spread over its sides, and white crappie (*Pomoxis annularis*) whose patches are merged into stripes across its back and sides. They often weigh up to 1 kg (2.2 lbs) and

Vital facts

Crappies thrive in lakes, ponds, and slow-flowing rivers or streams throughout the USA. Black crappie is most common in the northern states, while the white species occurs in the south. They enjoy clear water with vegetation and overhanging trees – mainly willows – where shade and protection are provided by rich plant life. Enthusiastic crappie fishermen thus often build shelters in the water, for example with mats made of reeds or branches.

The fish can be caught by either day or night, from some time after spawning until the autumn. Dusk, however, is regarded as the best hour. This is a popular quarry for ice-fishing, too. Like bluegill, crappies can overpopulate the water. They live on insects, worms, crustaceans, fry and small fish.

Catfish

A catfish is easily recognized by its flat head, which comprises 20% of the body – and by its "beard" of barbels, or feelers, which are a tenth as long as the body. Catfish occur on every continent, and there are hundreds of species in the world. Apart from the sturgeon, and carp species in the Amazon and eastern Asia, catfish are among the biggest of all fish in fresh waters. The European wels (*Siluris glanis*) grows largest, to over 200 kg (440 lbs), followed by other species in the Amazon and Mekong Rivers, while the smallest catfish in the group Silurodei are only a few centimetres long.

A further example is the electric catfish, *Malapterus electricus*, which can generate up to 350 volts. In the United States are several species, such as the flathead and the blue catfish, weighing as much as 25-50 kg (55-110 lbs). Channel catfish are also common, but they seldom weigh more than 8-9 kg (18-20 lbs).

The wels originally lived in Central and Eastern Europe as well as in Asia. It has spread to, and been implanted in, many countries – and today it inhabits a number of rivers in France, Italy, Spain and Germany. The northern limit of its distribution runs through southern Sweden and Finland and the Baltic.

Spinning for catfish

One can scarcely believe that catfish, with their relatively poor eyesight and dependence on dusk or murky water for much activity, will take a plug or spoon – but the fact is that they do. They are intrigued by preyfish that appear sick or move oddly, and this is a basic feature of spinning. Artificial baits should be brought in with jerks and, at the same time, hit the bottom. Two types of lure are most suited to such retrieval, plugs and large jigs, even though spoons and spinners can also trick catfish.

The colours are not very important when spinning, but strongly coloured or fluorescent plugs have proved effective. The plugs should be retrieved with regular impacts on the bottom. Large jigs, perhaps combined with fish strips, or whole fish on jig bodies, are superb as well. Moreover, whole fish on a tackle like the Drakovitch have become popular in spinning.

Catfish do not have "dangerous" teeth, so a leader of 0.50-0.70 mm is sufficient for spinning – as resistance to

Catfish can be very big and are then eager for large prey, so they are usually caught with natural baits – especially fish weighing up to about 3.5 lbs (1.5 kg).

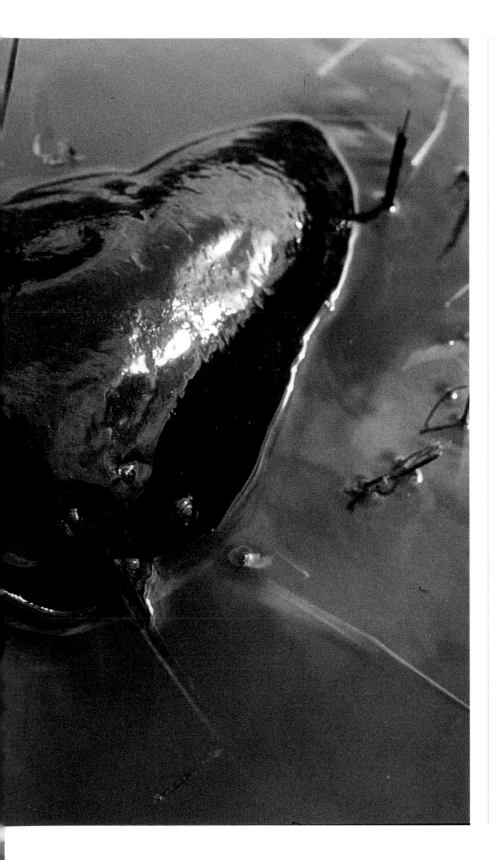

Vital facts

These fish are typically adapted to warm water and become most active in summertime. They spawn in shallow water when the temperature is at least 20° C (68° F). Their eggs are laid on branches, roots and plant remains. The fry grow rather fast, are 30-40 cm (12-16 in) long after two years, and measure 50-80 cm (20-32 in) after 3-4 years.

To begin with, the young eat mostly larvae, worms and fish fry. Soon they are big enough to consume water voles, frogs and the like. Catfish are also cannibalistic, but their greediness is debatable. They eat less in comparison to their weight than, for example, pike do – for catfish are not as active. It is known from fish farms that a catfish must eat 6-7 kg (13-15 lbs) of fish for every kilogram of weight it gains.

When the catfish attains a certain size, it occupies a territory and forms a stock there. Catfish are found in lakes, but rarely in very deep water. They occupy the calm parts of rivers and streams, although seldom the deepest holes. Avoiding currents, they are drawn to areas with fallen or overhanging trees that offer shade and shelter. Tributaries from other rivers are also attractive holding places.

While catfish can be caught by day, they are quite active at night. Traditionally good times for fishing are the evening, night and dawn. Their activity is notably dependent on the temperature, and increases primarily when it gets warmer, whereas less warmth can make them almost completely stop biting. Thunderstorms with rain and a rising level of unclear water, too, can heighten their activity. Then they enter shallow waters to feed – but with a sinking level of clearer water, they lapse into inactivity. Catfish are preferably caught with live or naturally dead bait, and spinning for them has become more frequent in recent years.

bottom stones and other obstacles, rather than to the fish's teeth. Often a catfish follows the lure and misses a few bites before it is hooked. You should cast repeatedly over a place where catfish are thought to be, since they are attracted by the lure's impact on the surface and its gait along the bottom. This fishing, of course, calls for strong spinning equipment and a reel that holds lots of thick line, such as 0.40-0.60 mm.

Catching catfish with natural bait

Natural baits are demonstrably effective on a night-hunter like the catfish, and are used by almost everyone who fishes for it. The bait may be dead or live fish, fillets or halves of fish, liver, earthworm snippets, leeches, and meat from mammals – even live or dead frogs, in countries where this bait is permitted. Among the classic types of bait are hen intestines and innards. Baitfish can weigh 100-500 grams, according to the size of fish you are after.

Bottom fishing with a sliding float and sliding tackle is the commonest method. At night, a bite indicator is used. When fishing from a boat, paternoster tackle is a standard accessory.

Many holding places of catfish are overgrown with vegetation, branches, roots and diverse hindrances. One fishes with a sliding float and fixed tackle, possibly of the paternoster type, and ideally somewhat above the bottom in order to avoid obstacles. Small catfish, in particular, often go higher over the bottom to take baitfish, and can thus be caught in the surface as well.

Observations show that catfish move away from their holding places twice each day – just before sunrise, and just before sunset – to hunt for food. Therefore, many fishermen concentrate on these times, unless they are familiar with a holding place and can serve the bait exactly on or near it.

The equipment must be strong, especially at places with plenty of obstacles. Frequent use is made of line up to 0.65 mm, on multiplier or spinning reels. A very strong, metre-long leader of nylon, steel wire, or kevlar may be needed to resist branches, roots and stones.

There is also a Hungarian attractor, the "kuttjer". It consists of a short cane with a handle and a little flat head, as big as a large coin. Used chiefly when fishing from a boat, it is swung down into the water with a regular rhythm, every 1.5-2 seconds. Its sound resembles the pop of a champagne cork, and brings up catfish to bite. This device has become common in many countries, on both drifting and anchored boats.

Striking, fighting and landing the fish

When spinning, you must give a strike as soon as you feel a catfish taking, or spitting out, an artificial lure. But if fishing with natural bait, you should delay the strike a few seconds. Since the catfish's mouth is hard, the strike must be stiff – and it may have to be repeated, so that you know the hook is driven in. Catfish are in the habit of immediately, after the strike, heading back to their shelter among fallen trees or branches.

The fish should be held strongly, as it is very tough and

persistent. During the fight, it often stays at the same place and can be difficult to get moving. You may succeed in making it swim by throwing stones at the place or otherwise frightening it with sounds.

An inexperienced fisherman can land a catfish with a large net, or a gaff in the middle of its lower jaw. The expert frequently uses a working glove to grip its lower jaw, with the thumb in its mouth. But a big fish requires extra man-power, for two hands are often necessary – one around the jaw and one in the gill.

Left: A "kuttjer" in action. This attractor is slammed repeatedly on the water, and its sounds apparently stimulate catfish to bite.

Above: A hefty catfish has been landed after a long, tough struggle. Specimens of this size can scarcely be landed by oneself, and at least two men are needed here.

Trout

The trout (*Salmo trutta*) has demonstrated great adaptability as a species. It occurs in clear, oxygen-rich waters, streams, mountain brooks and lakes, where several forms of it have evolved. In biological terms, the brown trout (*Salmo trutta fario*), the lake-run trout (*S. t. lacustris*), and the sea trout (*S. t. trutta*) belong to the same species. In many waters, all three of these develop from the same fish – depending on whether the offspring stay in flowing water, move into lakes, or migrate to the sea. They acquire different behaviour and colouring, but only a test of their scales can prove which is which.

Brown trout and lake-run trout were originally distributed in Europe – from the Mediterranean to northern Norway and Iceland, westward to the British Isles, and eastward far into Siberia. Trout were introduced to the eastern United States in 1883, then to New Zealand and other continents, such as South America, Africa and parts of Asia. However, these trout are not as tolerant of water temperatures as rainbow trout are. The ones implanted around the world derive from Loch Leven in Scotland, a lake north of Edinburgh that was once famous for its healthy, fast-growing stock of trout.

The size of brown trout varies widely according to their food supply. In European waterways, specimens of 2-3 kg (4.4-6.6 lbs) are unusual, while such weights are common in, for example, New Zealand. The maximum in flowing waters is 10 kg (22 lbs), but anything around 0.5-1 kg (1.1-2.2 lbs) is considered a fine brown trout.

Spinning for trout

The brown trout's manner of life differs between mountain rivers or brooks and the lowlands, whose nutritious, clear, oxygenated streams can make the fish quite selective about food. In flowing waters, the usual method is downstream fishing with spinners, spoons or small plugs. One then searches holding places – holes, furrows, banks of vegetation and so on. In a large waterway, you cast downstream toward the

The trout – which, in flowing waters, is a typically territorial fish – lives mainly on insects, but increasingly adopts a fish diet as it grows. Thus it becomes ever easier to fool with spoons, spinners and plugs.

Vital facts

Trout in the northern hemisphere spawn from October until December. The fry become territorial, and this trait is kept throughout their lives in flowing waters. Trout have diverse periods of activity, determined mainly by the supply of insects. Brown trout are active primarily in the morning, evening, and briefly at midday.

Trout consume insects, larvae, worms and fish fry. They usually also develop cannibalistic tendencies. In waterways, about 90% of their food comprises insects that drift with the current, and 10% of surface insects. When hunting, they use their eyesight and, as shown by numerous studies, their lateral line organ.

The holding places of trout are those that enable them to spend as little energy as possible in resisting the current, and where they can find plenty of food – at current edges, shorelines and holes. Brown trout often choose shady places, unlike rainbow trout which happily live in free water.

Trout also live in lakes of all sizes. In a small lake, they cruise about and frequently enter the shore zone. Here they live chiefly on insects, crustaceans, larvae and worms, as well as fish fry. Vegetated areas, promontories, shallows, and stream outlets attract them most. During the summer, they move out to deep water, but often approach land in the morning and evening. While the brown trout in flowing waters can be hard to catch, the fish in lakes are more willing to bite. Consequently, trout have been implanted in many lakes known as "put-and-take" waters, where the sport's quality is determined by the stock and the fishing pressure. In large lakes with inflows that allow the fish to spawn, lake-run stocks with big fish develop. Various European lakes contain lake-run trout, which are either shiny with black spots or bronze-yellow.

Far left: A spinner works very well in flowing waters, as it runs smoothly in the current and is easy to guide by moving the rod up, down or sideways.

A hooked trout often exposes itself at the surface by leaping and splashing. This habit obviously makes the fishing more fun, since you can see the fish during most of the fight.

opposite bank, let the bait swing into the current, and retrieve it. Thus you can carry the search metre by metre downstream.

The fish in flowing waters are often shy and see the fisherman at a great distance. It is therefore wise to fish cautiously and throw no shadows on the surface – in other words, make oneself "as little as possible". When fishing downstream, the bait comes from behind and the trout see it for only a moment. They probably do not aim very well at a lure and, hence, often miss the bite, or else follow it and become frightened.

Upstream fishing, which reaches beyond the fish, requires better contact with the lures. These should work in a lively fashion and are retrieved a bit faster than the current speed. The advantage is that the trout sees the lure soon, can "time" its bite, and is usually hooked securely. But upstream fishing is much harder than downstream fishing, because the current keeps the lure working.

A spinner is the best type of bait in flowing water. Its blade's rotation creates a high gait, while the spinner maintains a good "grip" in the water. If you lower the rod, or retrieve more slowly, the spinner goes deeper. When you lift the rod or slightly speed up the retrieval, the spinner will rise in the water. It can be steered in the right path at holding places by moving the rod sideways.

Spoons can also be used in flowing water, though they do not "grip" the water as well as spinners do. A spoon is therefore usually led away from the current – or up toward the surface.

Floating plugs are excellent for fishing in shallow currents. They cannot be cast so far, but you can let them follow the current to within a couple of metres from the holding place and then retrieve. A floating plug may also be weighted, a short distance up on the line. In deeper waterways with relatively strong currents, sinking plugs are used.

Jigs are less common for trout fishing in flowing waters. Yet a jig is easy to cast, sinks rapidly, and is suited especially to fishing in current furrows and deep holes.

The trout in flowing waters are both shy and fastidious. It is not unusual for flyfishing on a popular waterway to catch more trout than spinning does. However, spinning with flies is quite feasible. You weight the line 60-80 cm (24-32 in) up, for example with lead shot, and use a trout fly with a single or double hook – or a small tube fly. The fly can swing in the current, or be retrieved like a spinner.

Trout have good colour vision. The rules for bait colour exist to be broken, of course – but in general one uses silver, nickel, yellow, and fluorescent colours in murky water, high water levels, darkness, and strong winds with surface waves. In clear water, low levels, and bright weather, it is best to try subdued colours and copper, but also dark hues and black.

In lakes or put-and-take waters, the same types of bait are employed, and spoons may be equally profitable. A casting Buldo together with a fly is effective in lakes, too. The Buldo can be attached in two basic ways – sliding and fixed. In the first case, the stopper consists of a swivel, to which is tied a leader length of 1.2-3.5 metres (4-12 feet) depending, among other things, on the depth and on how shy the trout are. When the fish takes the fly, it can pull line without feeling resistance from the bubble. In the second case, favoured by many sportfishermen, the casting bubble and a quick strike are combined to hook the fish well.

When spinning in flowing water, it is normally best to cast the lure obliquely upstream. Once the lure has sunk, it is retrieved with a taut line along the bottom, and should more or less flutter along. If the current is weak, you may need to liven the lure by tugging with the rod tip, while retrieving slowly to make it bounce along the bottom.

Trout should be played with even pressure and relatively light force on the drag, so that the fish is not prevented from pulling line off the reel if it rushes.

Trout fishing with natural bait

In small flowing waters, no bait is more effective for trout than a drifting worm on an unweighted line. The worm is fished either upstream or downstream, and the current brings it down toward the trout. In wider or deeper waters, the worm tackle can be weighted with lead shot slightly up on the line.

But the simplest method is to fish with a float and a fairly long leader that is weighted according to the current and depth. The hook is baited with a worm. The float then drifts with the current while you walk downstream after it or "trot" out line. A pull on the float shows that the trout is biting, but only when it disappears under the surface do you strike.

Substantial waterways are often fished with a tackle that may have a three-way swivel, but using a leader of 80-120 cm (32-48 in) and a sinker on its end. Again the hook is baited with a worm. This tackle is cast obliquely downstream and swings in toward – or over – a holding place, so that you maintain bottom contact.

In a lake, there are two means of fishing with natural bait: the simple tackle with a float – fixed or sliding, depending on the depth – or using a casting bubble and worms, which is retrieved. Both methods are extremely effective in most waters.

Although worms are the classic bait, one can very well fish with larvae, insects, crustaceans, small fish, or other natural baits. During late summer and autumn, or early in spring, waterways can also be fished – where this is allowed – with salmon eggs or the roe of trout and salmon. Eggs and roe are fished with or without a float, or else on bottom tackle which moves in the current.

Fighting the fish

The leaps of trout are well known to all sportfishermen. Yet a trout goes wild only if your drag is set too hard. So you have to follow the strike with an even pressure, letting the fish pull out line if it wants. Then it is landed with a net, or slid up on land if the shore is smooth.

Sea trout

While the sea trout (*Salmo trutta trutta*) is biologically the same species as brown trout, it is anadromous – migrating between marine and fresh waters, swimming up the river where it was born just as salmon do. Originally sea trout were distributed in northern Europe. The stocks now in other parts of the world derive from implanted brown trout, which in some places have formed anadromous stocks – as in New Zealand, Argentina and the Falklands. In eastern North America, a smaller stock of sea trout inhabits, for example, Newfoundland, Nova Scotia, Maine, New York and Connecticut. A true stock of sea trout was first introduced to North America in 1958.

In Europe, sea trout are common in the British Isles, Iceland, the Faeroes, Norway, Sweden, Denmark, Finland, the Baltic region and Poland. There is also a small stock in northern Germany and northern France. Those in the Baltic Sea are notable for rapid growth, and the Mörrum and Emån are well-known streams with large and vigorous sea trout.

Different strains of sea trout vary in their development. At most places, they seldom weigh over 2-3 kg (4.4-6.6 lbs). Large specimens occur in only a few Norwegian rivers, the Swedish Baltic rivers, Danish streams, and some rivers in Poland, the Baltic states and Finland, where they may weigh up to 10-14 kg (22-31 lbs) although the rule is 3-6 kg (6.6-13.2 lbs).

Spinning for sea trout

The methods of fishing for sea trout differ widely in northern European rivers. But the clearer and brighter the water is, the more predominant flyfishing tends to be, while spinning and baitcasting has better chances in relatively dark, murky, deep waterways.

Spinning with spoons, plugs and spinners is done primarily for silvery ascending fish and strongly coloured sea trout. The fish select the same holding places as brown trout, and sea trout are then often caught by spinning downstream. In general, small artificial lures are used in small streams with

Sea trout live in the ocean during most of the year, but run up rivers in the autumn to spawn. The seagoing trout seldom weigh more than 4.5-6.5 lbs (2-3 kg), but in some places – notably the Baltic – they can be much heavier.

Vital facts

Sea trout spawn in the autumn, and the fry stay for 1-3 years in the waterway. When 16-22 cm (6-9 in) long, they migrate to the sea during March-April and, the same year or the next, return up the same waterway. Trout that have spawned go to sea in early spring, and some die – mainly males. Once in the ocean, they need a few weeks to regain their condition, becoming shiny and fat. Towards autumn, when ascending the waterway, they acquire spawning colours and the males develop a hooked lower jaw.

The ascent begins early in large waterways, but during autumn in small ones. Unlike salmon, sea trout ascend under cover of darkness – and they usually choose dark, protected resting places, whereas salmon often swim freely in the current. Sea trout do not normally feed in fresh water, and when they do it is not because of hunger. Their willingness to bite is connected with the development of spawning colours, milt and roe. The shinier a fish is, and the less mature in regard to milt or roe, the better its probability of biting in fresh water. Coloured fish do not bite eagerly – except those with strong dark colours, which can become aggressive as the spawning time approaches.

Sea trout ascend waterways in the greatest numbers when the water level is rising or high, so the fishing is usually best then. Newly run, silvery trout still have their bite-instinct from the period in salt water, and take bait regularly in large waterways. In smaller ones, fortune smiles during the evening, night and morning. The biting behaviour of sea trout also varies considerably with their environment. In Great Britain and Norway, fishing at night is common – but in Denmark and Sweden, for example, the fishing is excellent on dark, windy days with a high water level.

A sea trout obeys its instinct to bite for a short time after leaving the ocean and running up in fresh water. Flood tides and/or high water levels tend to provide the best conditions for hooking this fish.

little fish, while large baits come into play for big fish in wider waters.

Frequent choices of bait are spinners weighing 5-12 grams. Their substantial resistance in water makes them well suited to deep, slow retrieval, although fresh-run fish can be gluttonous and relish a spinner or other lure that is retrieved fast. Spoons are used less, but have long been reliable for sea trout in Swedish and Danish waterways. Early in the season, naturally coloured lures in silver/black or yellow/black are popular, but late in the season – when the fish are strongly coloured – fluorescent hues may have greater success.

During the winter, sea trout in the ocean do not tolerate normal salinity and low temperatures. They either move out to warmer deep water, or else migrate into fjords or up the lower parts of rivers. These fish are often small and not yet mature – in Scandinavia they are called "Greenlanders".

Their appetite is diminished by the cold water, but otherwise they are in fine condition. Only small bait can catch them, such as spinners, worms or – when spinning – little flies, as mentioned above for brown trout.

In some countries like Denmark, Sweden, Poland and the Baltic states, there is also spring fishing for out-spawned sea trout. It is best in mild weather, but can deteriorate rapidly with the slightest variations in water and air temperature. The condition of spawned-out fish is acceptable in certain waters, yet in others they may be very starved and should be returned.

Sea trout fishing with natural bait

Whether in a Norwegian river, a minor brook in the Hebrides, a Danish or Polish stream, fishing with worms is one of the safest methods for sea trout – from the newly ascended and coloured fish to the Greenlanders and the spawned-out emigrants.

One can fish in small streams with a worm, float, and no weighting. In large waterways, one uses single fixed floats that can carry sinkers of 1 to 10-15 grams, depending on the depth and current. A sinker on the end of the line, and a leader with a worm hook, allow you to make the hook glide in the current before the sinker – a more delicate presentation. A leader with 1-1.5 metres (40-60 inches) to the hook, and a short leader to the sinker, is quite common in rivers with comparatively great depth and good current.

However, worms are not the only type of bait applicable to sea trout. Cooked red shrimp are a superb alternative, especially in the spring and for Greenlanders. During the cold season and in spring, trout or salmon roe is used on single or treble hooks.

Right: A clump of worms, consisting of 3-4 lively earthworms on a single hook, can be extremely effective for sea trout in flowing waters. A bit of red wool yarn on the hook makes the morsel even more irresistible.

When fishing with worms, cast the bait obliquely upstream and let it bounce down along the bottom, while you follow it with the rod and reel in any loose line. The tackle combines a three-way swivel with one leader to the current sinker and one to the hook carrying the clump of worms. The same tackle and technique can be used if you fish with a spinning fly: just replace the hook and worms with, for instance, a tube fly.

Rainbow trout

The rainbow trout (*Salmo gairdneri*) originally inhabited North America, in the mountains north of Mexico up to southwestern Alaska and the Aleutians. It also occurs in Kamchatka. The first examples came to Europe by way of Germany in 1880. Next the species reached Denmark, inspiring many pond farms. As a pond fish it then spread to numerous countries, some of which implanted it in waterways. This has been done on several continents, since the fish is rather robust and tolerates higher temperatures than brown trout do. Today it lives in Africa – for example Kenya, Morocco and South Africa – as well as in Japan, New Zealand, Tasmania, Australia, and in South American countries including Ecuador, Chile, Peru and Argentina.

Hallmarks of the rainbow trout are its purple or pink stripes along the side, and lots of black spots on the back and fins – mainly the tail fin. It has thirty subspecies, but its progenitor is the cutthroat trout (*Salmo clarkii*) which occurs in North America, from Prince William Sound in Alaska down to northern California and several of the Rocky Mountain states. There are also various crosses between rainbow trout and the cutthroat, which itself has at least six subspecies in western America. Moreover, we find cutthroat which are anadromous. Those inland could once weigh nearly 20 kg (44 lbs), although seagoing cutthroat seldom exceed 6-7 kg (13-15 lbs). The cutthroat is not considered as interesting a species for sportfishing as rainbow trout.

The rainbow trout lives stationary in rivers and streams, where it rarely weighs over 2-3 kg (4.4-6.6 lbs). Further, it has a lake-living form that, during most of the year, remains in lakes and only migrates up the tributaries in order to spawn or feed, chiefly eating salmon roe. Perhaps best known are the rainbow trout in Alaska's Lake Iliamna, where they grow to more than 10 kg (22 lbs). The Kamloops trout becomes even bigger.

Anadromous rainbow trout – called steelhead – migrate between rivers and the ocean. In their home waters, the Pacific rivers of the American west and northwest, they approach weights of 20 kg (44 lbs) at some places, although 4-8 kg (8.8-17.6 lbs) is commonest.

Rainbow trout are recognizable by the pink or violet stripe all along the side, and the many black spots on the back and fins. This species occurs naturally in North America, from where it has been implanted in Europe.

Spinning for rainbow trout

The artificial baits preferred by rainbow trout are small ones, whereas brown trout take both small and large lures. Since rainbow trout stand more freely in the current, the same methods of spinning can be used as for brown trout. This is also true in lakes and put-and-take waters. Rainbow trout have a definite taste for red colours and fluorescent, or bright red or orange, lures – ranging from little red spinners to orange flies for spinning.

Rainbow trout fishing with natural bait

The manner of catching brown trout with natural bait can just as well apply to rainbow trout. It benefits, however, by

Vital facts

Unlike brown and sea trout, the rainbow trout spawns in flowing waters from January until early May. In waters with brown trout, the two species compete intensely. Where rainbow trout have been implanted or have escaped from farms, we often observe normal spawning behaviour – but without reproduction.

The rainbow trout does not seek the same holding places and territories as brown trout. It thrives in current edges and the main current, but in shallower waters, and it is more mobile than brown trout. In many North American rivers with ascending salmon, the stationary rainbow trout pursue the diverse salmon species (such as king, coho and sockeye), living at times on salmon roe. Also in contrast to brown trout, rainbow trout flourish in small groups or schools. They always feed on insects, larvae, leeches, crustaceans and so forth, though not as prone to eat fry and fish as brown trout are.

Appreciated as an implantation fish, the rainbow trout exists in numerous put-and-take waters, where it patrols pelagically along the shores. It often gathers at inflows and can also live in free water, even at fairly great depths.

Above: Compared with other trout, rainbow are more mobile and frequently swim in schools. They are also more attracted to shallow waters, both at current edges and in the main current. Further, they prefer smaller artificial lures with strong colours.

Left: Although rainbow trout usually eat larvae, insects and crustaceans, they can also, of course, be caught with baitfish such as sculpin. Worms, salmon eggs and roe are other natural baits that may appeal to them.

decorating the worm hook with a bead or a piece of orange or red wool thread. Fishing with salmon eggs or roe is also quite effective for rainbow trout, which eat roe during the winter regardless of whether they live in a western American or a Scandinavian river.

In put-and-take waters, these fish are often caught with diverse types of red or orange dough-balls that contain salmon-egg flavouring. Berkley's Power Bait assortment is the best-known type of dough for them. The balls are fished either stationary with bottom tackle, or with floats. In both cases, the baits become more lively if you retrieve them slowly with long pauses.

Steelhead

The seagoing form of rainbow trout inhabits rivers in western America. Also called steelhead by sportfishermen are the lake-living form in North America and the rainbow trout found in the Great Lakes. But the seagoing steelhead is silvery in the ocean and in lakes, as well as during its run upriver. At first sight, it can be recognized only by the many black spots on its tail fin, adipose fin and dorsal fin. After a short time in flowing water, its characteristic pink stripe becomes clearer. As spawning approaches, the fish grows spotty and acquires a pale purple stripe along the side.

Unlike sea trout and salmon, steelhead feed in fresh water and, moreover, they survive the spawning – in contrast to all species of Pacific salmon. Steelhead weigh 2-6 kg (4.4-13 lbs) but, notably in the rivers of British Columbia, they can reach 15 kg (33 lbs).

The rainbow trout that were brought to Europe have been genetically manipulated to yield the perfect farming fish. Yet some still have their instinct to migrate seaward. Plenty of escaped or implanted rainbow trout in northern Europe thus head for the ocean when they reach a certain size. Marine fish farms of rainbow trout have occasionally even caused accidents, with fish slipping out to wander along the coasts. At many places, they also migrate up waterways, though unable to reproduce.

Spinning for steelhead

In the rivers of western America and those flowing into the Great Lakes, steelhead run during almost the whole year. However, there are distinctive spring, summer and winter runs. As a rule, the fish ascend Pacific rivers all year round too, but with some variations depending on the latitude.

Steelhead are famous in flyfishing literature, especially with reference to small, clear rivers in the states of Washington and Oregon. But they also take different types of spinners, and roe in particular – a trait that is shared by the "steelheads" caught in Scandinavian rivers. Steelhead migrate upriver in small schools, and choose holding places in a manner that recalls salmon. Generally, they select neither dead water nor the fastest water. Current edges and middle furrows in a waterway are ideal stops for steelhead.

Here one can catch them on, for instance, small spinners

The steelhead is the seagoing form of rainbow trout. When fresh-run, it may look confusingly like a salmon, but is easy to identify by the numerous black spots on its tail, adipose and dorsal fins.

which are fished across the current or retrieved slowly over the bottom. It is important to fish near the bottom, especially in northern British Columbia; and many western American rivers are fished stationary with so-called Spin-N-Glo. These light spinners are "anchored" with a leader and a lead weight on the bottom, the line is pulled taut, and the rod is placed in a Y-shaped branch. When a steelhead passes the baits or sees them from its holding place, it usually bites. The treble hook on a Spin-N-Glo can also be provided with roe before it is "parked".

Some rivers in Washington and Oregon are fished with small shrimp-like crustaceans, weighted with light sinkers. In other rivers, and around the Great Lakes, fishing with salmon eggs or roe is extremely popular. Using one to three big salmon eggs on a little single hook, perhaps weighted with a couple of lead shot, is an easy and elegant way to catch steelhead. Elsewhere, bigger roe clumps are set on a correspondingly larger single hook.

In Scandinavian rivers and streams, steelhead are often caught as a by-product of fishing for brown trout, sea trout and salmon – on spinners, spoons, plugs and flies alike. Roe, too, is used to catch them in some Danish streams and southern Swedish rivers which are renowned for abundant ascents of rainbow trout.

Steelhead are fished near the bottom, ideally with small spinners. These are powerful, pugnacious fish and can cause hair-raising fights if challenged with the right gear.

North American lake trout

Cold, deep, big lakes in Canada, and the Great Lakes, are the primary habitat of North American lake trout (*Salvelinus namaycush*). This species also lives in Canadian rivers that flow through the lakes containing its stocks. Moreover, it has been implanted in some Rocky Mountain lakes and has been introduced to Europe – for example at lakes in Switzerland, Sweden and Norway – although without really managing to establish itself in any of these.

Lake trout may reach a weight of 30 kg (66 lbs), and individuals approaching 50 kg (110 lbs) have actually been caught in nets. The species can live at depths down to 70-80 metres, but is fishable only to about 20 metres, where it is taken chiefly by trolling.

Spinning for lake trout

Unlike other lake-dwelling trout, this species spawns in lakes, depositing its roe on stony bottoms in shallow water during the autumn. Only in spring, when the ice melts and the surface warms up, do lake trout move toward shore. At any other time they are virtually impossible to hook, except in very cold glacial lakes where they can usually be caught all summer from shore. In other lakes, they prefer deep water in summer and can evade ordinary spinning equipment – but they show up again in shallow waters during the autumn. However, in many states and provinces the fish is protected throughout autumn, when it spawns.

North American lake trout are cold-water fish that occur chiefly in large, deep lakes. They can be difficult to reach by spinning and baitcasting, since they stay too deep for most of the year. But in spring and autumn, they move up to shallower waters and are readily caught there.

Huchen and taimen

On the evidence of evolution, anatomy and kinship, the huchen (*Hucho hucho*) and the taimen (*Hucho taimen*) are really different developments of a single species. The taimen is distributed from the Volga and Amur Rivers northward, throughout Siberia to Kamchatka and Japan. Weighing up to 80 kg (176 lbs), it lives in clean oxygen-rich rivers and a few lakes. Its holding places are holes, current edges, and the deepest parts of waterways, where it eagerly takes all types of lures.

The huchen is native to the Danube River and its tributaries. Previously it could grow to 50 kg (110 lbs), but pollution and plentiful sportfishing have decimated the stocks, and today specimens of 5-10 kg (11-22 lbs) are reckoned as superb. It has also been implanted with success in rivers of the Atlas Mountains in Morocco – and in areas of former Yugoslavia, such as Slovenia.

Spinning for huchen

Depths and holes in rivers are preferred by huchen. This fish spawns in early spring, having migrated upriver to places with strong flows and fine bottoms. Only after spawning is it subjected to fishing in the Danube river system. Not many good fishing sites are left today, and sportfishermen defy death every winter by climbing in icy ravines to reach the huchen's hideouts. There it is caught with spoons, spinners, baitfish on tackle, and imitations of mice or water voles on diverse types of hook systems. The fishing becomes harder in spring and summer, but revives during early autumn.

Huchen are found mainly in the Danube and its tributaries, where they inhabit holes and other deep places. They tend to be caught after spawning, in late autumn and in winter.

Arctic char

Besides having a seagoing form, the Arctic char (*Salvelinus alpinus*) lives in cold clear lakes, mountain rivers and brooks with Arctic temperatures. Its distribution, spanning the whole northern hemisphere, includes northern Canada – for instance Baffin Island – as well as Greenland, Iceland, northern Norway, Sweden, Siberia and Alaska.

Furthermore, we find Arctic char in central and southern Norway, southern Sweden, Finland, the Lake District of England and Scotland, mountain lakes in the Alpine countries, and the former Soviet Union. Yet the stocks outside the normal area of distribution often have small fish, as in the Lake District and many Alpine lakes, where even dwarf forms occur. An exception is Lake Sommen in Sweden, which has yielded char of 8-9 kg (18-20 lbs). The fish usually weighs 0.25-3.0 kg (0.55-6.6 lbs), but the seagoing form can grow remarkably large, as on Baffin Island where examples over 12 kg (26 lbs) have been caught.

Arctic char belong to the numerous salmon species that evolved from the same progenitor at the same time – when a land bridge existed between Siberia and Alaska. This bridge caused the evolution of a southerly strain of char – the Dolly Varden (*Salvelinus malma*) – and of a northerly one which spread to Canada, Europe and Siberia. The two species are very similar, and are related to the brook trout, which – along with North American lake trout – is thought to share the same progenitor.

Spinning for char

Char live on small bottom animals, and sometimes on fish fry or larger prey. Precisely because their food comprises so few animal species, they tend to be selective. During the short summer, they may swim in the surface and take insects.

Curiosity is a trait of char, and they are easily tempted by artificial baits, but do not bite as eagerly as trout. A trout that follows the lure is immediately frightened if it sees the fisher-

Above right: Landlocked Arctic char are found primarily in areas with an Arctic climate. Typical of the species are its red-orange or red-pink abdomen, and its dark green back with green spots. These colours, already strong, are reinforced when the fish acquires its spawning appearance.

Below right: The seagoing form of Arctic char is shiny when it runs upriver. But after only a short time in fresh water, it becomes strongly coloured in the manner typical of landlocked Arctic char.

Within their region of distribution, Arctic char occur chiefly in lakes, but periodically also in rivers and tributaries. In a lake, the char patrol along the edges toward deep water. With colourful spinners and spoons, one can usually catch them during their hunting raids over the deep edges near land.

man, whereas a char seems less timid and often keeps after the bait for several casts in a row. The char in lakes are fished in deep water and above deep edges near land. Both spinners and spoons are fine baits, and should be retrieved in a varied manner upward over the edge, with numerous spin-stops. Small lures with red colours appear to be most attractive.

One of the surest ways to make char bite is to replace the treble hook on a spinner or spoon with a short leader of 20-40 cm (8-16 in), to which a trout fly is tied – for example, a simple, classic fly such as Red Tag Palmer or Black Zulu. Spoons and spinners are retrieved slowly with lots of short jerks and spin-stops.

Vital facts

Arctic char spawn in autumn and early winter. They grow slowly, as do many other Arctic fish. Schools are formed until the char weigh 300-500 grams, and bigger char live alone. Their diet includes insects, crustaceans, mosquito larvae, and snails. The char has a pink or red-orange abdomen, and a dark green back with yellow spots. Its colours become brighter when it spawns. It inhabits lakes, patrolling along the shores, but can also swim in the surface or enter the tributaries and wander up rivers.

The seagoing form, as fry, spends 3-7 years in a river. It emigrates between February and May, to grow briefly in the sea – often for just a few months. Still shiny, it begins to acquire colours after a short time in the river. Males acquire a hooked lower jaw, turning orange-red on the abdomen and green on the back, while females are less colourful. Unlike salmon and sea trout, all char are presumed to run upriver each summer. They eat little during their river journey.

The use of a casting Buldo and a leader with fly is also effective for fishing in lakes when the char hunt insects at the surface. Retrieval must be slow but at an even tempo. Char bite cautiously, and only when their resistance is felt should you strike.

In mountain brooks and rivers, char prefer the calmest areas. The lure is retrieved as in trout fishing. Possible holding places are searched, or the cast is laid obliquely downstream to let the spinner move in the current while you retrieve it.

The American Dolly Varden behaves in exactly the same way as the char, and can be caught by identical methods.

As for seagoing char, their willingness to bite has been found to differ across the Arctic region. In Canada, Greenland, Iceland and Siberia, they gladly take spoons – but in the clear rivers of northern Norway, they quite seldom take spoons or spinners. As mentioned, they eat very little when they run up rivers, and the longer they stay in fresh water the more enthusiastically they take artificial baits.

The fish are inclined to swim in the quieter parts of rivers, where they can hold in limited schools. Small spoons, possibly with a red hackle or red spots, are excellent for seagoing char. Retrieval has to be slow and deep, the spinner ideally going just over the bottom. When you manage to catch one char, others are likely to be at the same place. The fish rise with high water, so the fishing usually depends on the tides and melting snow.

As the fish migrate up through lakes, they grow more interested in biting. Here they patrol the edges toward deep water and frequently swim in the surface. They now increasingly resemble the stationary char in behaviour and way of life.

Char are caught with natural bait as well – for instance worms, larvae and maggots. However, it is primarily in spinning and flyfishing that the species has gained such popularity.

While Arctic char mostly eat insects, spinning with spoons can be rewarding, especially if the treble hook is replaced by a 10-cm (4-inch) leader and a little fly.

Eastern brook trout

The eastern brook trout, (*Salvelinus fontinalis*), has the same progenitor as do North American lake trout and Arctic char. Its natural distribution lies in eastern North America and westward to the Rocky Mountains, but it is readily displaced by rainbow and brown trout. The richest stocks of eastern brook trout are in Labrador, where the Minipi River with its tributaries is best known for one of the largest stocks of fish weighing up to 3 kg (6.6 lbs). Also famous for this species is God's River in Manitoba.

Eastern brook trout were introduced to Europe for pond-farming in the late 1800s, but were out-competed by the rainbow trout. Still, they have always been regarded as one of the most beautiful trout species, and were thus implanted in many of Europe's clear mountain rivers and streams, where they continue to thrive. They rarely become bigger than 30 cm (12 in), while those in ponds can reach 2 kg (4.4 lbs). Today, they are cultivated to some extent and the species is crossed with rainbow trout or ordinary brown trout. It has also been implanted in Argentina.

Spinning for brook trout

All traditional lures are applicable to these fish, with the same methods that catch other trout in brooks, rivers and streams. Big specimens in the northeastern United States,

Vital facts

Spawning occurs in autumn and winter. The fry grow slowly, living on insects, larvae and crustaceans; once larger, they add young fish to their diet. Eastern brook trout are characteristically found in sizeable rivers with calm currents. In the Minipi and God's River, they also take mice and lemmings. Small stocks of the species have proved to be anadromous, migrating between rivers and the sea, but seldom are as big as the stationary freshwater-living ones, or as pale and shiny.

though, are caught on large lures – mainly spinners and spoons. The retrieval should be relatively deep and slow, since the fish does not take food in the surface as often as rainbow and brown trout do.

The fish's lovely colours and deep red, fine-tasting meat

have made it a popular implantation fish in many put-and-take waters, whose temperature and clarity suit this much-liked species. Moreover, it can be caught with worms and other natural baits, in the same way as rainbow and brown trout.

The brook trout is a relative of Arctic char and lake trout. This beautiful fish is native only to North America, but has been implanted in Europe and other regions. Large spoons and spinners usually catch it, if fished deeply and slowly. Shown at right is a colourful pair of brook trout while spawning.

From the mid-19th century until some decades into the 20th, many well heeled English fishermen journeyed to Norway in quest of salmon. This painting from the same period still hangs in one of the socalled "English houses" where they lived during their visits.

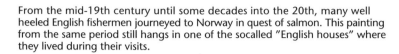

Atlantic salmon

The Atlantic salmon (*Salmo salar*) has given rise to a sport-fishing culture and history that no other species of fish can approach. It existed over a century ago in most European countries, but its stocks have declined due to dams, pollution, intensive professional fishing, and diseases – so much that, in central Europe today, it inhabits only a few rivers of northern Spain and France. Yet it still visits many rivers in Great Britain and Ireland, Iceland and the Faeroes, one river in Greenland, and hundreds of rivers in Norway, Sweden and Finland, as well as in various Russian rivers.

Salmon diseases come primarily from marine farming and, despite repeated efforts to restrict them, it has to be observed that the wild salmon in northern Europe face a risk of extinction in the near future. Probably even the genes of "wild salmon" will be strongly blended with those of cultivated salmon, which has serious implications for the wild salmon's survival, especially in Scandinavia and Scotland.

Atlantic salmon are also found in North America, running up rivers in New Brunswick, Quebec, Maine and Nova Scotia. Only in this region, during recent years, has it been possible to see improvements in the stocks – thanks to the buying up of salmon quotas from professional fishing in the North Atlantic. Perhaps one of the most virgin areas

The Atlantic salmon is often termed the "king of fish", as it is strong and full of fight, besides reaching weights over 65 lbs (30 kg). Fresh-run individuals are silvery and – unlike sea trout – tend to have only black, cross-shaped spots above their lateral lines.

with intact salmon strains is the Kola Peninsula, although the discovery of its world-class fishing in the 1990s has led to a minor decline even there.

Salmon strains develop differently. Some have genes

Vital facts

Atlantic salmon spawn in rivers and streams during autumn and early winter. The fry stay in the waterway for 2-3 years, and the silvery young salmon migrate to the sea during March-April. After 1-2 years at sea, each salmon returns to migrate up the same river, to the spawning bed and the brook where it was born several years earlier. This is one of nature's most astonishing feats, and has fascinated people for centuries.

The salmon ascent takes place from early spring until well into autumn, depending on the latitude. After a time in the river, the salmon become coloured, and males develop a strongly hooked lower jaw. The struggle for females and spawning places is hard for males, and some of them die after spawning – as do some females. How much of the stock perishes, though, we do not know for sure.

The surviving salmon descend to the sea and, at best, come back up the river once or twice in the following years. Compared to other species, the fry have a high survival rate – but things can go wrong, both during the spawning and while the yolk-sac fry are still in the spawning pit. Rain, melting snow and high tides, for example, can destroy the spawning banks or silt them over, so that the fry die. And if the fish do grow up, they occupy territories in competition with, among others, stationary trout. In many waterways, predatory fish such as pike may consume young salmon, especially when they travel toward the sea. Hydroelectric turbines and similar obstacles also reduce the stocks.

giving faster growth than others. Small salmon, or grilse, together with medium-sized salmon of 4-7 kg (8.8-15.4 lbs), predominate in all rivers, while large salmon of more than 10 kg (22 lbs) are common in few. The best-known rivers for big salmon include the Alta and Namsen in Norway, the Mörrum in Sweden, the Derwent in northwest England and the Tweed on the border between England and Scotland, besides certain rivers in the Kola Peninsula.

Spinning for Atlantic salmon

Salmon fishing involves a paradox: what is the point of serving food to a creature that eats nothing? Ever since the sport began, fishermen have wondered about this, for the fish do happen to bite. There are many theories about why they take bait. Fresh-run, silvery salmon often bite with frenzy at the start of the season. Some of us believe that this is because certain individual "springers" retain their biting instinct. Others think they are driven by a need to fight for resting and holding places in the river, chasing other fish away and, consequently, taking a fisherman's bait.

Later in the summer, the salmon accept small lures in the surface, such as a little spoon or a fly. These are presumed to revive an instinct of youth, when the fish lived on insects in the river. Once the salmon acquire their colours, the time approaches to compete over spawning places. They now become aggressive, and take bait for that reason.

Factors like the weather play, of course, a considerable role. Not the least important is the water level. When it changes, the salmon grow uneasy. Whether it rises or falls, therefore, the fisherman has a good chance – though a falling level is usually best. Both precipitation and melt-water influence the fishing in this way. The lower parts of rivers are also affected to some degree by tidal patterns in the sea, as the salmon ascend at high tide and migrate upriver in

Left: When the salmon migrate upriver to spawn, they are in good condition and thus a favourite quarry for sportfishermen. During their swim to the spawning areas, the salmon often have to pass serious obstacles such as wild rapids. River sections with these obstacles are normally good for fishing, since the salmon pause here before resuming their journey.

Right: Several theories exist as to why salmon bite in rivers even though they do not eat anything. Whatever the reason, it remains true that they can be coaxed to take artificial or natural baits. A time-tested method of salmon fishing is to put a piece of red wool yarn and a clump of earthworms onto the hook.

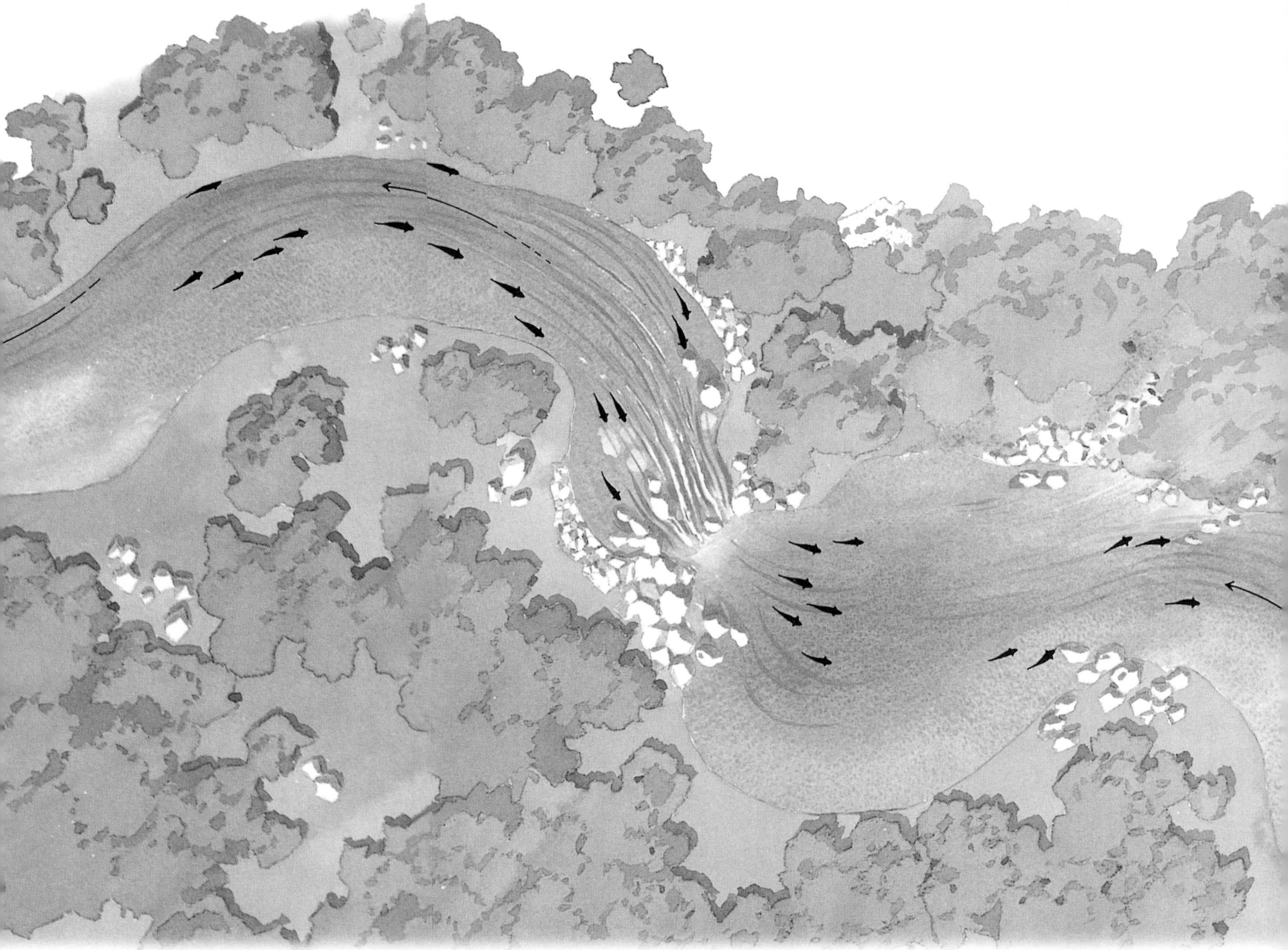

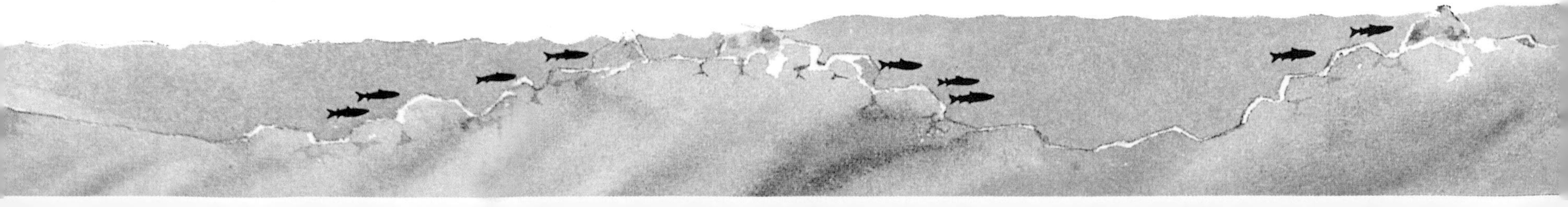

groups or small schools. Thus, one often finds that the salmon have distinct biting periods in the lower stretches.

The holding places can be very diverse. Large salmon choose the most suitable places, commonly in deep water, while those of medium and small size are banished to shallow water. Salmon often select a current edge, but the necks of rapids are excellent, and long current furrows are ideal.

Some places are more appropriate for flyfishing than for spinning. Yet if, for instance, you see only 2-3 metres of water at the opposite bank – or amid the current – and one metre at your own bank, this is a good site for spinning.

Early in the season, when the water is cold and the level high, you should fish so deeply and slowly in the river that you occasionally feel the spoon or plug hit the bottom. This can be done by casting toward the opposite bank, or obliquely downstream, and then lowering or raising the rod to keep the bait moving at the bottom. As a rule, shiny salmon at a given place will bite during the first two or three casts. To go on casting at the same place any longer is usually a waste of time.

In the middle of the season, the water has sunk and the holding places have changed. One seldom catches salmon in totally calm water, so the bait should move with the current, at the same speed or a bit faster. If the bait slows down, lift the rod or reel in a little line – and vice versa if it moves too fast, although in general it will do better if moving too fast than too slowly.

When the water level is low and the temperature exceeds 10-14° C (50-57° F), the salmon often go into faster water. While their holding places change during the season, so does the size of ascending salmon. The big salmon tend to arrive at the beginning of the season, followed by medium-size and small ones. However, large individuals sporadically run even at the end of the season in many areas. Also late in the season, the fish become coloured and more aggressive, frequently biting after several casts at the same place.

A typical river stretch, shown above, is illustrated below in cross-section. Salmon occur mainly at the inflows and outlets of pools. In relatively long and wide pools, however, the fish prefer to hold at the current's outer edges. Yet in shallow or fast-flowing areas, they take positions in the current lee near large rocks.

Salmon fishing in a river of average magnitude calls for strong spinning equipment: either a baitcasting reel or a spinning reel, with line of 0.40-0.45 mm, except later in the season when a line of 0.35-0.40 mm can be sufficient. But in small rivers, lighter equipment is used. Spoons, spinners and plugs are excellent bait throughout these months. Early in the season, spoons of 20-40 grams are often used, as the salmon then stand deep and the water level is high. Many people also fish with floating or sinking plugs of 11-13 cm. Once the water has sunk, spinners of 8-15 grams may be tried too.

Experience shows that, well into the season, salmon take small bait – chiefly flies. Spinning can be done with a fly aided by a casting bubble, or some other kind of casting weight. The flies are of the same type as in flyfishing, such as small single- or double-hooked ones of size 2-10. The leader should be 3.5-4 metres (11.5-13 feet) long, and the fly should swing in the current – as if you were flyfishing. A casting bubble works best in big, lazy rivers, where you can speed up the fly as it swings toward your bank.

Spinning is also possible with a fly and no casting Buldo. Instead you fish with a leader of 1-2 metres (3.3-6.6 feet) to the fly, and a leader of about 20 cm (8 in) to a suitable sinker. This tackle is superb during the whole season, and the fly can be fished exactly like a spoon. Early in the season, and in cold water, one often uses large bushy red-yellow tube flies of 12-16 cm (4.8-6.4 in) with simple patterns. Later on, black or dark tube flies are best. The fly may "hang" in the current, but it becomes more lively if, at the same time, you "pump" it forward and backward in the current – for example by lifting and lowering the rod with some quick movements. Here is an elementary method that can reward the newcomer, too. Yet remember that spinning with a fly is prohibited in, among other countries, Norway.

Fishing for Atlantic salmon with natural bait

Salmon will also take natural bait, though fishing with shrimp is not allowed in Norway. At many rivers in Great Britain, shrimp are still fished on hook tackle. A single hook is used in some places, and one or two small treble hooks elsewhere. Even whole, dead baitfish on hook systems were previously employed in salmon fishing.

Most common, however, is fishing with worms. In certain countries such as Ireland, fishing with a float is widespread, while worms on bottom tackle are used in other lands. The hooks are normally of size 1/0-3/0, baited with a bunch of worms. Attached to the hook are a leader 1-2 metres (3.3-6.6 feet) long, and a second leader that is weighted with a fairly heavy sinker, so that the worms swing in the current at the same speed as a spoon or fly.

Striking, fighting and landing the fish

Salmon bite in many different ways. Some take the bait explosively and hook themselves. Others are more cautious and require you to strike. If fishing with natural bait, both shrimp and worms, you may feel the fish either taking violently, or "chewing" on the bait for several seconds – perhaps up to a minute – before swallowing it, which is the signal for you to strike. Inexperienced salmon fishermen have notable difficulty in judging when to strike, if fishing with worms or shrimp. After the salmon bites, it should initially be allowed to run the show. This is true of all fishing – but in the case of salmon, patience is essential. A further paradox of the sport is how many people react when they hook their first salmon: as soon as it bites, they want to get it up on land immediately, since they are afraid of losing it. Instead, let the fish set the pace, and look for a place to land it only when it shows signs of tiring out, for example by turning its belly upward.

A salmon is landed with a firm grip on the tail. It becomes paralyzed and is quite calm when lifted out of the water. On smooth, shallow shores, the fish is best slid onto land. You walk backward and, every time the salmon thrashes, pull it a little up on land, until it lies on its side and can be lifted high and dry.

Many fishermen also use large nets, although these can be hard to handle. The gaff, too, is still used in some European countries. A tailer is a gentle landing aid, but it demands adeptness. In America and in the Kola Peninsula, there are special restrictions on fishing and rules for returning the fish to water. For instance, in Kola all the fish must be returned.

Powerful rushes may enable the fish to escape from the hook, or to break the line. The closer the fish is to the rod tip, the greater the risk of losing it. By quickly lowering the rod tip, you can prevent a rushing fish from tearing itself free. But the line should always be stretched taut, and the drag should not be set too hard.

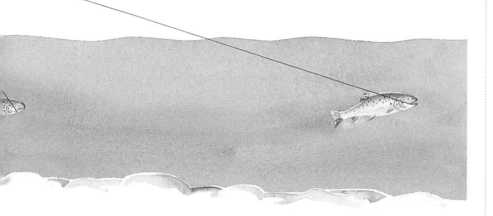

Even when the fish shows an urge to leap out of the water, it is best to lower the rod tip and, if possible, keep the rod parallel with the water surface. This reduces the pressure on the line, and usually makes the fish stop its acrobatics.

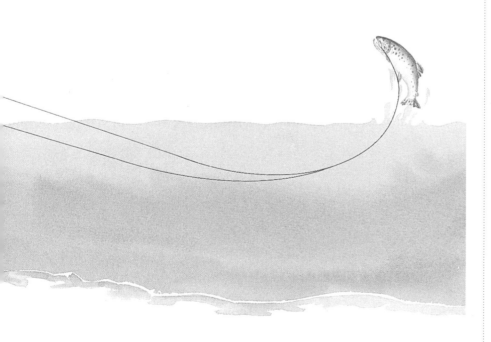

Above: In contrast to the majority of other fish species, a salmon can be gripped securely around its tail-fin root. It then becomes immobile, and lets itself be lifted or dragged ashore in a calm manner.

Left: Near long shallow shores, a played-out salmon is landed by sliding the fish onto land: you walk slowly backward and pull it gradually out of the water.

King salmon

The king salmon (*Oncorhynchus tshawytscha*) is the biggest among the six species of Pacific salmon. Five of these live on the American side of the Pacific Ocean, while the sixth – cherry salmon – exists only in Kamchatka and northern Japan. Other names for the king salmon are the chinook, quinnat, spring, and tye. Specimens of 30 kg (66 lbs) are not uncommon, and whoppers weighing over 40 kg (88 lbs) have been caught in rivers such as the Kenai in Alaska and the Skeena in British Columbia. But the average weight is 8-12 kg (18-26 lbs).

Unlike the other salmon species, king salmon are known for their migrations far up into river systems. In the Yukon River, they swim almost 3,000 kilometres. King salmon in the sea are silvery with irregular black patches, even on the back and tail fin. Moreover, they have black pigment on the mouth and throat. This species is distributed from northern Alaska to California and, on the Asiatic side, from Kamchatka to northern China. It has also been implanted in the Great Lakes, where it thrives and grows to 12-13 kg (26-29 lbs).

Spinning for king salmon

These fish bite much more eagerly than Atlantic salmon do – from the moment they approach the river mouth to the time they begin spawning. Trolling fishermen are busy already in the sea and estuaries, and fish are pursued with artificial baits and salmon roe as they run upriver. For holding places, they choose deep holes, current edges, brinks and backwaters. But unlike Atlantic salmon, they often prefer deep, dark, calm water. Many rivers are murky and partly muddy, so the inflows from clear tributaries can be counted on as holding places – especially at the creeks in which king salmon spawn. Only young king salmon, weighing up to 2-3 kg (4.4-6.6 lbs), rise to the surface for small bait such as flies.

Atlantic salmon usually betray their presence by leaping in the river, but king salmon almost always go to the bot-

tom and stay there. They often stand in dense schools, whereas the medium-sized and large Atlantic salmon are territorial and gather only at difficult passages or rapids.

During the fight, king salmon are considerably heavier and tougher than Atlantic salmon – yet by no means as wild and ungovernable. Just after biting, they normally show themselves once at the surface, while an Atlantic salmon may leap repeatedly as it struggles.

This fishing needs heavy equipment, often combining line of 0.40-0.60 mm with a very strong rod. Lures for king salmon include the Pixie, Spin-N-Glo, Tee Spoon, and diverse deep-going plugs that ideally contain rattles. Virtually all types of artificial lure work well, if fished deep and slow – almost crawling over the bottom, down to the salmon or among them. The salmon stand close together

Left: The giant of Pacific salmon is the king (chinook) salmon, which can weigh over 90 lbs (40 kg). Those that run upriver during the spring and early summer are silvery, but the ever later migrants become increasingly coloured.

Above: Robust equipment is needed to catch king salmon, as they are tough and heavy during the fight. In addition, they gladly choose deep holding places, where the lure has to be fished just over the bottom.

Vital facts

There are various strains of king salmon. They migrate upriver from January until late autumn, but the primary ascent in most western American rivers is made between May and early July. In contrast to coho salmon, the king salmon runs up large rivers, and it spawns from July until November. The fish that ascend during springtime often choose tributaries, whereas the autumn-running fish select the main river. A further difference is that the salmon ascending in early summer are always silvery, while the late ones are slightly coloured as they ascend. All the salmon die after spawning, as do other salmonoid species in western North America.

The fry feed on insects, crustaceans and larvae in the waterways. They migrate into the ocean during the next or the following summer. Dead salmon fertilize the basically barren waterways, so their fate is naturally beneficial. On reaching the sea, the young salmon grow rapidly, and 2-8 years later they return up the same rivers.

and, to avoid hooking them badly, it is only allowed in many rivers to use single hooks.

Nobody questions the power of king salmon – they are tough until the end. Since they usually form schools, one can catch several in the same place. Evidently they are not as shy as Atlantic salmon.

In the Great Lakes, fishing is also done from the shore around river mouths. Between early summer and early autumn, there are chances of catching king salmon when they migrate up the rivers. This is a typical wading sport, and succeeds best in the morning or evening, as the fish swim into deep water to eat during the daytime. One uses strong spinning rods, line of 0.30-0.36 mm, and spoons of 20-40 grams. Piers and breakwaters, as well as sand-banks and headlands near these ascent rivers, are other good fishing sites for king salmon.

Fishing for king salmon with natural bait

As the salmon approach the estuaries, they are subjected to intensive trolling – called mooching. The fish are caught with artificial lures, but whole or half herrings on hook tackle are also popular. When the fish run upriver, it is generally safest to use salmon roe, particularly if all else fails. Salmon roe is often packed in orange nylon net with fine meshes – as big as a walnut – and set on a single hook. Then the roe clump is fished with either a float, free line, or bottom tackle, allowed to swing in the current toward the salmon. In contrast to Atlantic salmon, which frequently bite on one of the first occasions when they are presented with artificial or natural bait, the king salmon is characteristically coaxed into biting by repeated casts with roe.

Left: A king salmon does not leap as often as an Atlantic salmon. During the fight, it shows itself at the surface only on rare occasions – like this!

Right: Once the king salmon have migrated up in spawning rivers, a cluster of salmon roe serves well as bait. A fine-meshed nylon stocking can be used to make clumps of roe. These are placed on a single hook and fished swinging in the current to entice a salmon.

Coho salmon

The coho or silver salmon (*Oncorhynchus kisutch*) is, along with king salmon, the most popular sportfishing species in western North America. It occurs from California to Alaska, besides Kamchatka and down the coast to Japan. It is entirely silvery, with small black patches over the lateral line, back and fins. Its average weight is 3-6 kg (6.6-13.2 lbs), although individuals are known to reach 12-14 kg (26-31 lbs). In 1967 these salmon were successfully implanted in the Great Lakes, where – together with other trout and salmonoid species – it has contributed to the region's impressive fishing. Coho salmon migrate upriver from July until early October.

Spinning for coho

Coho are also caught at sea, as are king salmon. Trolling or mooching for them is very common. They take spoons, or herring on tackle, at river mouths and in nearby marine waters. In the Great Lakes, spinning is done at the estuaries and from adjacent banks, headlands, piers and breakwaters, just as for king salmon.

However, the coho is more eager to bite than king salmon are. It migrates up small coastal rivers, often in sizeable schools, and then chooses quiet stretches of water or

current edges as holding places – but it keeps away from other salmon, such as chum. Unlike king salmon, it is content to stay in relatively shallow water. If the river flows through lakes, one frequently finds big schools of coho leaping at the outflows.

Coho are primarily a wonderful quarry for flyfishing, but they can be caught with small spinners of size 2-3, and on spoons of 5-12 grams. While king salmon are readily duped by bright red-orange spoons and spinners, in the case of

---

Vital facts

The coho runs up large rivers as king salmon do, but more commonly it chooses small coastal rivers when migrating into fresh water. In addition, it travels a shorter distance up the rivers than do king salmon, and thus exposes itself less to the dangers and difficulties faced by that species.

Coho are silvery during their run upriver, but later in the season one can also see lightly coloured fish ascending. The spawning takes place between October and February. The fry migrate into the sea either during the next summer, or 1-2 years later. They remain there for 2-4 years, although seldom wandering as far from the home river as do king salmon. In the ocean, coho feed on shrimp, cuttlefish and fish. The stock of silver salmon in western American waters has decreased in recent years.

coho it is better to use spoons and spinners made of silver or brass. Small baits should be retrieved slowly, as close to the bottom as possible – without losing speed. The bite is often cautious but resolute, and only when you start to put pressure on the fish does it begin to leap, approaching the surface much more frequently than a king salmon does.

Almost no fishing with roe is done for the coho, in contrast to king salmon. Thus, it is a distinctive spinning and flyfishing species.

Left: The greedy coho (silver) salmon normally weighs under 22 lbs (10 kg) and migrates up small rivers near the west coast of North America, ranging from California to Alaska. There it tends to remain in relatively shallow water, and eagerly takes small, colourful spinners and spoons.

Above: Coho are generally cautious biters, but become lively when they are hooked and feel the line's pressure. Frequently, they leap in the air and thrash in the surface more than they stay in the water.

Chum, sockeye and humpback salmon

These three salmon species are in no way as prominent for sportfishing as the king and coho salmon. The chum (*Oncorhynchus keta*), also called the dog or keta salmon, weighs 3-5 kg (6.6-11 lbs), but specimens of 6-7 kg (13-15 lbs) have been caught. Its habitats range from northern California to Alaska, and in 1956 it was successfully implanted in Siberia.

Chum are easily recognized by the stripes over their back and sides. The stripes become clearer after some time in a river. The chum migrates upriver during summer and autumn, to spawn in November-December.

Sockeye (*Oncorhynchus nerka*) are also known as red salmon. In the sea, this is the most important salmon species after the humpback, since it has the same size and its deep-red meat is tasty. The fish is silvery when in the sea, but acquires colours as soon as it runs upriver. The females become weakly or strongly red, and the males bright red with a slight hump. On the whole, sockeye do not occur south of the Columbia River. Farther north, they live in Alaska, Kamchatka and Japan.

The sockeye's life cycle differs from that of other salmonoids, as its migrations are almost confined to rivers which flow through a lake, in or near whose estuaries it spawns. It runs upriver early – from April until July. In some rivers, as at Bristol Bay, the run is so abundant that the river bottom is virtually coloured red. These fish weigh 2.5-3 kg (5.5-6.6 lbs).

Schools of sockeye are often found in calm, deep parts of a river, but chiefly at the estuaries in lakes. Unlike other salmonoids, red ones frequently break the surface. Sockeye are not as easy to tempt with bait, but small lures such as spinners or spoons – ideally somewhat red or orange – can get them to bite. Retrieve slowly and deeply, as near the bottom as possible.

The humpback, or pink, salmon (*Oncorhynchus gorbuscha*) is the leading salmon for professional fishing, but plays

Chum salmon, with their typical stripes across the back and sides, may weigh up to 33 lbs (15 kg) but often reach only 6.6-11 lbs (3-5 kg). They are also called dog salmon because of the large protruding teeth that the males acquire after running upriver. When fresh-run and silvery, a chum can be a fine fighter if fished on light gear.

quite a minor role in sportfishing. It occurs from northern California to northwestern Alaska – most commonly in British Columbia – as well as in Kamchatka, Korea and Japan. Weights over 1.5-2.5 kg (3.3-5.5 lbs) are rare. The humpback is silvery in the sea, and runs upriver from late June through July. After a short time in the river, it develops a clear hump and becomes reddish. It has a vigorous appetite and is one of the most bite-crazy salmon in the Pacific Ocean.

Humpback can be caught with flies, small spinners or spoons, which are retrieved slowly and deeply. Their holding places are at current edges, calm areas of water, little furrows and holes in shallows. In clear rivers, it is not unusual to find them in water only half a metre deep. The fishing is done with ultra-light gear, and this makes the humpback a fine fighter, happy to leap at the surface.

Above: The sockeye (red) salmon is also silvery when it begins its migration up a spawning river, but it soon turns red. Since it lives chiefly on small crustaceans, it may be hard to trick onto the hook. This can, however, be done by retrieving small lures deeply and slowly.

Below: The humpback (pink) salmon is named for the conspicuous bulge that the males develop after migrating upriver. It rarely attains weights over 11 lbs (5 kg), and is not considered very interesting as a sportfish. Yet it offers exciting experiences if fished with ultra-light equipment and small spinners, spoons or flies.

Fishing in Marine Waters

The saltwater fisherman's realm is enormous, and he or she must fish where the predators feed. Since many coastal waters are not very nutritious, the fish often concentrate in a few places. Knowledge about their ways of life and behaviour, as well as about good fishing places, is a prerequisite for choosing successful methods, techniques and baits. The best equipment, lures and tackle are useless without this "know-how" and a mastery of several time-tested, effective procedures.

∎

Cod

Throughout winter, English surf-fishermen challenge the cod (*Gadus morhua*) along their country's southern coasts. In Scotland, it is caught all year round. American coastal fishermen vanquish it during autumn and winter, from Cape Cod to Nova Scotia. Much-desired by practitioners of spinning in Norway, Denmark and Sweden, it has not surprisingly given rise to many of the traditions in coastal fishing.

The cod's main distribution covers the North Sea and the coasts of Norway, Iceland and the Faeroes, but it is also common on the east coast of North America. Its colours vary, though: on mixed bottoms in shallow water it is dark brown, while cod from sandy bottoms and deep water are paler. Red, or mountain, cod is the term for cod that live in shallow water and have a strong red-brown to deep orange colour, even on the abdomen.

Coastal cod seldom weigh more than 3-4 kg (6.6-8.8 lbs), except at some places in Norway – such as powerful tidal currents – which regularly yield specimens of 8-10 kg (18-22 lbs). But cod at sea can reach striking weights. In northern Europe, 20 kg (44 lbs) is not unusual and fish exceeding 30 kg (66 lbs) have been caught, for example, at Yellow Reef off northern Jutland, in Öresund and off Lofoten. In North America, boats have brought up cod that reach 40 kg (88 lbs).

Spinning for cod

Cod are caught by spinning from harbours, piers, long shallow shores and rocky coasts. They often prefer deep water and mixed bottoms. The spinning equipment must be robust and long-casting, such as rods of 9-11 feet with strong multiplier or spinning reels, line of 0.30-0.40 mm, and spoons or pirks of 20-40 grams in silver, copper, red or fluorescent colours. Since the cod is a bottom-fish and often goes into seaweed after being hooked, you can benefit by replacing the treble hook with a single hook, which causes much fewer bottom-snags.

One of the most frequent errors, when spinning in deep water, is to start the retrieval immediately after the impact. Spoons or pirks are then retrieved high over the bottom – without being seen by a single cod. Thus, the lure must be allowed to sink the whole way down, before you tighten up the line and begin to retrieve. The rod is lifted and lowered,

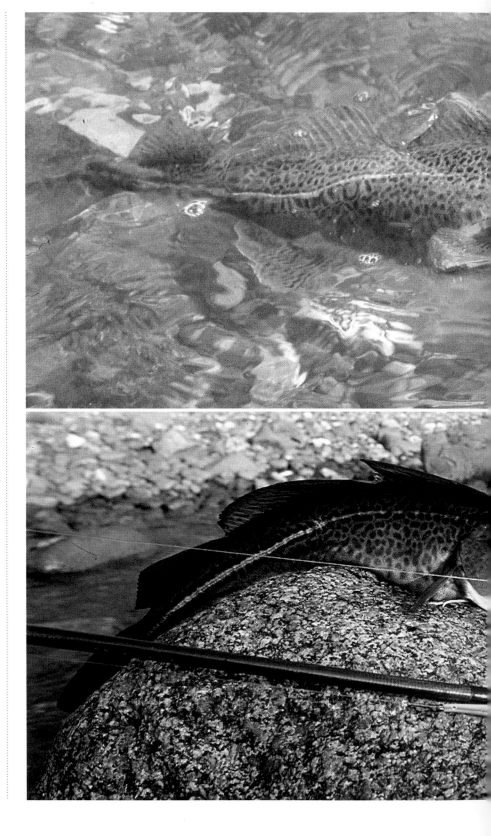

In many parts of Europe and North America, cod are caught regularly by coastal spinning. These fish are so widespread in some regions, especially in northern Europe, that traditional coastal fishing is based on them.

as you reel in the spoon or pirk so that it constantly grazes the bottom. In the shallows near land, these movements should continue but the retrieval is a little faster. This technique can be refined once you have a correct feeling for the given depth and bottom conditions: a retrieval that keeps the lure just above the bottom will soon seem natural.

Bottom-snags are almost impossible to avoid, but the worst ones are prevented by choosing the right weight on the spoon or pirk, combined with the right retrieval speed. Unfortunately, cod fishing often means lost lures. If you do not get a bite, the reason may be that no cod are present because the bottom is smooth, sandy or muddy. Cod are nearly always found on mixed bottoms with stones, seaweed, mussels and the like.

Dropper flies occasionally give results – due not to simultaneous bites on the pirk and dropper, but since the

Vital facts

There are many strains of coastal cod, often with different habits of migration and spawning. When the spawning time approaches, they head for certain marine areas with suitable temperature and salinity. Spawning proceeds from January until March and, in some places, also during April. Subsequently, the cod disperse to shallow areas and banks in the sea, or toward the coast, where their diet includes crustaceans, crabs, sand lance and herring.

The cod's senses of smell, sight and feeling are highly developed, and it uses them all when seeking food on the bottom. It can also be found in the middle layer or the surface, hunting sand lance and herring. The best season for coastal cod is from autumn until early spring. Yet at northerly latitudes, as in Norway, the warm months and especially autumn are thought most rewarding.

dropper is better at stimulating cod to take. You can use droppers made of feathers, plastic worms, or single hooks with jig tails. If fishing with a dropper, you must attach strong leaders of, for example, 0.45-0.60 mm line – or even stronger line in areas with big cod.

When the cod hunt herring or sand lance along the shores, rapid retrieval is most effective, as the cod frequently bite a little above the bottom or in the middle layer. At other times, cod are selective and may only swim at the bottom to eat crabs. It is then especially important to spin with good bottom contact, and make the spoon or pirk almost crawl across the bottom to imitate a crab. Under these conditions, red-coloured spoons are superior. Generally, cod in deep water enjoy taking spoons and pirks with bright yellow and red colours.

However, in shallow water and along gentle shores with 2-4 metres of water, varied bottom vegetation, seaweed and stones, it is wrong to use the above technique of retrieval. Strong spinning equipment is still used here, such as a rod of 9-11 feet, line of 0.30-0.40 mm, and a pirk or spoon of 15-30 grams. As soon as the lure hits the water, you start to retrieve at a uniform tempo, possibly with a few spin-stops, so that the lure goes in the middle layer – neither in the surface water nor too near the seaweed.

Regardless of whether you fish in deep or shallow water, there are often more cod where you catch one. The area can be searched with casts in a fan pattern or, along shallow shores and cliffs, by walking for some metres and making parallel casts outward. In such places, the times before and after sunset are good for fishing, as the cod then move toward land.

If you fish from a boat over shallows, it is best to drift across promising current edges or areas known to have cod. This method involves two principal techniques. First, the pirk or spoon can be let down on the side that the boat drifts away from – the wind side – and the rod is continually lifted and lowered, maintaining bottom contact. Second, you can cast with the wind from the lee side and retrieve while jerking the rod up and down. The latter method

Spinning for cod is often done from rough coasts with breakers. The essential equipment includes long rods, strong reels, 0.30-0.40 mm line, and long-shafted nets. Shown at far right is a much quieter form of coastal spinning, from a float-ring close to the shore.

demands good contact with the spoon or pirk, since you must also compensate for the boat's drift.

Cod fishing with natural bait

Scandinavians traditionally spin for cod with artificial bait, either from a boat or from land. In other countries such as Germany, Holland and Great Britain, natural baits are used to catch cod.

The given marine or coastal environment dictates the choice of methods and baits. Bottom fishing with natural bait at cliffs, piers and harbours can employ simple equipment. A strong rod of 9-11 feet, line of 0.35-0.45 mm, and a suitable casting weight, as well as paternoster tackle with one or two leaders, and hooks of size 1/0-3/0, are about all the items you need.

Cod are omnivorous, but some types of bait are preferred: lugworms, ragworms, herring strips, mussel meat, shrimps and cephalopods. After baiting and casting the hook, you can either hold the rod in your hand or lay it, within view, on a cliff or place it in a rod-holder. As soon as a cod bites, you make a strike.

At open coasts with sandy beaches, hard current and waves, surfcasting gear is essential. The rods are 11-13 feet long, specially designed for this rough environment. Most people prefer baitcasting reels, but spinning reels work well too. Due to the wear on the line when casting, it is necessary to have an extra-thick line tip, which must be long enough to form 5-6 turns on the reel spool before the cast. The cast itself requires a lot of training and, not least, familiarity with the equipment and how it is loaded.

Fighting the fish

When a cod bites, it heads for the bottom to hide itself among seaweed or stones. A superficially placed treble hook will thus easily catch in the weeds. You must therefore quickly put pressure on the fish, to lift it off the bottom. This is called "pumping in" the cod. With hard lifts of the rod, it is forced upward, while you reel in line each time the rod is lowered. The fish can be landed with a gaff and net, or slid up onto land where this is allowed by the coastline.

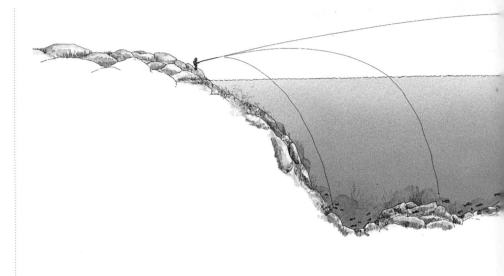

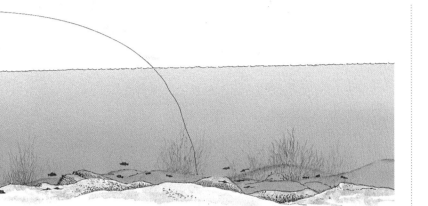

Left: Cod often occur where the water is deep even near shore and the bottom is thus not influenced by weather, wind and tides. Here they can hunt close to land, so a relatively short cast is sufficient.

Above: A cod usually weighs 1-5 kg (2-11 lbs). It is seldom a hard fighter, but appeals greatly to gourmets. By quickly "pumping" it up from the bottom after it bites, you can avoid bottom snags.

Left: Since the lure must be retrieved just over the bottom, snags may be hard to prevent. But as illustrated here, it is easier to lift the line over seaweed and other vegetation with a long rod than with a short one – especially when the lure approaches the shore.

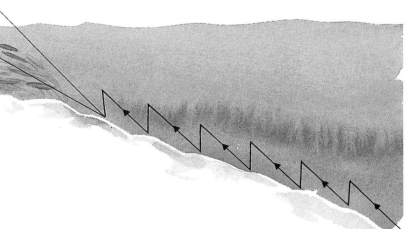

203

European pollack

The European pollack (*Pollachius pollachius*) is one of the greatest challenges along rocky coasts of the Northeast Atlantic, where the chances are best of catching this beautiful fish. It is easy to recognize from its bronze-yellow, torpedo-shaped body, big brown hunter's eyes, strong underbite, and notably the dark lateral line that distinguishes it well from the coalfish. Although a type of cod, it has no barbels.

Pollack occur from the Faeroes and northern Norway to Morocco and the Mediterranean, but are chiefly distributed around the British Isles as well as southern and central Norway. They prefer rock coasts with good current and water circulation, living mainly at depths of 4-5 to 50 metres but found as far down as a hundred metres. They are drawn primarily to wrecks, sunken rocks and underwater cliffs. At the coasts, they weigh 0.5-2 kg (1.1-4.4 lbs), and examples up to 4-5 kg (8.8-11 lbs) are seen. Farther out to sea, wrecks have yielded pollack of 9-10 kg (20-22 lbs), which is the maximum.

Pollack are a type of codfish but often live pelagically. They are fast and strong, and large pollack can offer exciting sport with powerful rushes toward the bottom.

Vital facts

Known spawning grounds exist off southern Norway and in the North Sea, where the spawning lasts from February until April. When the young are a few centimetres long, they wander toward the coasts, where they grow up, living on worms, crustaceans and fishfrye. Once larger, they eat small fish – mostly sand lance, herring and sprat – but sometimes also mysis shrimp and other small crustaceans. The pollack is not a bottom-fish like cod, but holds a bit over the bottom. At sundown and on dark, windy days with disturbed water, it usually moves up to the middle layer. It may even be found in the surface at dusk.

Spinning for pollack

Since they tend to hunt somewhat up from the bottom, at rocky cliffs or in surface water, pollack can be caught with relatively light spinning equipment. Exposed rocky coasts with strong currents and deep water are ideal places.

When spinning, it is most important to search all water layers with light, lively spoons or pirks, preferably in sub-dued colours such as copper, red/copper or green/blue. Pollack are occasionally rather fastidious, and may only take a certain bait of a special colour, size or type. Jigs are often superb for pollack. A little compact pirk with a single hook, carrying a fish strip, is also very lively and inviting.

The retrieval can be made with accelerations ending in long stops. Then the bait sinks through the water and can be reeled in again. It is during the pause, or when the bait resumes moving, that the pollack usually bites. The bite is hesitant and heavy, followed by a violent rush toward the bottom – which means your drag must be finely adjusted.

Droppers are effective, too, particularly in daytime when pollack take small lures. However, the risk is that the leader will snap if the fish dives and the pirk catches in seaweed.

Pollack fishing with natural bait

The pollack is a distinctly predatory species suitable for spinning, but it can very well be caught with natural bait that is fished with a float in breaking waves. A small float with a hook of size 1-1/0, baited with attractive fresh-cut sand lance, herring or mackerel, and swaying irresistibly in the swells, is excellent for pollack. Nor is it uncommon to catch these fish while float-angling for wrasse, which thrive in the same coastal environments.

Above: Jigs can be the right medicine for evasive pollack. Pirks baited with fish strips are also attractive when the pollack are choosy.

Below: Pollack are commonly found along rocky coasts where the water is kept moving by, for example, currents. In this case the pirk and droppers have crossed the path of a school of pollack.

Coalfish

The coalfish (*Pollachius virens*), widely called pollack, is another member of the cod family. Characterized by a dark-grey back, white lateral line and shiny tin-coloured abdomen, it lacks barbels and has a clear underbite. Its distribution resembles that of cod, but the southern limit goes through the Bay of Biscay, the northern boundary passing Iceland and southern Greenland. Coalfish also occur along the eastern coast of North America, from Newfoundland to New York.

Small specimens are often encountered off rocky coasts, and in deep water close to land – even just a few metres away. Large coalfish, weighing from 5-6 kg (11-13 lbs) up to the maximum of 25 kg (55 lbs), swim as far down as 400 metres.

Spinning for coalfish

These are extremely greedy creatures. Small coalfish, in particular, bite almost anything that moves. Spoons, pirks and droppers are therefore outstanding lures for them. Since the fish often hold in free water, you have to search it from top to bottom when working from a rocky coast, pier or breakwater, and remember that they may be right in the surface when evening or cloudy weather comes. Their hunting for small fish in the surface is commonly revealed by seagulls.

The retrieval must be quick and varied. Keep in mind

Vital facts

Coalfish spawn in the open sea, between January and April, at certain places with suitable temperature and salinity. The fry consume plankton but, as soon as this stage is over, the fish approach land. Weighing from a couple of hundred grams up to 1-1.5 kg (2.2-3.3 lbs), they may appear in enormous schools offshore, especially at rocks. The young coalfish feed occasionally on shrimp, otherwise on fish fry – mainly herring and sand lance – while the latter species are eaten by larger coalfish. Throughout their lives, coalfish form schools and seldom stay at the bottom, usually swimming some metres above it and nearly reaching the surface. As with European pollack, they rise at evening and night or in cloudy, windy weather.

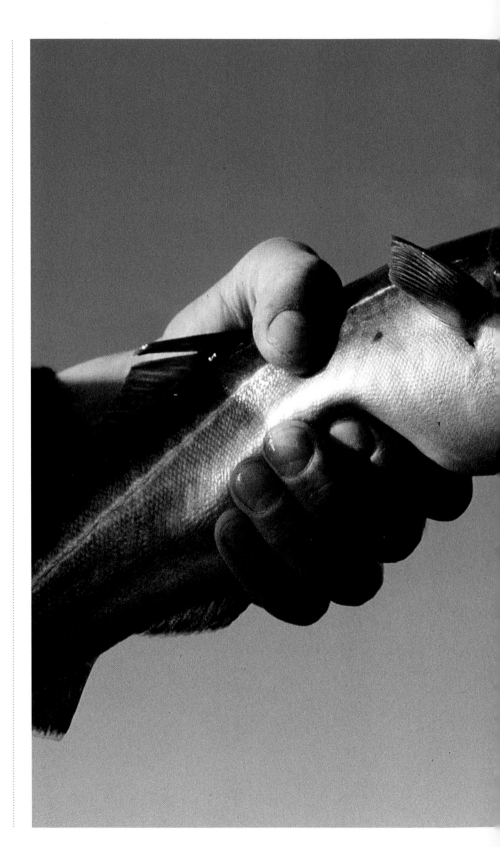

that coalfish, like pollack, may also bite when the spoon or pirk leaves the surface for a new cast. This fishing is not at all difficult, and anybody can land a fine catch of coalfish with no problems after locating them. While good places for pollack tend to be permanent, schools of small coalfish are frequently found by chance.

Large coalfish rarely swim next to land, so examples of 2-3 kg (4.4-6.6 lbs) are regarded as superb along coasts. But one area where big specimens can be caught from the coast is Saltströmmen, at Bodö in northern Norway. Local fishermen have brought up coalfish weighing over 20 kg (44 lbs) in November and December, a time when few people are out with spinning equipment at that latitude. Such prizes are taken with powerful rods, line of 0.60 mm, baitcasting reels and 200-gram pirks.

Left: The coalfish is a beautiful, gluttonous codfish that gladly takes a pirk, spoon or dropper.

Below: At rocky coasts, small coalfish often swim near land, but they may hold almost anywhere between the bottom and the surface. Varied retrieval, preferably with the countdown method, is therefore important in locating a coalfish school.

Mackerel

The mackerel (*Scomber scombrus*) is the ocean's mini-tuna. Its torpedo-like body puts it among the speed demons of the deep. A pelagic predator, a school fish, and a summer guest in the northern part of its distribution – from the top of Norway, past the Faeroes and Iceland, to Newfoundland – it occurs as far south as the Mediterranean and, in America, Cape Hatteras.

The native North Atlantic mackerel lacks a swim-bladder. An almost identical species, the Pacific mackerel (*Scomber japonicus*), lives from Alaska to Baja California, as well as on the Asiatic side of the Pacific and in the Indian Ocean. It resembles the former species, but has a swim-bladder. A third species is the Spanish mackerel (*Scomberomorus maculatus*), which ranges from Chesapeake Bay to Cuba on the American side of the Atlantic, and along the North African coast to the Canary Isles. Mackerel normally weigh up to 1 kg (2.2 lbs) and sometimes over twice as much.

There are several species of mackerel. This is the North Atlantic variant, which has no swim bladder and can move easily between different depths. To find the depth at which it is hunting, one must often fish all levels according to the countdown method.

Vital facts

Mackerel overwinter at depths of 400-600 metres in the Skagerrak and west of the British Isles. Those west of Ireland swim toward the Irish, English and Scottish coasts, whereas mackerel in the North Sea and Skagerrak approach the coast of Norway and enter the Skagerrak and Kattegat during springtime. Before then, they have spawned in deeper water, and spawning proceeds in free water near the coast.

The stocks of mackerel have suffered great changes, and the fishing was poor for many years in the 1960s and 1970s. Professional fishermen discovered their overwintering areas in the deeper parts of the North Sea, and could double the catches – which has irreparably harmed these stocks.

Spinning for mackerel

When the first mackerel head for the coast, between May and early July, they are hungry and tend to attack any moving object – including spoons, pirks and droppers. But later in July, having fed on sand lance and the young of herring and sprat, they become less eager to bite. It is then chiefly in the morning and evening, as they approach land to hunt, that fishing pays off. Their presence is often shown by gulls and other seabirds, which dive at the mackerel hunting small fish in the surface.

Spinning is done from cliffs, piers and breakwaters, where the water is deep and vigorous. Long-casting equip-

ment with line of 0.30 mm, a shiny pirk of 20-50 grams, and a leader tied of 0.35-0.45 mm line, with a couple of little droppers made from feathers – in white, blue and green colours – suits the work perfectly. The water is searched from the bottom to the surface. Mackerel hunt in all water layers, but at dawn and dusk they swim in the uppermost layer and can frequently be seen in the surface.

Mackerel fishing with natural bait

Float-fishing for mackerel can be done wherever the fish exist. However, primarily in the later summer when they bite less greedily, natural baits usually yield results – even at midday as they go deeper.

Since the mackerel prefer to swim at 2-5 metres of depth, this fishing makes use of sliding floats. A float that carries 5-15 grams of lead is suitable, together with a leader having a hook of size 4-8 and a small fresh-cut strip of herring or sand lance. The fishing depth is adjusted by means of a stop-knot or a rubber stopper. For example, you can fish first at 4-5 metres and, if unlucky, try higher up in the water. When the fish bites, you are seldom left in doubt – but on some days the float only shakes a bit, and you have to strike immediately or the monster goes missing.

Garfish

The garfish (*Belone belone*) lives along the European coasts from the Arctic Circle, past the Faeroes, down to Morocco. It, too, is a summer fish in Scandinavian waters. The Mediterranean and the Black Sea also contain garfish. Yet its main habitats lie around the British Isles. Some closely related species inhabit tropical and subtropical seas.

Spinning for garfish

This is a marvellous sportfish, slender and beautiful, often seen more in the air than in the water when it has been hooked. One rarely meets a predatory fish which occurs so abundantly and is still so hard to catch.

Garfish frequently pursue a spoon or pirk without taking. Such "imitators" are noticed especially in the early part of the season, before their spawning has finished. After spawning, however, the biting begins and the fish can be sought at headlands or banks, from piers or breakwaters, and off coastal rocks, preferably where the current is strong.

These fish are ideal to challenge with light spinning equipment and spoons of 8-25 grams. Elongated, silvery spoons are best. Treble hooks of thin metal have proved to

Vital facts

After overwintering to the south of Ireland, garfish arrive at the Scandinavian coasts in April or May. First come the big ones, often weighing about 1 kg (2.2 lbs), soon followed by the rest. Garfish spawn among seaweed and eel grass in shallow waters, once the sun has warmed these up. The spawning takes place in May and June, although it may last until August in some areas. Early during the season, garfish swim in schools, and small schools are commonly observed in the shallows. But when spawning is over, they spread out and appear both in the surface and in deep water. Here they eat fish fry, shrimp and stickleback. Late summer and early autumn find them retiring to the west.

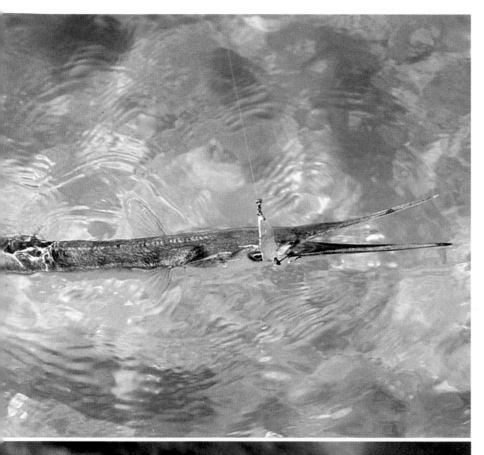

give superior results. The garfish's mouth is small and not always easy to hook. Therefore, many of us remove the treble hook and tie it to a short nylon leader. This should not be longer than the spoon, since otherwise the hook may get caught in the main line during the cast.

The retrieval should be even and rapid. Do not be surprised if the fish follows the lure time and again. Once the fish bites, avoid delivering a strike and just tighten up the line well, to fight the fish with a softly set drag.

Catching garfish with natural bait

While the species is quite suitable for spinning, it also falls for natural bait. All you need is a fixed float with 1-1.2 metres of line to a small hook of size 4-8, carrying a small fresh-cut strip of herring or mackerel. Cast out and let the float lie still or drift with the current. The garfish swallow the bait with no trouble, and then you strike.

Left: The garfish is a slender, rapid swimmer with a long, hard "beak". It can be difficult to hook, but fights admirably and often leaps into the air.

Below: Light equipment, sharp treble hooks, and fast retrieval are the three rules of thumb for conquering garfish. They frequently travel in schools and, once found, can yield an abundant catch.

Sea trout

Equally exciting to match wits against are the ocean's silvery racers, sea trout (*Salmo trutta trutta*). Catching them in salt water is a Danish national sport – though also done with flies and Buldos at, for instance, estuaries in Orkney and the Shetlands after World War I. Coastal spinning was started by Danish sportfishermen during the inter-war period, but it developed mainly in the 1950s, at the same time as the equipment became ever better and could cast farther. In

Vital facts

Sea trout hunt along all shallow sections of coast that have rivers or waterways which the fish can run up to spawn in. After they spawn and return to the sea, they are emaciated and begin to eat worms, fish fry, herring and sprat. They become shiny and silvery, regaining their weight after a few weeks.

These fish stay along the coasts almost all year round, and can be caught in any month. But some periods are better than others, spring and autumn being excellent. During autumn, though, sea trout are not as willing to bite as in the spring.

The fish prefer mixed, varied bottoms with current, weeds, sand, stone and mussels. Consequently, good fishing places include banks, headlands and rocky points. From May throughout summer, the coastal water in many areas is too warm, so the sea trout move into deeper water, returning to the coast from evening until morning.

Some sea trout migrate up in streams and rivers as soon as June, while others head for fresh water during the autumn and early winter. The winter also brings many shiny non-spawning fish into coves and estuaries with lower salinity – and here they are found on soft, rather uninteresting bottoms.

Coastal spinning for sea trout should be done by presenting the lure just above the bottom. The retrieval must be varied and lively, with regular jerks and spin-stops, in order to entice sea trout.

Fishing with a casting bubble and flies enjoys wide popularity. The Buldo is a great aid especially in winter and early spring, when cold water prevails or when the fish are mostly focusing on a single type of food, such as ragworms. It is also worth using a casting bubble in summer until August-September, when sea trout are less eager to bite.

Fishing for sea trout with natural bait

Natural baits are often served to sea trout. Most simply, where the water is deep enough and a stony shore exists, you can fish with a fixed float and a short line to a hook with worms. But the absolutely best method is spinning with a Buldo and a leader of 1.5-3 metres with a single hook and worms.

The baits employed are earthworms, ragworms and herring strips. In some areas, small fish such as sprat and sand lance are preferred. Spinning with a casting bubble and natural baits is done all year round, with a slow retrieval and ideally some pauses so that the bait and hook can sink. If you want them to go deeper, the leader may be lengthened and weighted with a couple of lead shot, or a short piece of sinking fly-line can be tied to the line tip.

Slender spoons weighing 10-20 grams, and a dropper on a short leader of 20–30 cm (8-12 inches), are a combination that not even big sea trout are likely to resist.

215

European bass

The European bass (*Dicentrarchus labrax*) is the star species of sportfishing in Great Britain. Hardly any other fish around the British Isles has meant so much for the development of coastal fishing, surfcasting, and their equipment. Rods, reels, lines, leaders and other accessories have undergone enormous refinement in recent decades due to the fish's popularity.

These bass live chiefly around the British Isles, in the Bay of Biscay, on the Atlantic coast of the Iberian peninsula, off

Vital facts

Open, surf-filled shorelines are the primary habit of European bass. Along beaches interrupted by rocky outcrops and breakwaters, they hunt sand lance, herring and crabs. Often they wander about at only half a metre of depth. Being attracted to river mouths and fresh water, they can also be caught from piers and barriers that give them shade on bright days in clear water.

Both on coasts with surf and in estuaries, the first hours after an ebb tide are considered good for catching bass. But no other firm rules exist for the fishing. They move to deep water in wintertime, and can be harvested almost all year round in Ireland. The spawning lasts from March until June in the British Isles, and takes place during late winter in the Mediterranean. These fish are widely prized by professional fishermen, and are universally regarded as fine food.

Fishing for European bass can be highly diverse. In some periods it is incredibly easy to get them to bite – on simple bottom tackle, a spoon or a mackerel tackle. At other times, particularly in clear water, they may become extremely shy and suspicious of any bait. Occasionally they fight like crazy, even in water just a few inches deep, or else become very lazy and virtually swim up on land by themselves without pressure from the rod.

Morocco and in parts of the Mediterranean. They also occur in the Black Sea, and some are found at the coasts of southern Norway and western Sweden. The latter region has lately received ever more bass.

Weights of 5 kg (11 lbs) are seldom exceeded, and 1-2 kg (2.2-4.4 lbs) is most common. Professional fisherman, though, have landed bass weighing more than 10 kg (22 lbs). The species belongs to a family with several hundred representatives in subtropical and tropical waters.

Spinning for bass

This fish is caught mainly with natural bait. Despite being a genuine predator with well-developed eyesight, it does not attract direct efforts at spinning in most places. Such spinning is practiced, however, along the Dutch coast at many wrecks in relatively shallow water – with good results on pirks and spoons. In Great Britain, the species' homeland, spinning for it is not so common. To make it bite, the fisherman needs clear water, and thus has little success under murky conditions. The best season for spinning is from June until October. Classic spoons and pirks such as the Toby are excellent for bass. Bridge pillars, piers and breakwaters should be fished from, besides rocky headlands and underwater shoals in shallow water.

Fishing for bass with natural bait

When natural bait is used, these fish can be tempted at all sorts of places – river mouths and fjords, shore structures, open beaches and stony coasts. The fishing is easiest where the cast length does not matter much, as in estuary areas and from piers. Often, though, an acquaintance with the tides is essential, because bass are known for hunting over large shallow areas when the tide comes in. As mentioned, one does well to fish soon after the low tide.

Standard equipment for bass on open coasts is a rod 10.5-11.5 feet long, with a casting weight of 50-90 grams and line of 0.30-0.35 mm on a baitcasting or spinning reel. A thick line tip is also necessary. Bass are usually fished with a paternoster tackle – either fixed, which is most

European bass are extremely popular in, for example, Great Britain – where they have strongly influenced the development of coastal fishing techniques and equipment. Normally they weigh 1-2 kg (2.2-4.4 lbs), but individuals over 5 kg (11 lbs) have been caught.

A number of bass have been landed at last. This voracious predator tends to prefer relatively shallow waters, taking both artificial and natural baits.

simple and effective, or sliding – and a single hook of size 1/0-3/0. Since the fishing often occurs amid currents or waves, most people use a breakaway weight that is anchored on the bottom. The baits include lugworm, sand leeches, cuttlefish, sand lance, or small peeler crabs.

The great majority of bass fishermen need only be able to cast 40-90 metres. This is quite enough, as in many places one can wade into the surf – wearing waders. Moderate surf is best, and so is cloudy weather in general, although the fishing can be superb even in strong sunshine. A bite from a bass may show itself in various ways – ranging from a couple of tugs on the rod tip, to a slack line or a ferocious pull on the line.

Left: Breakers and rocky coasts are favourite spots for the coastal fishermen who go after bass. The first hours after the ebb tide are usually most rewarding.

Right: Bass are temperamental fish – sometimes very easy to catch, but shy and wary during other periods. Here, a slender spoon has given good results.

Striped bass

The striped bass (*Roccus saxatilis*) is a favourite of sport-fishermen along the eastern coast of America, from St. Lawrence Bay down to northern Florida, and in the Gulf of Mexico from western Florida to Louisiana. Yet the most famous stretch is from South Carolina to Massachusetts. This fish was introduced on the Pacific coast towards the end of the last century, and is thus also found from the Columbia River mouth in Washington to the Los Angeles area in California. Here the best-known place is San Francisco Bay, whose fishing is far better than on the east coast.

Striped bass resemble the European bass in many ways, but can grow much bigger. Examples approaching 50 kg (110 lbs) have been caught by professional fisherman, and up to 30 kg (66 lbs) by coastal fishermen. The commonest

Vital facts

During the eastern winter, striped bass stay in Chesapeake and Delaware Bays. From there, a minor emigration of bass occurs in the winter. The fish spawn in river mouths from April until June, depending on the latitude. One renowned spawning area is the Roanoke River in North Carolina. They weigh scarcely half a kilogram (1 lb) when two years old, and 10 kg (22 lbs) when aged seven. The females grow bigger than the males. Striped bass are more or less omnivorous: their diet includes grey mullet, flatfish, herring, anchovy, lobster, crabs, shrimp and mussels. In spite of that, they eat selectively – when offered a certain type of food, they often concentrate on it and may therefore be unwilling to bite. Some bass stocks migrate locally, and there are two long major migrations every year: northward in springtime along the coasts of New Jersey, New York and New England, then southward in autumn. These occasions, especially the latter, provide the best coastal catches.

weights, however, are 3-8 kg (6.6-18 kg). On the east coast, striped bass have been fished hard by professionals for long periods, suffering serious stock reduction. Still, this spectacular fish is available if you are on the coast at the right time and place. Moreover, it has been implanted successfully in large lakes in North and South Carolina.

Fishing for striped bass

Spinning is done with very strong spinning or surfcasting gear, and large plugs or spoons. Rods of 10-11 feet, and ample spinning or multiplier reels filled with 0.35-0.45 mm line, are standard. Wind, weather, currents, migrations and, not least, the supply of preyfish are influential – and suddenly these bass may appear for a short time near land, where they can be caught. Early morning and the evening are profitable, but night fishing with natural bait is also common.

Bottom fishing with natural bait is as frequent as spinning. Among the baits used are small fish, worms, crabs, fish fillet, and sand lance. But the leaders, hooks, and other equipment must be adapted to the widely varying conditions of this fishing, from the surf on open coasts to the rocks and breakwaters where spinning is possible. It is tough work, and can prove demanding indeed.

Striped bass may be up to 2 metres (6.6 feet) long, and then weigh about 50 kg (110 lbs), but specimens of 3-8 kg (6.5-18 lbs) are most common. These are distinctive predators and call for comparatively strong gear, combined with either artificial or natural baits. In the tough fishing along wave-worn coasts, surfcasting is the usual method.

Bluefish

The bluefish (*Pomatomus saltatrix*) lives in nearly all sub-tropical parts of the Atlantic region: the Black Sea and Mediterranean, the Iberian peninsular and northwest African coasts, the Canary Isles and Azores, and the American coasts all the way from Massachusetts to Argentina. Nor is it strange to the waters of South Africa, the Indian Ocean, Southeast Asia and Australia.

Bluefish are coastal hunters and weigh up to 10 kg (22 lbs), the norm being 3-6 kg (6.6-13 lbs). Directed coastal fishing for them is done only along eastern North America, from North Carolina to Maine, and mostly with boats. The season lasts from April until September, beginning in the south, and peaks during the summer off New York and New Jersey. Sadly, like so many other marine species, this one has been subjected to hard professional fishing, and the sport is very uneven with good and bad years.

Catching bluefish

Schools of bluefish may hunt in the surface, near current edges, and at headlands or banks. Their presence is indicated by leaping small fish and wild splashing, which attract gulls and terns. The best times for fishing are morning and evening, since the small fish then move toward land. Bluefish are known for having a violent mouth with awfully sharp teeth, so it is useless to fish without a leader. A steel leader of 50-80 cm is common, but on some days the fish are quite shy of a leader and call for one of strong nylon.

Spinning is done with plugs, spoons or pirks – and sometimes whole baitfish on tackle, such as eels. Bluefish are masters at taking artificial lures and immediately shaking free of them. Live bait is amazingly effective, but difficult to handle for a coastal fisherman. Chumming gives additional opportunities when fishing from piers and breakwaters.

The choice of equipment desies general advice, as there is a huge difference between catching small bluefish in a Florida bay and casting against the wind or waves on an open coast in New Jersey. At all events, the bluefish is an exciting, quick and wild opponent if you have the right gear. Still, it seldom pays off to cast straight into a school, which causes fright. Instead, fish the school's outer edges and make several casts at the same spot. The first bait may not be seen, but the next will be, and the third is bound to bring a bite.

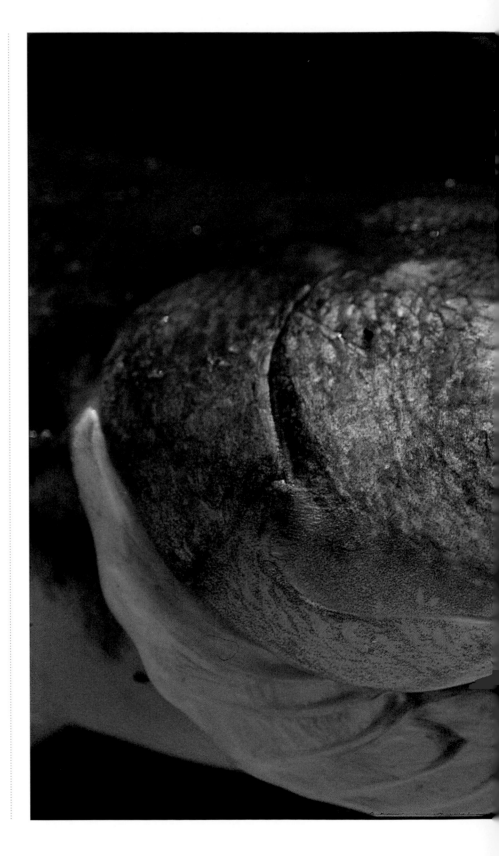

Weakfish

The weakfish (*Cynoscion regalis*) is encountered along the eastern coast of the United States, from New England to Florida, but is most abundant off New Jersey and New York. It inhabits shallow waters in, for example, surfs and coves, river mouths and tidal currents, but does not run up in fresh water. Its weight is not impressive but averages 2-3 kg (4.4-6.6 lbs), sometimes reaching 7-8 kg (15-18 lbs).

The fish is elongated with an often green-blue back and paler sides. Its back and tail have black patches and the abdomen is pale. Weakfish also go by many other names, such as sea trout, specked trout, and spotted weakfish. They are close relatives of the spotted sea trout, which occurs off Florida and along the coast in the Gulf of Mexico.

Weakfish live on worms, crabs, crustaceans and small fish. They may hold anywhere from the bottom to the surface. This is a popular species, frequently easy to catch with bottom tackle, and in many places also suited to spinning with spoons, pirks and plugs. The better you manage to imitate the ways of its natural preyfish, the finer your success at spinning.

Regardless of whether spinning or fishing with natural bait, you should deliver a strike only when the fish's weight is felt clearly on the rod. Weakfish have a habit of thrusting at the bait, tasting it and then spitting it out. They are caught chiefly during the summer half-year, and are a culinary delight.

Bluefish are an aggressive species and should be treated with a certain respect. They are even said to have attacked people swimming, and caused serious injuries with their sharp teeth. Hence the fishing should always be done with a steel leader, regardless of whether you use a wobbler or natural baitfish.

Red drum

On the coasts of southeastern America and the Gulf of Mexico, red drum (*Sciaenops ocellatus*) are also called red-fish, or channel bass – and coastal fishermen even flatter them with the name "bulldog". Red drum are similar in shape to the striped bass, but more powerfully built. Bronze to red in colour, they have a black patch on the tail – which distinguishes them from the black drum, despite some confusion between the two.

Red drum weigh 3-20 kg (6.6-44 lbs), and bigger examples have been landed in the past, such as one of 40 kg (90 lbs) from a pier in North Carolina. Along the Texas coast, stocks of red drum have varied due to low water temperature, algae blooms, and changing salinity. Here the fish do not migrate much, either, in contrast to the Atlantic coast where annual migrations are common.

The red drum is a bottom-fish, living on crustaceans and grey mullet. Fishing is best in the morning and evening. Catches are made over mixed and sandy bottoms – from open coasts and piers, or in harbours and tidal channels. Larger red drum are caught along the Atlantic coast, while the fish off Texas are modest in size.

Both artificial lures and natural bait are used to catch red drum. Diverse jigs, spoons, pirks and sinking wobblers are excellent lures, whereas the main baits are worms, crabs, mussels and fish strips. When choosing bait, the rule is to let the current and wind dictate the equipment, but one is often forced to employ strong gear. Many bottom-fishermen place their rods in holders and, meanwhile, spin with jigs in shallow water for small red drum.

Above left: When fishing for red drum in the "Texas style", one wades out with a big lure until chest-deep. Then the lure is let down and one wades back to shore, to await the fish's bite.

Below left: Red drum are often fished in the dark hours. These fish live in shallow water – eating smaller fish, mussels and crabs, for instance – and thus take both natural and artificial baits.

Right: Tarpon are characterized by their many silvery scales and their bone-hard mouths. They are also, of course, famous for high leaps in the air and for being able to snap the strongest lines...

Other great sportfish

Numerous species of famous sportfish have yet to be mentioned. Among them is the tarpon (*Megalops atlanticus*), found throughout the Caribbean and along the coasts of many equatorial West African states – from Gambia southward to the Congo. It is mainly known as a target of flyfishing, but probably more tarpons are landed by spinning and trolling or with natural bait. The tarpon weighs from a few to a hundred kilograms, and both its fighting qualities and hard charges are uncompromising. Hence, too, most hooked tarpons are lost.

No matter which equipment and bait you use, the strike is the high point of the fishing. A tarpon's tough moth, way of biting, and manner of fighting leave an impression that it is almost impossible to hook. The fishing is often done from a boat, primarily by casting out plugs or natural bait. However, many enthusiasts have gained their first experience of small tarpon from a bridge, pier or breakwater, at night in the glow from street-lamps.

The snook (*Centropomus undecimalis*) is another superior sportfish. It also occurs in Florida, along the entire Gulf coast, and down the shores of Central America and the Atlantic coast of South America. Close relatives of the snook live in

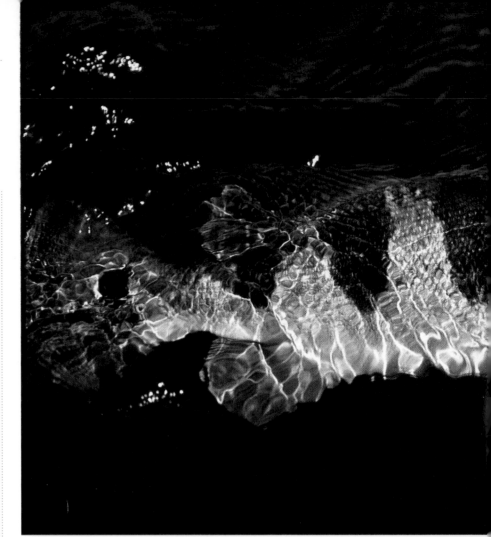

The peacock bass is a lovely species, related to the bass and found in South America. It has built a reputation with its capacity for fighting to the bitter end.

Southeast Asia and Australia. It can weigh up to 20 kg (44 lbs), but fish of 2-5 kg (4.4-11 kg) are commonest. Like the tarpon, it is often encountered on the mangrove coasts and in river mouths. Snook are caught with plugs and spoons, or with tackled baitfish such as grey mullet. They react only to fast, varied retrieval – whereas a tarpon, for example, frequently wants the bait served very exactly in relation to its patrolling and hunting routes.

The bonefish (*Albula vulpes*) is reputedly the ultimate challenge in flyfishing, but plenty are caught by spinning and with natural bait. This species is found all over the Caribbean, and in the Pacific Ocean – especially around Christmas Island – as well as in Southeast Asia and the Indian Ocean. Mostly, though, it is in shallow waters of the Caribbean and the Florida Keys that we see this shimmering jewel. Spinning is done with ultra-light equipment and small jigs. The art lies in locating the fish and serving the jig without scaring them. Many bonefish are also taken with natural baits such as small crabs, snails and shrimp, placed in line with the fish's course of travel.

Pompano (*Alectis ciliaris*) occur along the eastern coasts of the Americas and in the Caribbean. This is one of the most popular small species off the eastern United States and Gulf coast. It seldom weighs more than 1-2 kg (2.2-4.4 lbs), examples over 3 kg (6.6 lbs) being rare and easily confused with the permit. Natural baits are used almost exclusively – only under peculiar conditions do pompano fall for small spoons and jigs.

Permit (*Trachinotus falcatus*) are found from Massachusetts to Brazil, and resemble the pompano. These fish normally weigh at most 5-10 kg (11-22 lbs), but specimens of nearly 25 kg (55 lbs) have been recorded. Permit occur in shallow coastal areas, such as the Flats, where they lurk in deep holes and tidal channels. At flood tide, they may move into shallower water. The species is popular among flyfishermen, but can be caught with light spinning equipment.

Thus, every continent has distinctive fish species and "great sportfish" that attract practitioners of spinning. The same is true of South America where the dorado, piranha and payara are instances of very popular fish in rivers. Venezuela and Colombia are best known for peacock bass, or pavon –

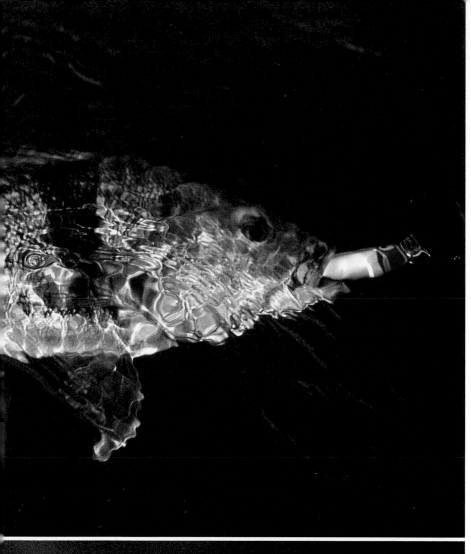

a relative of the bass, with beautiful colours, black stripes and a red spot on the tail, and impressive fighting abilities.

In Africa, tigerfish inhabit many rivers such as the Zambezi, Blue Nile, Niger and Volta, besides numerous large Central African lakes. Tigerfish are notorious for their terrifying jaws, which can destroy most artificial lures. They may weigh up to 15 kg (33 lbs). The Nile perch occurs in lakes of the Great Rift Valley including Lake Victoria, in the upper Nile sources at Murchison's Falls in Uganda, and below the Aswan Dam in Egypt. It commonly weighs 10-30 kg (22-66 lbs) and sportfishermen have caught examples approaching 100 kg (220 lbs).

In Asia, the huge beluga or sturgeon in the Caspian Sea is also conquered with artificial baits, along the rivers it migrates up for spawning. Fish attaining 150 kg (330 lbs) have been taken by sportfishermen. And in the rivers of northwestern Australia we find the barramundi – a close relative of the snook, and yet another fantastic fighter.

Tigerfish are found in numerous African lakes and rivers. Their impressive jaws have terrified countless sportfishermen, and chewed up at least as many lures.

Sport-fishing in North America

No matter how you measure it, North America has the greatest sportfishing in the world. Blessed with fresh water throughout most of its land-mass, and surrounded by warm and cold oceans, North America has an incomparable variety of esteemed gamefish, from trout to tuna, bass to bonefish, salmon to sailfish, bluegill to bluefish, and pike to permit.

Its abundant opportunities range from the water-rich frozen tundra of the Arctic to tropical islands surrounded by reefs, from fjord-like Pacific Northwest coastal bays to mid-Atlantic barrier beaches and lowland marshes, and from Rocky Mountain coldwater streams to Florida's reclaimed sea-level phosphate pits. These opportunities provide great, almost- great, and just-plain-good angling from inlet to ocean, river to lake, highlands to lowlands, and region to region.

This fishing is, remarkably, publicly accessible with very few exceptions, although some excellent North American waters – Alaska and northern Canada in particular – are difficult, and relatively expensive, to reach because of their remoteness.

Abundant waters, diverse species, and easy access put sportfishing into the category of the third most popular recreational activity in North America, surpassed only by the number of people who annually swim or ride a bicycle. A U.S. government survey in 1996 indicated that 35.6 million Americans over the age of 16 fished annually, and the value of their purchases relative to sportfishing – equipment, travel, jobs, wages, taxes, etc. – exceeded $108 billion dollars.

Although similar figures for Canada are not known, it can be assumed that they are proportional, and it is known that angling is a major component of tourism in Canada, with hundreds of thousands of nonresidents fishing while on vacation there each year. It is no accident that 75 percent of all people vacationing in the United States head to the water, and that two out of every five Americans on vacation will do some sportfishing.

A great deal of that angling is done from boats, perhaps more so in the United States and Canada than in any other country. It is estimated that more than 16 million recreational boats are in use by Americans (1997), and more than 12 million of these are large enough to be powered and/or to require state registration. A lot of recreational boat owners trailer their boats, and many of these are anglers for whom the ability to be mobile and to sample different places is very important.

Self-sustaining attractions

The greatest amount of angling effort in North America is devoted to freshwater fishing, in part due to geography; most states and provinces are located far from marine environments. In freshwater, bass – specifically largemouth and smallmouth varieties – are the most popular species.

Largemouth bass are a highly adaptable fish, and widely available in large and small bodies of water alike, including lakes, reservoirs, ponds, rivers, and streams, as well as some low-saline tidewater environments. They are found in forty-nine out of fifty states, the lone exception being Alaska. The states of Texas, Florida, and California are especially noted for bass, in part because they have in the past produced, or currently produce, the larger specimens. However, many states, especially in the central and eastern portions of the U.S., have excellent largemouth bass populations and fish of good proportions.

Almost all sportfishing for bass is done by casting with lures, the vast majority of that from boats. The wide array of habitats and cover preferences of this species, as well as its predatory ambush nature, lends itself to virtually all types of lures and diverse presentations. There is very little trolling done for the species and a comparatively small amount of fly-fishing, with spinning and baitcasting tackle vastly preferred.

Smallmouth bass, which inhabit cooler and rockier envi-

In the Bassmasters Classic, the year's forty best professional bass fishermen compete during three days for the title of Classic Champion. The weighing-ins attract some 100,000 spectators and are accompanied by laser lights and firework displays. Shown at far left is Ray Scott, founder of the organization B.A.S.S.

Northern pike have a good following, but are less widely available than the foregoing species, and muskellunge attract a small but ardent coterie of anglers who devote a lot of effort to what are generally modest catch results. Muskies are perhaps the least widely available major freshwater gamefish in North America and considered difficult to catch; as with bass, the majority today are released by anglers. Muskies are most prominent in and around the states and provinces bordering the Great Lakes, with special attention given these fish in Minnesota, Wisconsin, and Ontario. Pike overlap muskies in many of the same waters and do not grow as large on average, but are much more numerous and susceptible to a variety of lures, which are popularly caught on spinning and baitcasting equipment. Large pike are consistently caught in Canadian lakes and rivers, especially in the central and northern waters of the southern tier provinces, and in the southern parts of the northern territories.

It is the various species of panfish – crappies, bluegill, sunfish, perch, white bass, and the like – as well as the various catfish and bullhead species, that collectively rank second to bass in total angling interest and provide a lot of satisfaction (as well as good eating) to many anglers, but which do not have the glamor or get the publicity that is typical for other species. However, these fish are generally abundant, widely available, and accessible to people of all skill levels and abilities. Spinning (open face) and spincasting (closed face) tackle are almost exclusively used for panfish, with a great emphasis on angling with small natural baits and jigs.

All of the species previously mentioned are largely self-sustaining in their respective environments, although there is some supplemental or introductory stocking by government agencies.

Other popular fish

Trout are widely available in the United States and Canada, with a great deal of variety in both species and habitats. Brook trout, native to the continent, are favored by many small-stream and high-pond aficionados, especially in the midwestern and northeastern regions, though they are

rons than largemouths, are less widely distributed and on average smaller in size; they are predominantly found from the southerly regions of Canada to the middle of the United States, but are lacking in warmer latitudes. A belt from southwestern Ontario and Minnesota eastward to southern Quebec and Maine has long held the premier smallmouth fisheries, but some rivers and impoundments in the central U.S. are notable for big specimens.

A similar overall range exists for walleye, a species highly coveted for its flesh and one that attracts legions of anglers with the beginning of the open-water season each spring. However, walleye have expanded westward to develop significant fisheries in some waters, including the mighty Columbia River in Washington State. In recent years the major emphasis in walleye fishing has shifted to the largest lakes and river systems, which tend to produce the bigger fish and abundant numbers of this species, which take advantage of prolific baitfish populations in large waters. Unlike bass, little directed casting is done for walleyes, and the major emphasis is on trolling, jigging, and natural bait presentations.

rarely found in large sizes. Light spinning and fly tackle is commonly used.

These fish are actually char, and their family relatives, lake trout, do grow to large sizes although they inhabit the cold waters of large northern lakes. One of Canada's primary sportfish, and the object of many far-north fishing trips as well as outings on the Great Lakes bordering the two countries, lake trout are primarily caught by trolling with medium to medium-heavy spinning or baitcasting tackle, shallow when the water is cold early in the season, then deep as it warms. The Great Lakes offer the best opportunities for numbers and size of lake trout in the United States, while numerous waters in Canada are productive, with big lakes in northern Saskatchewan, Manitoba, and Ontario, as well as the Northwest Territories, favored for trophy specimens. Most of the lake trout in remote Canadian waters are released alive, as these giant fish are old and take a long time to grow big in such relatively infertile waters.

Rainbow and brown trout, which are more tolerant of warmer and less pristine waters than brook and lake trout, are more widespread and thus a greater part of the angler's catch. They are the primary river and stream trout species, although circumstances and sizes and fishing methods vary widely. Small specimens, the product of regular stockings, inhabit the waters where these fish cannot sustain themselves. The largest specimens, some over 20 pounds, exist in large lakes and rivers, and may also be the product of stocking.

Excellent rainbow trout and/or brown trout fishing exists in the highlands of various regions of the continent. In the United States, this includes northern California, the Rocky Mountain states, the Ozarks of Arkansas and Missouri, the Catskill and Adirondack Mountains of New York, and the southern Appalachian Mountains, but very good fishing also exists in Michigan, Pennsylvania, Washington, Idaho, British Columbia, Ontario, Quebec, Alberta, and other areas. Big rainbow (or steelhead) and brown trout also exist in some lakes scattered around the continent, most notably in the Great Lakes, where they are caught by trolling in spring and summer, and bank or wade fishing in tributaries from fall through winter.

Salmon are intensely popular in the regions where they occur, but, as anadromous coldwater species, are not available to the vast majority of Americans and Canadians without incurring substantial travel. They are restricted geographically to naturally occurring Pacific stocks, with the greatest populations existing in Alaska and British Columbia, and naturally occurring Atlantics being confined mainly to the eastern maritime provinces, especially Quebec, Newfoundland, New Brunswick, and Nova Scotia.

With the exception of Pacific salmon (coho, chinook, sockeye, pink, and chum salmon) in Alaska, native North American salmon have been under tremendous pressures due to environmental changes, especially damming of rivers and water quality issues, and to excessive commercial harvest in the oceans. However, thriving fisheries for transplanted salmon in the Great Lakes have provided exceptional angling in both lakes and major tributaries; this is sustained by extraordinary levels of stocking and is not subject to commercial fishing pressures.

Angling for sea-run Atlantic salmon in North America is almost entirely restricted to flyfishing, although landlocked populations exist and can be pursued by various methods, including casting spoons with spinning tackle and trolling with various tackle types. Pacific salmon are caught on all

Largemouth and smallmouth bass are undoubtedly the most popular species in fresh waters. Most states in the central and eastern USA offer excellent fishing especially for largemouth bass.

types of tackle in rivers, and entirely on spinning and bait-casting tackle in lakes and coastal waters.

Spinning in salt water

Saltwater fishing in North America varies considerably be-tween West and East Coasts and the Gulf of Mexico as well as the Caribbean, where the Bahamas, although not techni-cally part of the continental landmass, are a major light tackle fishing destination for North Americans.

Along the East Coast, anadromous species such as shad and striped bass are major spring attractions in large coastal rivers, and striped bass are one of the most important coastal species from the Carolinas to Maine. Although striped bass were imperiled as recently as the mid-1980s due to com-mercial fishing and water pollution, stiff commercial controls and improved water quality have allowed their numbers to rebound dramatically, and they have regained their place as the primary sportfish in the cooler Middle and Northern

Atlantic waters, where they are caught on various tackle with both bait and lures, and with most fish being released due to regulations.

Stripers, incidentally, although a saltwater species, have been widely transplanted into freshwater rivers and lakes, and huge landlocked populations of these fish occur in many impoundments throughout the middle and southern regions of the United States; few are naturally self-sustaining. In many locations hybrid striped bass, the result of cross-breeding a pure strain striped bass with a pure strain white bass, are stocked by state fisheries' managers and provide a fast-growing and aggressive sportfish that can be completely controlled for management purposes, as they are sterile.

Bluefish, weakfish, spotted sea trout, flounder, and assorted bottom fish are also major species in the same inshore region as striped bass, and, to some extent also drum; these are all suitable to lighter tackle presentations with either spinning or baitcasting equipment. The upper East Coast also offers opportunities offshore for big game species, including marlin, tuna, dolphin, and shark, but this is a heavier tackle game.

Further south the emphasis is more on a different mix of species, as the warmer climate leads to more tropical condi-tions and the coastal sweep of the warm Gulf Stream Current comes closer to the shoreline. This is why sailfish and dolphin are caught on spinning tackle and live bait not far from the southern Florida coast, as well as king mackerel and other species.

Inshore, however, attention turns to drum (redfish), sea trout, snook, tarpon, and bonefish, as well as the occasional permit. Wade fishing and casting with spinning and bait-casting tackle for redfish and sea trout along the Gulf of Mexico is very popular, as are poling and stalking fish along shallow grass flats. Snook are probably the least abundant of these species, mainly found in the brackish backwaters, but they are very much favored. Tarpon are very abundant and one of the premier light tackle fish, both on the flats and in the bays, eagerly pursued by anglers with lures and live bait, and almost universally released alive after capture.

Bonefish are the glamor species and hotly pursued by anglers fishing from flats skiffs. In Florida waters they can run

The opportunities for North American sportfishermen are almost endlessly diverse. Most of the desirable species are found here, and in many places the chances of a catch are superb – both from boats and from land.

to large sizes but are more solitary and skittish, while in some parts of the Bahamas they are more abundant in schools, and often not as wary as elsewhere. They, too, are virtually all released alive, and spinning gear is used by many anglers who are not proficient with flycasting tackle, especially when a stiff breeze occurs and makes fly presentation very tough.

On the West Coast, coho and chinook salmon have long been the premier catch in the Pacific Northwest region. However, these fisheries have been depressed in recent years due to low populations and the plight of these fish has drawn much attention in northern California, Oregon, and Washington, as well as in British Columbia, although the latter location, and especially Alaska, has good coastal salmon fisheries as well as excellent angling for the deep-dwelling halibut, which is a heavy tackle game.

California is a hotbed for saltwater fishing, and its opportunities range from imported striped bass and shad fisheries in northerly coastal rivers, to offshore pelagic species and to the ever popular yellowtail, albacore, and a great diversity of surf and bottom-dwelling species. In Southern California, assorted rockfishes, lingcod, and eels are always popular and available, while the occurrence of warm, bait-laden currents is necessary to produce good catches of bonito, barracuda, yellowtail, albacore, and other tuna, some of which are pursued on heavy tackle, others on light gear.

With a considerably different topography, the West Coast does not have the shallow flats fishing characteristic of the southeastern United States, and thus none of the same species; however, there is no lack of challenging opportunity for light tackle users, with light revolving spool saltwater reels the main tackle preference.

Vast fishing territories

Visitors to North America will find that there are plenty of guides, charter boats, and services catering to anglers, especially in the more well-known and publicized areas. In fresh water, major lakes, rivers, and areas with abundant waters have many guides (with and without boats), and charter boats are plentiful on the largest waters (restricted to four to six anglers on a limited reservation basis). All of the major coastal ports have fleets of party boats (capable of accommodating a large number of anglers) for bottom fishing and charter boats for inshore and offshore forays. Smaller guide boats, usually taking no more than three anglers, and primarily used for near-shore, estuary, and flats fishing activities, are available as well, and especially numerous in southern regions. Lodges, camps, and other facilities dedicated to serving anglers are plentiful, and are widely advertised in major outdoor publications, of which there are many. Outfitters exist who cater to canoe camping and fishing trips, houseboat vacation and fishing trips, horse or foot pack trips, and so forth.

If anything, the United States and Canada are so large, and there is such a plethora of angling opportunities in both, that it can be a bit bewildering for the visitor who aspires to do some fishing. Therefore, a prospective angler needs to focus on either the region that he or she is planning to visit (perhaps on vacation) and discovering both the opportunities available there and the common means of angling, or to focus on the species that he or she wishes to catch and then decide what place(s) to visit in order to catch either many of that species or large specimens (at some places it may be possible to do both).

Sportfishing in North America is most popularly pursued from early spring through fall. Numerically, far fewer people fish during the cold weather months, although ice fishing is very popular in the more northerly regions of the U.S. and in Canada, and the most southerly areas of the United States (Southern California, South Texas, and Florida) provide the most comfortable winter fishing due to a normally mild winter climate.

There are regulations that restrict sportfishing by season, usually to protect spawning fish or fragile populations; these are more prominent in fresh water than in salt water. During a limited time frame, the season will be "closed" for a particular species. This is especially prevalent for trout and salmon species; it also occurs for bass, walleye, pike, and muskie, especially in the more northern states and in Canadian provinces.

For the most part, regulations regarding seasons, methods of fishing, catch limits, and licensing are governed by state and provincial governments. There is no national or federal

sportfishing license in either the United States or Canada, although each of the fifty American states and fourteen Canadian provinces and territories requires a license issued by their government to fish in fresh water. In some places, the same license also applies to saltwater fishing in their governmental jurisdiction; in some places there is a separate license required for saltwater fishing; and in a few places there is no license requirement for saltwater fishing.

A fishing license issued by a state, province, or territory is only valid in waters within that jurisdiction, and in no jurisdiction is there a test or examination required to obtain a sportfishing license. Any person, whether resident or nonresident, can purchase a fishing license, although the fee for nonresidents is higher. Licenses can usually be purchased for varying time periods (a full year, a week, three days, and, in some cases, per day). They are most commonly acquired at stores selling fishing tackle, but are also obtainable at some government offices, marinas, lodges, etc., and are becoming increasingly available by telephone purchase via a credit card.

A license is valid for all waters within a jurisdiction, whether they are public or private. The vast majority of waters are publicly accessible, but a license does not grant permission to cross private property to reach or leave the water. Ingress and egress must be accomplished at places that are provided for such purpose. In waters that are privately owned, or which are inaccessible because all of the land around them is in private ownership, permission must be received to fish. There is no private licensing arrangement as exists in Europe, although an access fee may be charged by the owners of private land or waters who run a commercial business (such as a private marina or boat dock where people launch a boat, or a pay-to-fish facility).

There may be regulations pertaining to the manner of fishing; examples include a waterway where only barbless hooks are permitted, or where the use of live or dead bait is prohibited. These and other issues are addressed in a brochure or booklet that is provided with the purchase of a fishing license.

Though from afar there may seem to be a complicated maze of regulations, species, waters, and opportunities associated with North American sportfishing, a newcomer can get guidance at local bait and tackle shops (which are sadly fewer in number these days), or from organized clubs, or while attending the numerous regional outdoor shows that are held all around North America during winter months.

Index